Donald Trump Explained

A Special Education Perspective of the
Forty-Fifth President of the United States

by

Mr. Jarvis

The contents of this work, including, but not limited to, the accuracy of events, people, and places depicted; opinions expressed; permission to use previously published materials included; and any advice given or actions advocated are solely the responsibility of the author, who assumes all liability for said work and indemnifies the publisher against any claims stemming from publication of the work.

All Rights Reserved
Copyright © 2019 by Mr. Jarvis

No part of this book may be reproduced or transmitted, downloaded, distributed, reverse engineered, or stored in or introduced into any information storage and retrieval system, in any form or by any means, including photocopying and recording, whether electronic or mechanical, now known or hereinafter invented without permission in writing from the publisher.

Dorrance Publishing Co
585 Alpha Drive
Suite 103
Pittsburgh, PA 15238
Visit our website at *www.dorrancebookstore.com*

ISBN: 978-1-6453-0311-4
eISBN: 978-1-6453-0838-6

Contents

Foreword

When people hear the term Autism or its full name of Autism Spectrum Disorder, they almost universally think of the children highlighted by Autism Speaks and other advocacy groups of those individuals who present with the most severe and profound "shades" of the spectrum. It is this power of negative cultural association that often makes an announcement that a child should be evaluated for Autism agonizing for not just the parents, but also for the person making the statement. When I pointed out to my youngest sister that her second child was further advanced in both socialization and language than her first child, and that both myself and another sibling in education had remarked at the atypical and sensory behavior we had both observed in our nephew as being possible signs of Autism, she flipped out as it just couldn't be true. She did manage to take him to the doctor, who promptly laughed it off, looked him over and said he didn't see signs of Autism. As my sister took all the steps I had recommended on her own to help my nephew, including explicit instruction and replacement techniques for his odd behaviors, his needs as a child with the disorder would still be met without a diagnosis. Fewer meltdowns, better communication and a reduction of sensory-oriented behaviors were a gradual result and my nephew flourished. I did find it hilarious that a medical doctor "looked" my nephew over and saw nothing. Most people do. Autism generally has few common physical characteristics, but they aren't generally known or understood unless you are privileged to work with these wonderful and unique individuals. It is the behavioral, emotional and social aspects that are most documented.

Autism is a spectrum. That simply means that individuals who share a group of common characteristics, will likely be as unique and varied along with the severity of their disorder. One child can be blazingly brilliant, able to see patterns and express seemingly superhero powered senses with extreme levels of giftedness, while another child fails to connect socially and emotionally with their peers. They all have differences, yet they all have behavioral and social characteristics that distinguish their educational needs being different from the general population.

What does all this have to do with President Trump? People have been asking the same question about Trump since he emerged as a Presidential candidate as they began noticing and recording the many hundreds of odd things associated with him. That question was why does Donald say and do the things he does? As a Special Education teacher with more than fifteen years of experience working with children similar to our President the answer is obvious. Donald Trump likely has Autism Spectrum Disorder.

I say likely as I am not qualified to diagnose, as that responsibility falls on others with more schooling and higher certification than I. I do consider myself expert enough based solely on experience that my observations might be helpful to others in properly identifying if Trump has Autism as I suggest or perhaps another disorder drives his behavior. I spent eight of my years in education specifically tasked to conduct behavior observations for children suspected of having a disability. These observations would then be given to our school psychologist who would then observe that child also before taking all the documentation together and reaching a diagnosis. Donald Trump, while not directly observed, has provided a plethora of indirect evidence including recorded interviews, pictures, writing samples, etc., of his behavior and ability that make indirect observations substantial enough to pull together a very thorough analysis that supports an eventual diagnosis by more highly trained professionals than I. It is my hope and purpose to open up professional dialogue into whether or not our President has Autism using existing documentation that I believe supports a qualification under the Diagnostic and Statistical Manual of mental disorders, volume five, known as the DSM-V, should Trump be properly evaluated.

You are just an SPED teacher, why do you believe Trump is Autistic?

The easiest response is that Trump, if evaluated by the diagnostic criteria needed for an Autism Spectrum Disorder, using the DSM-V standards by the appropriate experts, qualifies as having the disorder based on the evidence I will be providing, documenting and detailing in this book.

In order to reach a diagnosis, an individual must be evaluated by a highly qualified individual such as a medical doctor, pediatrician or psychologist and meet set qualification criteria as specified in the DSM-V. Although I do not meet the threshold to diagnosis being a Special Education teacher, I can record my observations and submit them to other professionals who can. I do understand my manner of disclosure is highly unusual, however given the severity of the suspected disorder and the impact that the individual has standing in as President of the United States, creates a moral obligation to come forward and to disseminate this information in as public a manner as possible.

As I have many of these same behaviors, being somewhat on the spectrum, but not sufficiently enough to warrant a diagnosis, I felt my position as a Special Education teacher with added personal insight made me uniquely qualified to bring this story together for the benefit of the public and finally explain why Trump acts and says the things he does that are so inconsistent with the Office which he presently holds.

Why are you speaking out now?

I had considered keeping this information hidden as Trump is over twenty-one and I am only required by law to report a suspected disability of children under twenty-one to an appropriate agency under Federal Child Find requirements. However, the suspected disability, what I have observed and what has been reported, has compelled me to release this information despite not having the appropriate certification to definitively say that Trump has Autism. The overseeing agency for Donald Trump should feel fully obligated to investigate my claims through verification of the noted behaviors and draw their own conclusions after consultation with medical professionals as to whether Donald Trump should remain in his position, or should be required to step down for reasons of incapability to perform the required responsibilities of the Office of the President of the United States.

What is required to "have" Autism?

There is a difference between an educational distinction of qualifying under the Individuals with Disabilities Act and a psychological or medical diagnosis. I am most familiar with the educational distinction, which I am able to do so as part of the IEP team.

From the IDEA, Individuals with Disabilities in Education Act, comes the following:

Sec. 300.8 (c) (1)

(i) Autism means a developmental disability significantly affecting verbal and nonverbal communication and social interaction, generally evident before age three that adversely affects a child's educational performance. Other characteristics often associated with autism are engagement in repetitive activities and stereotyped movements, resistance to environmental change or change in daily routines, and unusual responses to sensory experiences.

(ii) Autism does not apply if a child's educational performance is adversely affected primarily because the child has an emotional disturbance, as defined in paragraph (c)(4) of this section.

(iii) A child who manifests the characteristics of autism after age three could be identified as having autism if the criteria in paragraph (c)(1)(i) of this section are satisfied.

To qualify for the Autism classification in an educational setting, an individual must have deficits for communication, both verbal and non-verbal and social skills that impact their overall functioning in the classroom. Generally "red flags" such as patterns of stereotypical behaviors, engagement in repetitive acts, showing restricted patterns of behavior, and/or demonstrating unusual responses to sensory input support the classification but are not always evident nor required in each child to receive the classification to qualify for services.

There is an evaluative process, including observation, formal testing, interviews, surveys and developmental records gathered before a meeting is scheduled to discuss the child's needs. The IEP meeting includes the parents or guardians of the child and education and/or medical professionals. The committee must state that the child qualifies for Specialized Education services under the classification of Autism.

An educational distinction for Autism is easier to obtain than receiving a medical diagnosis for the disorder. For Donald Trump to receive a diagnosis for ASD, he must be formally evaluated by appropriate professionals using the DSM-V as a guide. He must meet the following criteria as outlined in the Diagnostic and Statistical Manual of Mental Disorders (5th edition), 2013[1]:

American Psychiatric Association. (2013). Diagnostic and statistical manual of mental disorders (5th ed.). Arlington, VA: American Psychiatric Publishing.

A. Persistent deficits in social communication and social interaction across multiple contexts, as manifested by all three of the following, currently or by history:

1. Deficits in social-emotional reciprocity, ranging, for example, from abnormal social approach and failure of normal back-and forth conversation; to reduced sharing of interests, emotions, or affect; to failure to initiate or respond to social interactions.

2. Deficits in nonverbal communicative behaviors used for social interaction, ranging, for example, from poorly integrated verbal and nonverbal communication; to abnormalities in eye contact and body language or deficits in understanding and use of gestures; to a total lack of facial expressions and nonverbal communication.

3. Deficits in developing, maintaining, and understanding relationships, ranging, for example, from difficulties adjusting behavior to suit various social contexts; to difficulties in sharing imaginative play or in making friends; to absence of interest in peers.

---

[1] "DSM-5 Criteria." *Autism Speaks*, 2019, www.autismspeaks.org/dsm-5-criteria.

B. Restricted, repetitive patterns of behavior, interests, or activities, as manifested by at least two of the following, currently or by history.

1. Stereotyped or repetitive motor movements, use of objects, or speech (e.g., simple motor stereotypies, lining up toys or flipping objects, echolalia, idiosyncratic phrases).

2. Insistence on sameness, inflexible adherence to routines, or ritualized patterns or verbal nonverbal behavior (e.g., extreme distress at small changes, difficulties with transitions, rigid thinking patterns, greeting rituals, need to take same route or eat same food every day).

3. Highly restricted, fixated interests that are abnormal in intensity or focus (e.g., strong attachment to or preoccupation with unusual objects, excessively circumscribed or perseverative interest)

4. Hyper- or hyporeactivity to sensory input or unusual interests in sensory aspects of the environment (e.g., apparent indifference to pain/temperature, adverse response to specific sounds or textures, excessive smelling or touching of objects, visual fascination with lights or movement).[2]

In my professional opinion as a Special Education teacher, Trump meets the broad requirements of having persistent deficits in socialization and restricted patterns of behavior for each and every category listed in the DSM-V, as well as matching criteria for an Educational placement under the classification of Autism. It is my recommendation Trump should receive a psychological examination and independent determination from the appropriate healthcare professionals.

---

[2] "Individuals with Disability in Education Act." *Individuals with Disabilities Education Act,* sites.ed.gov/idea/regs/b/a/300.8/c/1.

Chapter One

"Is He Crazy or Is That Just the Way He Acts"

Flat Affect

Autism is not typically spotted by identifying physical characteristics, though one notable presentation exists. This is within a person's affect, or their facial expression. For many children with this disability they do not develop a full range of emotional expressions. The facial muscles appear relaxed and the entire face has very little expression similar to what one would see on a newborn. For most individuals social interaction helps to tighten and develop facial muscles as they develop, laugh, smile and grow. For a child with autism, they may not make sufficient eye contact or have enough socialization to develop more typical expressions, and thus maintain this baby-like expression known as a flat affect throughout most of their lives.

Donald Trump has demonstrated a flat affect facial expression since early childhood. Look at nearly any picture or video of Donald Trump. Note his relaxed cheek muscles, his wide open eyes and his lips not frowning or smiling. Very little expression isn't too uncommon in young children; however those with Autism may miss developmental steps that open up a wider range of emotional expression that we tend to see in older children and characteristically in adults. Donald Trump as an adult, one of the most photographed and videoed individuals in our time, still hasn't developed typical emotional facial expressions. I have estimated that about ninety-percent of the recorded material and more than two-thirds of the photographs that I have observed of Donald his expression is mostly that of a flat affect. He looks as if he is staring oblivious into space most of the time.

Flat affect is also associated with Schizophrenia and mental retardation. As neither is readily apparent in Donald's behavior or demeanor, they likely can be ruled out as root causes for his flat affect. Additionally, some individuals with brain injuries may present similar persistent facial expressions and autism-like behaviors. As these flat affect presentations are consistent throughout Donald's lifetime as evidenced by nearly all his pictures from early childhood to present day demonstrating the same blank facial expression, Autism is still the most likely explanation.

Stereotypical Behaviors

Stereotypical repetitive behaviors are observable signs that strongly suggest that an individual has autism. These are very developmental, seen in very young children and usually disappear naturally as the child matures. Walking on tippy-toes, putting inedible things in the mouth, sticking arms/hands out away from the body for balance, flipping on and off the light switch or water, and doing things over and over and over again are normal for toddlers. When they are still ongoing in school aged children, the behavior is considered markedly atypical.

Tearing Paper

Donald has been observed and/or recorded engaged in several of these stereo-typical behaviors. The most daunting behavior has been the paper ripping he engaged on camera after the third Presidential debate, October 19, 2016, against Hillary Clinton. At the end of the debate, Trump grimacing picked up his yellow notepad, wrenched the end of multiple pages and vigorously tore them out while the cameras were still rolling. While this behavior was fine as a candidate, as President destroying documentation which must be preserved under the Presidential Records Act is illegal.

We haven't seen a repeat of this behavior on camera as of this writing, however stories that this is an ongoing problem continue to surface. On June 10, 2018, multiple connected stories about Trump ripping up documents emerged after two career government employees, Solomon Lartey and Reginald Young Junior, who were part of a group of those tasked with piecing back together and taping documents Trump had destroyed to comply with

Federal law, were interviewed months after each were terminated without explanation.

Trump sometimes rips documents in half. Other times he rips paper into small tiny fragments. Trump's penchant for tearing paper after he is "done" with it likely fills a sensory need. The act of pulling and ripping the paper flexes muscles and releases tension, while the paper shredding makes a sweet, delightful crackling sound as the fibers snap and pull apart with each tug. From the June reports, it appears that staffers have found creative ways to reduce Trump's destructive impulses against paper.[3]

With how often Trump has obliterated paper, the behavior is likely a compulsion and repeated often enough is most certainly a stereotypical behavior. Some likely will argue that this behavior is more an element of Obsessive Compulsive Disorder. OCD is generally present as comorbidity with Autism Spectrum Disorder as elements of restricted behaviors and compulsion are key elements that define ASD.

Self-Hug

I noted many children I have had contact on the extreme side of the Autism Spectrum frequently engage in a self-hug, rocking their bodies back and forth or side to side repeatedly. The rocking movement, often referred to as stemming and provides proprioceptive feedback, isn't readily present in Trump's behavior; however the same close to self-body contact hug is. The only time Trump slightly sways left and right of center, is when he walks, and while awkward in appearance isn't likely to have been noticed by other observers as it is slight. Generally the rocking must also be evident when the individual is otherwise standing still for the behavior to be stemming, so even though he waddles a bit, it isn't significant enough to be described as a stereotypical behavior. However the hug is.

Trump frequently hugs himself, sometimes awkwardly high on his body, arms crossed with his right arm over his left arm. This behavior is most often expressed when he is sitting. The unusualness of his self-hug is how tight and close to his body he holds his arms, and has the appearance that many associate with a stubborn toddler.[4]

---

[3] Karni, Annie, et al. "Meet the Guys Who Tape Trump's Papers Back Together." *POLITICO*, 10 June 2018, www.politico.com/story/2018/06/10/trump-papers-filing-system-635164.

[4] Dem, Tex. "Mojo Friday - Mr. Self Hug Knows He's Over His Head - Edition." *Daily Kos*, 2019, www.dailykos.com/stories/2019/2/1/1831427/-Mojo-Friday-Mr-Self-Hug-Knows-He-s-Over-His-Head-Edition.

There could be many reasons for this learned behavior to be so pervasively expressed. One theory is that Trump's body language indicates that he is guarded and defensive. This isn't likely the case as he has that same posture during times he is seemingly in his element and enjoying himself as the center of attention receiving adulation from the cabinet or other officials flattering him.

Another suggested reason is that his self-hug is a learned strategy or re-placement behavior to prevent him from doing something else. I tend to vi-brate excessively when seated, so I developed a coping strategy of sitting on my right foot to stop the shaking as the movement often led to public notice and embarrassment on my part. Trump may have done something when he was younger that the self-hug acted as a restraint and stopped.

A third explanation is that Trump's compulsion to avoid germs, a reason he avoids shaking hands and prefers drinking through a straw, may be why he hugs himself so tightly. Only Trump knows why he does the self-hug. What we do know is he likely can't help himself from doing it, meaning it is a com-pulsion and often repeated stereotypical behavior.

Trump's self-hug is so pervasive that there are countless memes of each indelible image, especially the one on June 9th, 2018, at the G7 where he is seated looking upwards with arms crossed at Merkel and other standing world leaders asking him to sign a communique the international community had agreed upon. Trump said he would sign (which he didn't), took out Starbursts from his pocket, throwing them on the table before leaving, telling Merkel, *"Here, Angela. Don't say I never give you anything."*[5]

Band Conductor Hand

Trump's odd mannerism of holding his right hand up in the air, with his arm bent with his index and thumb touching forming the okay sign at his eye level, could be another stereotypical behavior as he does it multiple times at each of his recorded speeches where he is standing. He looks as if he is about ready to swing a baton leading a band. [6]

---

[5] CBS News. "Bremmer: Trump Threw Starbursts on Table, Told Merkel 'Don't Say I Never Give You Anything.'" CBS News, CBS Interactive, 20 June 2018, www.cbsnews.com/video/bremmer-trump-threw-starbursts-on-table-told-merkel-dont-say-i-never-give-you-anything/.

[6] Bishop, Rollin. "The OK Sign Is Becoming an Alt-Right Symbol." *The Outline*, The Outline, 24 Apr. 2017, theoutline.com/post/1428/the-ok-sign-is-becoming-an-alt-right-symbol?zd=1&zi=cruevc64.

Clearing Space

Trump has this odd quirk of moving objects sitting nearby when seated, clearing the space immediately in front of him or moving an object from one place to another. He does this repetitive behavior enough that others such as Mike Pence noticed and began doing it to hide the oddness of it, or because they felt socially uncomfortable when Trump did it. Unusual behavior does that to people. [7][8]

What is particularly unusual about this behavior is how developmentally inappropriate it is. Very young children pushing things around or off the table is something I think most parents with toddlers understand. I am constantly reminding my almost two-year old to sit down each time she stands on her chair and reaches for the centerpiece, cup or other object to push it aside. It certainly isn't the only pervasive developmental issue that Trump has been recorded doing.

Where Does Trump Fall on the Spectrum?

Before the current DSM-V came out in 2003, there were five categories under that fell under ASD, Asperger's, Autism, Pervasive Developmental Disorder not otherwise specified, Child Disintegrative Disorder and Rhett Syndrome. Now there is one category, Autism Spectrum Disorder. With the old categories it was a bit easier to categorize based on the severity of the behaviors on communication and socialization.

Rhett Syndrome is a genetic disorder that affects some girls. As it is the only known genetic based cause of the behaviors it is no longer considered to be part of the Autism Spectrum.

Childhood Disintegrative Disorder is when a child has normal development up till age two, and then demonstrates clinically significant loss of skills.

Asperger's is where most of the high functioning individuals are classified. Sheldon from the hit show *The Big Bang Theory*, Napoleon Dynamite, and Dr. Shaun Murphy from *The Good Doctor* are all incredible characters with an Asperger bent to them. Generally those with Asperger have extreme giftedness accompanied with extreme sensory or social difficulties.

---

[7] Bishop, Rollin. "The OK Sign Is Becoming an Alt-Right Symbol." The Outline, *The Outline*, 24 Apr. 2017, theoutline.com/post/1428/the-ok-sign-is-becoming-an-alt-right-symbol?zd=1&zi=cruevc64.

[8] "Internet Mocks Pence Copying Trump - CNN Video." *CNN*, Cable News Network, 8 June 2018, www.cnn.com/videos/politics/2018/06/08/donald-trump-mike-pence-water-bottles-moos-erin-pkg.cnn.

Autism under the DSM-4 was where individuals with the most severe difficulties with language and socialization were evident had been classified. Unfortunately, this is where the stigmatization for the disorder originates as most connect Autism with extreme difficulties due to Autism Speaks and other advocacy groups' work, and it is the only official category still recognized by name specifically in the DSM-V.

The last category was the catch-all classification for those who showed many Autistic traits but didn't quite fit Autism or Asperger, is Pervasive Developmental Disorder Not Otherwise Specified. Trump communicates well enough that classic Autism does not fit, and although he functions independently, is reasonably intelligent, Asperger doesn't quite fit as he socializes and interacts too well despite obvious deficits. What behaviors he does have, other than the social and communication difficulties described in later chapters, appear to be persistent developmental issues, making Pervasive Developmental Disorder Not Otherwise Specified as the most appropriate category to describe Donald Trump's present functioning. [9][10]

Pervasive Developmental Deficits

Trump has done a fine job of compensating for most of his skill deficits throughout his life that he could no longer hide under the intense scrutiny that comes with choosing to run for the highest public office. At this point there are copious amounts of recorded evidence of pervasive developmental deficits including proprioceptive or sensory needs, poor adaptability and lack of sufficient development for many skills and tasks requiring coordination.

Trump has been recorded twice holding a drink similar to how a toddler would on November 15, 2017, and then again on December 18, 2017. The first incident he was mid-speech about his Asia trip and his mouth got dry. He paused, grabbed a bottle of Fiji, holding the cap in one raised hand, while the other hand raised the bottle to his mouth and drank. Both hands were on the same level though only one hand appears to hold the beverage. This was noticed more because Trump had criticized Marco Rubio for taking a drink mid-speech, and not for the unusualness of how he held the container until the second incident.[11]

<hr>

[9] Rudy, Lisa Jo. "9 Different Names to Describe One Autism Spectrum." Verywell Health, www.verywellhealth.com/what-are-the-different-types-of-autism-260611.

[10] "Tools: DSM-IV Criteria for ASDs." *DSM-IV Criteria for ASDs* | Autism Research Institute, www.autism.com/tools_dsm4.

[11] Ward, Pat. "President Trump Stops His Speech to Search for Watercc: @Marcorubio

On the second occasion, while giving another speech in Washington, D.C., Trump with a grip on both sides of a glass lifted and drank. While this only lasted a few seconds it was on camera and astute media folk recalled the previous odd drink. The internet lit up at the President's infantile behavior. Some said this may be a sign of dementia or some cognitive difficulty. It is more easily explained under the overall description of a Pervasive Developmental Disorder (Autism), as clusters of these behaviors are frequently observed while following forty-five. [12]

Is it hard to correctly flip a coin? Actually it can be for some, such as Trump who sort of chucked the coin straight up and down at the start of the Army-Navy game on December 7, 2018. Many behaviors that are genuinely easy for most of the population must be taught explicitly, step-by-step with plenty of practice for individuals with ASD to master a skill that is unfamiliar to them. [13]

How about closing an umbrella? Having wrestled with the challenging nature of umbrellas when I was a small child, I can definitely relate to the difficulties Trump must have had when he was using an umbrella and didn't even attempt to close it. I avoided using one till I was about ten and figured how easy it was to push a lever and close the umbrella. On October 27, 2018, Trump ascended to the top of the stairs of Air Force One and tossed an opened umbrella to the side entering the plane. When someone went to retrieve the discarded umbrella they closed it with one quick motion in less time than it took for Trump to pitch it on the small platform. [14]

There are other skills expected to have been learned by now that Donald hasn't appropriately mastered. Failing a skill that is novel is understandable; failing when the skill is required every day isn't. Trump struggles with correctly tying his necktie, as it consistently dangles well below his waistline. A necktie should hang no further than one's belt, requiring Trump to adjust where he begins his knot. The back side of the tie should be one to two inches shorter

---

Pic.twitter.com/26hR5w7Zle." *Twitter*, Twitter, 15 Nov. 2017, twitter.com/WardDPatrick/status/930899999092887552.

[12] "Trump Drinks Water with Two Hands like a Child during Big Speech on National Security." *YouTube*, 18 Dec. 2017, youtu.be/sTqTFnzkaJU.

[13] "President Donald Trump Doesn't Know How To Do A Coin Toss | All In | MSNBC." *YouTube*, 12 Dec. 2018, youtu.be/3dapw_EB4xo.

[14] "Trump Dumps Umbrella at Door of Air Force One." *Reuters*, Thomson Reuters, 28 Oct. 2018, www.reuters.com/video/2018/10/28/trump-dumps-umbrella-at-door-of-air-forc?videoId= 477744202.

than the front part, and slide into the loop attached to the front section. This keeps the tie properly aligned. Trump adjusts his tie so poorly he has at least on one occasion been spotted with scotch tape fastening the back of his tie to the front. He was photographed on December 1, 2016, in Indianapolis, Indiana, leaving a plane with his taped-up tie flailing in the wind. That Don hasn't been successful in this everyday task may have to do with restricted patterns of behavior which will be discussed in another chapter.[15]

Trump failed to accurately draw the stars and stripes of the American Flag while visiting a kindergarten class, on August 24, 2018, in Ohio. Health and Human Secretary Alex Azar posted the clip on Twitter, which went viral for the Trumpian mistake. Donald incorrectly colored the first stripe red, leaving the second white and coloring the third blue. The error makes sense in that Trump alternated red, white and blue, a common phrase used to describe the US flag. It didn't make sense because Trump is over seventy and should know what the US flag looks like. MOST children can do this independently. Those that need assistance have developed coping skills to help solve the problem, such as looking at what a peer is doing (social referencing) or finding a model in the room to copy. Most individuals with Autism Spectrum disorders have to be taught social skills using role-play in small groups and then are taught to generalize that skill to other situations. Trump likely has had little intervention to help him overcome this glaring deficit.[16]

Our President also failed to sing along with the National Anthem when making a show of "patriotism" staged before an NFL game on January 9, 2018. Trump at times joined in and then dropped out of the singing. It wasn't clear what was going on with forty-five.[17] The event wasn't the only time Trump didn't follow accepted social protocol. The First Lady had to remind her husband to hold his hand over his heart on April 17, 2017, standing on the White House balcony as the National Anthem played.[18]

---

[15] Landsbaum, Claire. "Donald Trump's Tie Is Held Together by Scotch Tape." *The Cut*, The Cut, 2 Dec. 2016, www.thecut.com/2016/12/donald-trumps-tie-is-held-together-by-scotch-tape.html.

[16] Azar, Secretary Alex. "The Opioid Crisis Is One of Our Top Priorities at HHS, with a Drumbeat of Action on the Full Range of Efforts Where We Can Assist Local Communities. Today, I Joined @POTUS & @FLOTUS in Ohio to Learn How States and Communities Are Responding to the Challenge of Opioid Addiction. Pic.twitter.com/NwxSoeNznA." *Twitter*, Twitter, 25 Aug. 2018, twitter.com/SecAzar/status/1033142676424679425.

[17] "President Trump Half-Sings the National Anthem." *YouTube*, 9 Jan. 2018, youtu.be/vuUWJ8WAeH0.

Trump's failure to pick up on social cues isn't limited to task-oriented activities. He fails to do so while on the world's biggest stages where he represents the American people. These will be discussed further in another chapter.

Lack of Spatial Awareness and Wandering

Probably the most confounding and potentially risky behaviors that President Trump has displayed and is readily documented are his inexplicable and frequent wandering off right in the middle of an event or interview. The job of Secret Service is to protect the President, and when he is unable to stick to his designated area, like he did in Poland on July 5, 2017, and meanders from behind the bullet resistant barrier directly onto the stage in front of the crowd and just stands there, the adults assigned to security appear very nervous as they recognize dangers that the President is unable to. The thing is most parents can identify with the fear of a child wandering away like that because young children haven't developed the ability to recognize the potential for problems if they wander. It is developmental having spatial and body awareness, and wholly lacking in most of the behaviors we are seeing on full display in President Trump at nearly every foreign trip as well as some domestic visits.[19]

Really young children and older people with dementia or altered states do frequently wander, so it shouldn't be too surprising that people have questioned the cognitive abilities of Trump. It isn't dementia or other degenerative issues that cause this behavior. Donald lacks spatial awareness, the ability to recognize where his body is in relation to other things.

Lack of spatial awareness while the President visited Queen Elizabeth at Buckingham Palace on July 13, 2018, marked the moment that convinced me I was observing was indicative of Autism related behaviors, as I have seen this awkwardness and inability to properly socialize and connect with so many times from my own students. I actually pointed to my computer screen and said, "That looks just like so and so," referring to the name of a former student. Trump at one point appears to forget where he is, moves in front of the queen blocking her off. She moves around him from behind to his right side while

---

[18] "First Lady Nudges Trump to Raise Hand at Anthem." *YouTube,* 22 Apr. 2017, youtu.be/ghpNYDi72f0.

[19] "Trump Wanders Outside of Bulletproof Glass After Speech in Poland, Looks Like a Sad, Lost, Old Man." *YouTube,* 6 July 2017, youtu.be/1XPKDw6kkTE.

he peers to his left, possibly looking for her. When he sees her on his right the two continue up the path. [20]

What should have been the first indication Trump was developmentally different than any political candidate before him occurred during the third debate, October 19, 2016. Hillary Clinton was speaking. Trump wandered for a bit then moved positioning himself behind his opponent reasonably close, staring quietly and looking down on her. In the SPED world we often teach our students about personal space, and how important it is in keeping out of others' "bubble" when we interact with them. This interaction likely was wholly unintentional on Trump's part as he has continued throughout his Presidency to do these sorts of poor spatial awareness things. The internet lit up about how creepy or dominating it appeared to be. The reality is that Trump hasn't had proper intervention and explicit behavioral training to reduce the frequency of these behaviors.[21]

The Hillary debate brings up the subject of personal space, which many children on the Spectrum struggle with. I often refer to this comfort zone as a person's bubble. Teaching children to not enter someone's bubble starts in kindergarten and is learned by normal functioning children by second grade. Those with persistent deficits for spatial awareness may take longer. Trump's awkward handshakes and lack of awareness for personal space mark him as extremely atypical.

While visiting with Israel's Prime Minister Benjamin Netanyahu on May 27, 2017, during a press junket, Trump abruptly stood up from his chair and began to wander off away from Netanyahu without recognizing a handshake was verbally being offered. An aide corrected the social error and returned Trump quickly where the two shook hands and finished the picture taking.[22]

On July 4th, 2017, Trump deplanes and walks past the security detail standing by the Presidential limo parked directly in front of the stairs further out onto the tarmac. Someone signals him, and he turns around surprised, points to the car, smiles and begins walking back to the vehicle. His showing humor to the situation is an appropriate coping skill, one that gets him by for the most time. This sort of coping skill behavior has helped Trump gloss over his lack of ability countless times.[23]

---

[20] "Trump Breaks Royal Etiquette, Walks in Front of Queen." *YouTube*, 14 July 2018, youtu.be/tyBKS-rV4eE.

[21] Reuters. "Presidential Debates." *Reuters*, Reuters, 19 Oct. 2016, i.ndtvimg.com/i/2016-11/hillary-clinton-donald-trump-debate-reuters_650x400_61478453820.jpg.

[22] "Donald Trump Wanders Off." *YouTube*, 28 May 2017, youtu.be/nAjE1e8FG18.

[23] "Donald Trump Wanders Off Again." *YouTube*, 4 July 2017, youtu.be/5fumChF0Skg.

Who can forget the G20 Summit December 1, 2018, in Argentina where Trump entered stage right and exited quickly stage left leaving the host country's President standing alone and confused while an aide went and retrieved the missing world leader? The President in this instance either didn't read or understand the directions and expectations of the task he needed to fulfill.[24]

Trump has had multiple televised signing ceremonies where he has to be reminded of the task expectation-signing the document. When he isn't reminded quickly, he may leave without signing like he did on March 31, 2017, failing to publicly sign either bill that the photo op was created for.[25] A repeat mistake was avoided on October 12, 2017, when Pence succeeds in calling back the wayward leader before he disappeared after speaking to the press.[26] On October 24th, 2017, Melania saves another bill-signing ceremony by redirecting the wayward elder.[27]

Trump's inability to complete tasks independently is a sign of poor executive functioning skills. Executive functioning is a person's overall ability for organization, planning and work completion. Generally when a young person has poor executive functioning the inadequate skills can be targeted. With Trump's overall poor executive functioning having likely never been directly addressed, it is certainly putting a drag on his entire administration giving Bob Corker's catch phrase of *"alert the daycare staff"* profound meaning and implication erupting from the chaos and disorganization of a White House run by an atypical and developmentally different President.

---

[24] "Trump Leaves Argentinean President Alone on Stage at G20." *YouTube*, 2 Dec. 2018, youtu.be/KOnfiFOCwH0.

[25] "Watch Trump Leave Executive Order Ceremony Without Signing." *NBCNews.com*, NBCUniversal News Group, www.nbcnews.com/video/trump-forgets-to-sign-executive-order-911564355790.

[26] Giaritelli, Anna, and Evan Vucci. "Mike Pence Chases Down Trump after He Forgets to Sign Executive Order: WATCH." *Washington Examiner*, 12 Oct. 2017, www.washingtonexaminer.com/mike-pence-chases-down-trump-after-he-forgets-to-sign-executive-order-watch.

[27] "In Opioid-like Daze, Trump Nearly Forgets to Sign Opioid Bill." *Daily Kos,* www.dailykos.com/stories/2018/10/25/1807262/-In-opioid-like-daze-Trump-nearly-forgets-to-sign-opioid-bill.

Chapter Two

"Low Energy" Don and Executive Functioning

Executive functioning is the overall ability to organize oneself and to complete tasks. With many individuals on the spectrum, these skills are either lacking or learned through effective and precise interventions. Trump appears to have developed sufficient executive functioning to live seemingly independently. However, that may not actually be the case as he relies on aides, family and trusted advisers to get anything done, and has likely done so in his business dealings considering reliance on people such as Hope Hicks, a cadre of family lawyers and staff throughout his career as a real estate magnate and celebrity. A great deal of executive functioning requires three components-literacy, writing skills and organization to be adequately able to function.

It is my professional opinion that Trump independently lacks the overall executive functioning ability to handle the tasks required of the office of the President. In the last chapter I discussed how Trump frequently employs coping skills to cover up his inadequacies and deficits. Others have hidden his inadequacies as well long before he entered the White House. The only thing that has changed for the President is the people who now are covering for him.

Everyone probably knows Trump from his time on the hit show *The Apprentice*. The producers were personally invested in making their show work with Trump as the centerpiece. Trump was just as incoherent and rambling as we presently see him in his unedited and unscripted glory representing all of the United States according to producers and others who worked on the show. To make the program work someone had to be a clever editor, while other staff placated the petulant and bossy prima donna star to keep him happy and preoccupied.

The Apprentice like many reality shows was mostly staged to make it palpable to drive viewership and ratings. Trump looked smarter, wealthier and more powerful than he was in real life and public perception of the man was morphed positively because of their efforts. This made the show, Trump's main launching point to American and world audiences, responsible for making Trump into something he truly is not able to do. He wasn't easy to work with, didn't read and would improvise or fire someone impulsively without consulting the producers. Erratic behavior and impulsiveness does not make an effective or efficient leader, nor does someone who struggles with task oriented behavior.[28][29][30]

Time Management

Being able to effectively manage time is a vital element of executive functioning. Trump has proven so poor with having to work within a structured schedule that former Chief of Staff John Kelly created the term "executive time" to describe unstructured time set aside to meet Donald's needs of watching TV, calling friends, Tweeting and otherwise being unproductive. Stories of the President's schedule were first revealed by Politico in an article by Eliana Johnson and Daniel Lippeman published on October 29, 2018, at 5:09 A.M. EDT. The article reviewed the Presidential record of activities for the five-day work week of October 22-October 26.

Trump had three- to four-hour work scheduled in with late start times to the day at 11 or 11:30 A.M. for a briefing or meeting. The rest of the time was unstructured. During some unstructured time, Trump did hold some unscheduled meetings and may call a foreign leader. He also tweeted in real time to what was featured on TV on the Fox News channel.[31]

---

[28] "'What We Did Was a Scam': The Apprentice Creators Give Behind the Scenes Reveal of Trump's Show." *PEOPLE.com,* people.com/politics/apprentice-creators-donald-trump-scam/.

[29] Baysinger, Tim. "'Apprentice' Staffers Had to 'Reverse Engineer' Episodes Because 'Unprepared' Trump Would Fire Contestants on a Whim." *TheWrap,* TheWrap, 27 Dec. 2018, www.thewrap.com/apprentice-staffers-had-to-reverse-engineer-episodes-because-unprepared-trump-would-fire-contestants-on-a-whim/.

[30] Keefe, Patrick Radden. "How Mark Burnett Resurrected Donald Trump as an Icon of American Success." *The New Yorker,* The New Yorker, 28 Feb. 2019, www.newyorker.com/magazine/2019/01/07/ how-mark-burnett-resurrected-donald-trump-as-an-icon-of-american-success.

[31] Johnson, Eliana, et al. "9 Hours of 'Executive Time': Trump's Unstructured Days Define His Presi-

Axios followed up on the executive time reporting with an article by Alexi McCammond and Jonathan Swan on February 3, 2019, this time with a larger sampling of the leaked internal schedules of the White House, of fifty-one days. Trump averaged sixty percent of his time on unstructured executive time. The first block of time, up to 11 A.M. generally, Trump wasn't at the White House according to sources despite being on the official schedule as being there. Instead he was believed to be at his residence on most of these days.

So what does Trump do when he actually works? Donald attends rallies, signing ceremonies and meets or calls advisors or other people. These are the more enjoyable aspects of the job, and the ones he is both visible and enthusiastic about doing. When it comes to policy and detail, Trump's schedule like his actual accomplishments are rather light.[32]

Planning

There has been little evidence given to support Trump being able to articulate and execute a detailed political plan independently, another element required for adequate executive functioning. This extends beyond the Presidency into his personal life and the overall Russian investigation. He announces something on impulse, and others get the job done for him or he throws a fit.

Trump so far has presented no real plans, only the bigger idea of what he wants, and expects others to work out the details for him. He has been much like the boy who becomes President in one of my favorite children books, *Big Plans* by Bob Shea and Lane Smith, first published in 2008. In that book that oddly foreshadowed Trump's rise to the White House, a young boy who says he has big plans forces others to follow him blindly all the way till he reaches the White House, then the moon. The conclusion of the story is great. The boy receives a much needed time-out from his teacher.

This inability of Trump's to lay out a plan and see it through has been consternation to political allies in Congress like Senator McConnell and Paul Ryan. Congress looking for guidance expects a plan from the guy who campaigned on being both a deal maker and a winner. Trump hasn't lived up to the hype. Meanwhile, GOP leadership essentially conceded authority to the

---

dency." POLITICO, 29 Oct. 2018, www.politico.com/story/2018/10/29/trump-daily-schedule-execu-tive-time-944996.

[32] McCammond, Alexi, and Jonathan Swan. "Scoop: Leaked Private Schedules Show Trump Spent 60% of Last 3 Months in 'Executive Time.'" *Axios*, 3 Feb. 1970, www.axios.com/donald-trump-pri-vate-schedules-leak-executive-time-34e67fbb-3af6-48df-aefb-52e02c334255.html.

White House after Trump pummeled those willing to speak out into submission. Gone are Bob Corker, John McCain and Jeff Flake, while others like Lindsey Graham who once criticized now work as enthusiastic cheerleaders and sycophants. So is the power of an adult who knows how to meltdown when he doesn't get his way.

The first legislative item on the 2017 schedule was the repeal and replacement of the Affordable Care Act, something both Trump and the GOP promised as their most pressing responsibility throughout the years leading up to the 2016 election. Trump said he wanted to get rid of Obamacare, but clearly didn't understand the process of a bill becoming a law. On May 4, 2017, Trump took the celebratory victory lap of the repeal effort when the House once again voted to repeal the ACA. Standing in a grand ceremony in front of the White House and the press were members of the House receiving adulation and praise for their great work in finally ending Obamacare. [33]

There was a problem, easily predicted by anyone who had paid attention during fifth-grade history class. According to the Constitution, the process which a bill must take to become a law requires that both the House and the Senate must pass the same bill, and then it must be signed by the President to become law. Celebrating the victory on the first lap of a mile race was not the winning strategy Trump had envisioned to start his momentous Presidency. He had genuinely thought the deal was done despite the history of repeal efforts prior to his term ending in the same inglorious manner. The repeal and replace effort died in the Senate humiliating an unsuspecting President, when the late and honorable John McCain sensed the bill's folly and gave a thumbs-down response from the Senate floor on July 28, 2017.[34]

Throughout the legislative effort, Trump was more a bystander leaving the details to be hammered out by Congress, then as a lobbyist and cheerleader. As it was the first major legislative piece of his administration it was understandable he didn't contribute to the policy formation and planning that would be expected later down the road.

---

[33] Press, The Associated. "Trump Celebrates House Vote on Obamacare." The New York Times, *The New York Times*, 4 May 2017, www.nytimes.com/video/us/politics/100000005080570/trump-obamacare-repeal.html.

[34] Narjas Zatat @Narjas_Zatat. "The Moment John McCain Killed Trump's Flagship Bill." *The Independent*, Independent Digital News and Media, 28 July 2017, www.independent.co.uk/news/world-0/john-mccain-vote-video-no-obamacare-repeal-bill-us-senate-arizona-republican-healthcare-a7864231.html.

Tax reform was up next, and with Trump having "impressive business acumen," he was expected to take lead on crafting the policies. On September 27, 2017, the Treasury submitted a short document entitled UNIFIED FRAMEWORK FOR FIXING OUR BROKEN TAX CODE. The document was titled with all caps, adding a flourish that signifies Trump's a personal touch in crafting the messaging. The nine-page document was criticized as being sparse on details and more of a wish list, which was curious, considering that by the time it was published people had been meshing out the details trying to get the big reveal approved by the President for months. The resulting bill encompassed a whopping 1,097 pages and was passed December 22, 2017. This was the only significant piece of legislation ushered in during Trump's first full year in office where his party, the Republican Party, had control of the House, Senate and Presidency.[35]

The Beginning of the Trump Shutdown

The chaotic nature of Trump's poor planning was perhaps felt the most during the Christmas season of 2018, when facing the reality of investigations and checks on power as the House was wrested away from the GOP decisively in the midterm election, tuned into the heated news waves of Fox News. Trump had agreed to a Congressional plan to fund the government keeping it open, and someone launched an effective influence campaign to cause Trump to change course. When Trump turned on the tele and went to his favorite safe place in TV land, Fox News, he was likely in a good mood feeling successful with what he had accomplished during the day. Instead of his normal dose of tailored positive messaging that had generally been supportive and enthusiastic about what he was doing, while berating real and imagined political foes for good measure, what Trump saw and heard was intended to set him on a different course.

Ann Coulter, Sean Hannity, Rush Limbaugh and other rightwing pundits convinced Trump that he must close down the government in order to build the wall he had fervently campaigned on. Coulter made the argument that failing his wall promise would mark the end of his presidency. Trump had been convinced, and he would soon take decisive action that led to the longest government shutdown in US history of thirty-five days.

---

[35] Mnunchin, Steve. "Press-Release." Www.treasury.gov, 2017, www.treasury.gov/press-center/press-releases/documents/tax-framework.pdf.

Trump met with Schumer and Pelosi in a televised event on December 11, 2018, in the White House. Mike Pence was also in attendance. Pence did his best impression of Bernie in the 80s classic *Weekend at Bernie's*, sitting as stiff as the titular character seated blissfully and unmoving disconnected from the ongoing discussion in the room. The optics and one-liners of the made for TV political event left such an indelible impression even after the left and rightwing media put their spin on what happened for their respective audiences. Trump with his essentially lifeless VP didn't stand a chance as Chuck and Nancy controlled the narrative expertly, even getting Trump to trigger on camera, declaring this:

> *"I am proud to shut down the government for border security, Chuck, because the people of this country don't want criminals and people that have lots of problems and drugs pouring into our country. So I will take the mantle. I will be the one to shut it down. I'm not going to blame you for it. The last time you shut it down, it didn't work. I will take the mantle of shutting down."*

There was a lot of interesting banter throughout the meeting. Trump's idiosyncratic language and inability to fully follow the conversation was readily apparent during many of the exchanges, both difficulties associated with Autism and more fully explained in a subsequent chapter. As a brief example of idiosyncratic language, a speech pattern that is repetitive with frequent pragmatic and syntactic errors, here is a section of what Trump replies to a reporter asking when he would make a decision on Chief of Staff shortly after owning the shutdown:

> *"Thank you very much. Yeah, we're interviewing a lot of—we have a lot of great people for Chief of Staff. A lot of people want the job. A lot of people want the job. And I have some great people. A lot of friends of mine want it. A lot of people that Chuck and Nancy know very well want it. I think people you'd like. We have a lot of people that want the job—Chief of Staff. So we'll be seeing what happens very soon. We're in no rush. We're in no rush."[36]*

---

[36] MarketWatch. "Transcript of the Heated Meeting between Trump, Pelosi and Schumer." *MarketWatch*, 11 Dec. 2018, www.marketwatch.com/story/transcript-of-the-heated-exchange-between-

That repetitive stereotypical simplistic phrasing Trump employed is very idiosyncratic. Before the DSM-V, there was more of an emphasis that using idiosyncratic language was evidence of the disorder. Now, while still associated with the disorder for issues with communication, it isn't required specifically for a diagnosis. [37]

Trump on December 22, 2018, with full control over both sides of Congress, closed down the US Government for the third time with no semblance of a plan and only a big idea of what he wanted to accomplish.

Literacy

Saying President Trump lacks required literacy and writing skills needed to complete Presidential duties are no longer far-fetched nonsense statements when that appears to be the consensus of those who know Trump's habits. It isn't that he can't read. Trump has successfully read script from the teleprompter or enlarged script notes with adequate fluency on numerous occasions. It is that Trump likely hates to read.

When someone with a spectrum disorder dislikes a given task, they often demonstrate avoidance behaviors to get out of what they find uncomfortable. The two most common tactics I have seen for avoiding reading are missing glasses and lost reading materials. Trump does the *"I don't have my glasses"* shtick in a recorded deposition on June 16, 2016, 10:30 A.M., appearing before a judge when asked to read documents regarding a case.

Trump admits he doesn't review the leases, instead relying on others to do so which is a very understandable response for an executive. When asked to read he first complains that it is long, which the interviewer responds by asking him to read just one section, the section on monetary damages. Trump then points out he doesn't have his glasses and the text is very small. Donald then proceeds to read silently at first then audibly, correctly summarizing the details demonstrating comprehension.

I chuckled at Trump's audible sighs and complaints about how long the material is. I had never seen an adult behave like that, but I have seen hundreds of students do the same things. I will give him kudos for persevering and successfully reading, as he genuinely appeared to want to please the interviewer

---

trump-pelosi-and-schumer-2018-12-11.

[37] "Tools: DSM-IV Criteria for ASDs." *DSM-IV Criteria for ASDs* | Autism Research Institute, www.autism.com/tools_dsm4.

despite his lawyers objections heard in the background of the tape. This we call "teacher-pleasing skills" in the world of education.

When the President has been seen with written instructions, they are always printed in a large font size which appears to be at least size 24, making it easier for him to see. Two conclusions can be drawn from this. First, Trump doesn't wear glasses in public settings, but may do so in private. Trump not wearing glasses is similar to Roosevelt not using his wheelchair, and may have similar reasons for his choice of not wearing his glasses. Second, Trump read and demonstrated some literal comprehension of the lease he read, identifying what the main idea of the section given was. Literal comprehension is answering the "who, what, when and where" questions of any given text. They aren't that hard and are developed by most fourth graders. What isn't known is how well Trump understands inferential comprehension tasks, which are the "why" types of questions from his reading.

Someone who can read but doesn't is essentially functionally illiterate. As the President receives copious amounts of information in writing, and forty-five is known to avoid lengthy reading, he has to get his information another way in order to "do" his job. For Trump that source is the TV. [38]

Pete Davidson spoke on *The Opie* with Jim Norton radio show about Trump's time hosting the television show *Saturday Night Live*. In that interview dated November 16, 2015, Pete explained how Trump improved everything because he doesn't really know how to read.

"Yeah. So during like the table read he like—before, like, we were gonna read each before he had to read each line, and he's the host so he's in everything. He would go, uh, I'm not gonna say this. I think I'm gonna say it the way I want to say it. Is that okay? Is that okay, Lorne? Is that-everything-And everybody's like, what? And then this is my favorite part is there was a sketch that we wrote where he's at Disneyland with his daughter and the line is, uh all right, let's get out of here. Turkey legs? Like, let's go get turkey legs? And he doesn't know how to read, so he went, All right. Let's get out of here, Turkey Legs. He called his daughter Turkey Legs. And then he looked up. Like, he doesn't get it. Like, he thinks if everybody's laughing with him but we're all laughing at him.[39]

---

[38] The Chris Lapakko - The King of Earned Media. "Can Donald Trump Read?" *YouTube*, YouTube, 1 Oct. 2016, www.youtube.com/watch?v=WfaXILOSEf0.

[39] Radio, Opie. "Donald Trump CAN'T Read Says SNL Pete Davidson to Opie - SUBSCRIBE @OpieRadio PODCAST." *YouTube*, YouTube, 16 Nov. 2015, www.youtube.com/watch?v=PR7cQAjZsJI.

There is a social language and rulebook, full of idioms and hidden meaning that often our kiddos with severe disabilities do not have. Pete's comment on Trump is more correctly understood in that Trump is unable to read socially and expressively. Donald thinks very literal, while everybody else around him understands figuratively and more in depth than he does. This lack of pragmatics skill and judgment is a severe social impairment where he can't pick up that everybody is laughing at him. Trump does not get it—the social code and rules he cannot access.[40]

There certainly are other executive skills Trump seemingly lacks. His desk in many pictures mostly prior to his ascendency to the Presidency appears highly disorganized with piles of documents, books and other things haphazardly strewn all over. Occasionally, we see some of this on the Desk of Resolute, but more often than not, someone is likely cleaning up after the President as they already sort through the trash and pick up torn or shredded documents needing to be taped together and achieved anyway.[41]

Trump's poor executive functioning skills usually mean the United States isn't being adequately represented at world meetings. He doesn't listen, he doesn't pick up on cues and he doesn't report back to Congress and his cabinet sufficiently. At times, there are no witnesses or recorded notes to verify what was said or promised, such as with all his meetings with Putin. That has consequences when the American public must then trust foreign countries accounts of what happened as our President has proven incapable of doing his job. [42]

---

[40] Show, David Pakman. "Uh-Oh: Does Donald Trump Know How to Read?" *YouTube*, YouTube, 2 Feb. 2017, www.youtube.com/watch?v=bd79UsXSLWg.

[41] Hosie, Rachel. "Donald Trump's Messy Desk Could Be a Sign of Something Much Worse." *The Independent*, Independent Digital News and Media, 16 Feb. 2017, www.independent.co.uk/lifestyle/donald-trump-desk-messy-what-is-says-about-him-expert-opinion-a7583711.html.

[42] Cummings, William. "President Trump Went to 'Extraordinary Lengths' to Hide Details of Putin Meetings, Report Says." *USA Today*, Gannett Satellite Information Network, 14 Jan. 2019, www.usatoday.com/story/news/politics/2019/01/13/trump-putin-meetings-interpreter-notes/2565471002/.

Chapter Three

"Covfefe" Idiosyncratic Language and Cognitive Filtering

A *Newsweek* article written by Nina Burleigh on January 8, 2018, outlined a study of former Presidents and their language skills. Donald scored on a 4.6 grade level, the lowest of any modern President. The study took the first 30,000 spoken words of each President and used the Navy's Flesch-Kincaid scale to access where each President communicates when speaking. Trump scored at the bottom tier for every metric, from unique words uttered to fewest average syllables. What the article didn't specify was why. Our President's language is idiosyncratic a marker that strongly suggests Trump has an underlying developmental disorder. [43]

Idiosyncratic language is simplistic speech with repetitive patterns often including pragmatic and/or grammatical errors. Donald Trump's language has the errors, the simplicity and pragmatic disconnects that clearly define what he says and writes himself as idiosyncratic. Take this example of Trump's border security speech given on *January 10, 2019*:

> *"They say a wall is medieval. Well so is a wheel. A wheel is older than a wall. And I looked and every single car out there, even the really 'expensivest' ones have (pause) the secret service uses them.*

[43] Burleigh, Nina. "Trump Speaks at Fourth-Grade Level, Lowest of Last 15 U.S. Presidents, New Analysis Finds." *Newsweek*, 26 Feb. 2019, www.newsweek.com/trump-fire-and-fury-smart-genius-obama-774169?fbclid=IwAR14Uq43k-2Tp2TL-OKGUw-u0UaUtuFL65dOScQ7sHfOMTzmAVnl-GXJjWhs.

Believe me they are expensive. I said do they all have wheels? Yes.
Oh, I thought that was medieval. The wheel is older than a wall,
you know that? And uh there are some things that work, you know
what? A wheel works, and a wall works."[44]

Trump wasn't intending to talk about a wheel. It just happened, likely because he made an association with "medieval" in his previous statement. He made a grammatical error, caught himself and paused after saying "expensivest" indicating awareness he had said something wrong. He then identifies how he got off topic by saying, "Yes, oh, I thought that was medieval." This is an example of a pragmatic error, as it left out key information explaining how Trump connected walls and wheels. Both are medieval.

In the second of James Comey's memos about his interactions with President Trump, dated 1/28/17, James had this to say about their conversation at dinner:

> *"The conversation, which was pleasant at all times, was chaotic,*
> *with topics touched, left, then returned to later, making it very dif-*
> *ficult to recount in a linear fashion. Normally I can recall the pieces*
> *of a conversation and the order of discussion with high confidence.*
> *Here, given the nature of it, there is a distinct possibility that, while*
> *I have the substance right, the order was slightly different. It really*
> *was conversation-as-jigsaw-puzzle in a way, with pieces picked up,*
> *then discarded, then returned to."*[45]

In a nutshell, what James was describing, is how I also sometimes speak, which is circuitous in nature, one of my autistic flickers. Trump does this all the time, which from a pragmatic standpoint confuses most people as they can't follow the connectivity or critical details needed to understand the story or the context are left out. I worked and still work on this.

Trump's *January 2, 2019,* Cabinet meeting was more than an hour long and quite entertaining due to the plethora of language misuse, and Trump's near complete lack of filter before he speaks. Below are a couple examples.

---

[44] Factbase. "Transcript Quote - Remarks: Donald Trump Holds a Roundtable on Border Security in McAllen, Texas - January 10, 2019." *Factbase*, factba.se/transcript/donald-trump-remarks-round-table-border-security-mcallen-texas-january-10-2019.

[45] Day, Chad, and Associated Press. "Ex-FBI Director James Comey's Memos." *DocumentCloud*, www.documentcloud.org/documents/4442900-Ex-FBI-Director-James-Comey-s-memos.html.

"Okay. Thank you very much. Thank you all for being here and joining the first Cabinet meeting of 2019. It's going to be a very exciting year. I think it's going to be a very good year. Some people think it'll be controversial and tough, and it probably will, but we're going to get a lot done. I think we can work with the Democrats, actually, and get quite a bit done. And we're looking at infrastructure, we're looking at many things that can happen and I think that both sides want."

Note the stereotypical pattering of how he launches into his off-the-cuff speech. He repeats his welcome and how he thinks the year will be with little variation each over the first four sentences. This is often how emerging writers in the early grades express themselves, repeating the same idea with sleight repetition. By fourth grade, they have typically developed deeper communication skills and phase out the redundancy. For an adult to express such frequent patterning is clearly marked as atypical. Here is what Trump said later that got the most coverage.

"I mean, I'll give you an example. So, Taliban is our enemy. ISIS is our enemy. We have an area that I brought up with our generals four or five weeks ago, where Taliban is here, ISIS is here, and they're fighting each other. I said, 'Why don't you let them fight?' Why are we getting in the middle of it? I said, 'Let them fight. They're both our enemies. Let them fight.' 'Sir, we want to do it.' They go in and they end up fighting both of them. It's the craziest thing I've ever seen. I think I would've been a good general, but who knows. But you know what? These are two enemies that are fighting against each other, and we end up going in and fighting. And what are we doing?"[46]

Note the self-assuredness in saying maybe he would have been a good general. That got a lot of attention, and rightly so as a leader rarely blurts out such statements. The reason Trump does is that he lacks the ability to cognitively

---

[46] Factbase. "Transcript Quote - Remarks: Donald Trump Holds a Cabinet Meeting at The White House - January 2, 2019." *Factbase,* factba.se/transcript/donald-trump-remarks-cabinet-meeting-january-2-2019.

filter before speaking. Most adults have developed social inhibitions that filter out inappropriate things. We may think, *Hey, honey, you are looking fat and tired today.* What we actually say hopefully is entirely different and maintains our relationship with our spouse. To someone who doesn't filter, they will just blurt out the fat and tired comment and often do not understand why others are upset or throwing objects at them.

Rambling in front of the cameras in front of the devastation of the wildfires in California on November 17, 2018, Trump goes on-the-record with another gem:

> *"We're all committed, I'm committed, to make sure that we get all of this cleaned out and protected, take care of the floors. You know, the floors of the forests, very important. You look at other countries, where they do it differently, and it's a whole different story. I was with the President of Finland and he said, we have a much different—we're a forest nation. He called it a forest nation, and they spent a lot of time on raking and cleaning and doing things, and they don't have any problem, and when it is, it's a very small problem."*[47]

Eighty people died between the multiple fires that swept through the state that month. Trump, who may not spend much time in the wilderness judging by what he said, may not know how quickly forest debris gather, particularly in the fall time when leaves drop. The President of Finland story was made up but the anger and resentment for what he said in light of many deaths lingered.

On January 12, 2019, Trump in New Orleans was the key note speaker for the American Farm Bureau Federation's 100th Annual Convention. Trump spends a good part of his opening speech noting who was in attendance. When he identifies Steve Scalise, a GOP Congressman who had been shot and Trump had visited in the hospital, Trump can't help himself, due to lack of filter and overwhelming cognitive association of who Steve is in respect to Trump, to then blurt out the following:

---

[47] Canty, Jennifer. "Transcript Quote - Remarks: Donald Trump Discusses Wildfire Damage in Paradise, California - November 17, 2018." *Factbase*, CantyMedia, factba.se/transcript/donald-trump-remarks-paradise-fire-damage-tour-november-17-2018.

"And the legend from Louisiana—a man who's got a lot of courage. He was playing second base and it didn't work out so well for him that day, but I have never seen anybody with more strength and really more courage than Steve Scalise. Steve Scalise. (Applause.) He got hit hard. He got hit hard. He never even thought about quitting."

"He—I was there the night, in his hospital. And they didn't think he was going to make it. And I looked at him; he wasn't looking too good, I have to tell you. This is the first time I'm telling you this, Steve; you weren't looking too sharp. And his wife loves him, because she was a mess. She had tears pouring down. I'll tell you a couple of these little facts. Your family loves you, Steve." [48]

Trump tends to fixate on things. Does Steve need to be reminded of his being shot in front of thousands of people? Does Steve being shot have anything to do with farms? The answers are no, but Trump can't help it, and Trump had to let everyone know what happened to Steve replete with frequent repetition and errors that mark what he says as idiosyncratic. The reason Steve Scalise and his being shot is such a strong association for Trump is that he visited Steve in the hospital, forever connecting the shooting to the man.

Lack of cognitive filtering isn't limited to blurting things out. It explains why Trump in the shutdown was unable to predict possible outcomes of many of his biggest failings as President. Trump sat in his hotel in Paris for Armistice Day instead of attending an event at a mostly American cemetery due to rain while others traveled and attended in a car. Trump shut down the Federal Government for thirty-five days and ended with less than what he had agreed to prior to the shutdown when he found no one willing to give in to his demands. When cognitive filtering is as poor as Trump's is, the results of his actions will generally appear rash and impulsive and generate poor results.

Perhaps the most entertaining example of Trump's inability to properly filter was a 2005, published on February 3, 2016, previously unreleased clip from the Conan O'Brien show. Trump was asked to pour some water. He did the expected behavior, pouring the water into a glass, then went and did the

---

[48] Factbase. "Transcript Quote - Speech: Donald Trump Addresses the American Farm Bureau Federation Convention - January 14, 2019." *Factbase*, factba.se/transcript/donald-trump-speech-american-farm-bureau-new-orleans-louisiana-january-14-2019.

autistic unexpected thing of pouring water directly onto the table. This complete lack of inhibition is typical for preschool-aged children, and generally isn't observed by grade two for normally developed children. It is extremely off putting seeing an adult that has not developed normal cognitive filtering that would tell him that this was not a correct thing to do socially, as is seen in Trump's behavior. Here is what Trump said after a brief pause and looking up into the camera:

> *Trump: "You didn't think of that did you, huh? Alright is that okay with you?*
> *Unknown: "Sure."*
> *Trump: "Why not?"*
> *Unknown: (inaudible)*
> *Trump: "Do you like it or not?"*
> *Unknown: "We'll keep that as an option."*
> *Trump: "I thought that was very funny."*[49]

What was intriguing is Trump's reaction just after he had poured the water all over the table as it reminded me of my toddler. She looks up that same way when caught playing in the toilet, bath or sink as she loves fooling around with water. It is a developmental stage I have enjoyed immensely. Trump, a grown man, still playing with water is no longer cute, even if he covers his mistake with self-deprecating humor.

Trump's Fox interview with Maria Bartiromo on April 12, 2017, the President describes telling Xi that he just launched an attack using fifty-nine missiles while eating the most delicious piece of chocolate cake. Who knew that chocolate and death would fit so perfectly into a presidential conversation?

> *Trump: "I will tell you. Only because you treated me so good for so long I have to tell you, right? I was sitting at the table, we had finished dinner, we're now having dessert and we had the most beautiful piece of chocolate cake that you've ever seen and President Xi was enjoying it, and I was given the message from the generals that the ships are locked and loaded, what do you do? And we made a determination to do it.*

---

[49] "Donald Trump Secrets Very Funny Outtake (2005)." *YouTube*, 3 Feb. 2016, youtu.be/nzPEwaN4bGM.

So the missiles were on the way and I said, Mr. President, let me explain something to you. This is your dessert. We just fired 59 missiles all of which hit, by the way, unbelievable from, you know, hundreds of miles away, all of which had—
Maria: Unmanned.
Trump: So incredible, it's brilliant, it's genius. Our technology, our equipment is better than anybody by a factor of five. I mean, what we have in terms of technology, nobody can even come close to competing. Now we're going to start getting it because, you know, the military has been cut back and depleted so badly by the past administration and by the war in Iraq which was another disaster. So what happens is I said, we just launched 59 missiles heading to Iraq.
Maria: Headed to Syria.
Trump: Yes. Yes, heading toward Syria. And I want you to know that. Because I didn't want him to go home, we're almost finished, it was a full day in Palm Beach. We're almost finished and what does he do? Finishes dessert and go home and then they say, you know, the guy you just had dinner with just attacked—
Maria: How did he react?
Trump: So he paused for 10 seconds. And then he asked the interpreter to please say it again, I didn't think that was a good sign. And he said to me, anybody that uses gasses, you could almost say or anything else but anybody that was so brutal and uses gasses to do that to young children and babies, it's OK. [50]

There is so much in this dialogue to digest. First, Trump made a very strong association with *"the most beautiful piece of chocolate cake that you've ever seen."* These powerful cognitive associations Trump drops out on the fly add a great deal of character, though often comical, to the persona Trump wants to convey as an everyday man. These connections come up quite frequently in his communication, and generally do not logically fit, often due to the connection being socially inappropriate or some other oddity. In this case, Trump should have waited till after the cake to tell Xi.

Second, Trump named the wrong country he just sent death to. Trump has not had the best record on being accurate in his interviews or his speeches,

---

[50] Factbase. "Transcript Quote - Fox Business: Maria Bartiromo Interviews Donald Trump - April 12, 2017." *Factbase*, factba.se/transcript/donald-trump-interview-fox-business-april-12-2017.

and that should be most concerning as a misspoken word or action by our leader could lead to a diplomatic or other crisis.

Third, Trump makes personal connections, at least to his understanding he does, quite well. Note how at the beginning he talks about being "treated so good" by Maria. The correct word should have been "well," not "good," just another one of Trump's grammatical errors. However, that positive treatment happens to be the key to manipulating a person as socially vulnerable as Donald is and getting him to do what you want. Once someone has earned his trust, Donald will do something in return. In this case he shares a story.

I have seen this happen so often with unsuspecting students with social deficits. People "earn" their trust, use them and then walk away while the consequence of whatever they did stays mostly with the unintentional accomplice. I'll delve further into that manipulation both by Donald and using Donald in later chapters.

Addressing a packed room of Law Enforcement July 28, 2017, in Long Island, New York, Trump reminisces about the "biggest" brigade he had in Chicago with likely excessive exaggeration of 300 motorcycles. Trump has a strong tendency to use certain words or phrases, and "biggest" whether he is talking about parades or crowd size is Trump's way of conveying deep meaning with his limited lexicon.

"But we're in Chicago, and we had massive motorcycle bridges, and you know those people have to volunteer. I don't know if you know that, but from what I understand, they have to volunteer. And I had the biggest brigades. I had brigades sometimes with almost 300 motorcycles. Even I was impressed. I'd look ahead and it was nothing but motorcycles because they'd volunteer from all over various states."

Trump then continues his roundabout journey to his main point, about killings in Chicago, in an entertaining manner connecting some nameless "rough" cookie—instead of tough cookie—he suggested to the mayor to fix the problem:

"But this one guy was impressive. He was a rough cookie and really respected guy. I could see he was respected. And he said, 'All right, come on, get over here. Get over here. He's got to get to work. Get over here.' And I said, 'So let me tell—you're from Chicago?' 'Yes, sir.' I said, 'What the hell is going on?'

"And he said, 'It's a problem; it can be straightened out.' I said, 'How long would it take you to straighten out this problem?' He said, 'If you gave me the authority, a couple of days.' [Laughter] I really mean it. I said, 'You really think so?' He said, 'A couple of days. We know all the bad ones. We know them all.' And he said, the offi-

cers—you guys, you know all the bad ones in your area. You know them by their names. He said, 'We know them all. A couple of days.'

"I said, 'You got to be kidding.' Now, this is a year and a half ago. I said, 'Give me your card.' And he gave me a card. And I sent it to the mayor. I said, 'You ought to try using this guy.' [Laughter] Guess what happened? Never heard. And last week they had another record. It's horrible."

Note the repetition of phrases and words. Ask yourself, is there missing information needed to understand what Donald is saying? The name of the officer isn't that necessary, but what the problem the officer was talking about, the key missing element of the story is. Donald had mentioned it earlier in the speech before sidetracking on the brigade obscuring the point of what he was talking about.[51]

Pragmatic errors like this are still my bane. As I have been working on this since I became aware it was a problem in my teens, I am able to follow and understand what Trump is saying, especially when I can read and listen to it over and over again, more so than media types.

On *The Howard Stern Show*, April 12, 2010, Trump mentioned attending a funeral for yet another "unnamed" employee of forty-seven years that had worked for him. Stern then asked what he had died from, Trump responds:

Trump: *"Well, probably went to the dentist's. You ever hear the dentist's stuff? You remember, Steve Floria right from [inaudible]? He went to the dentist and you get an infection and it affects the heart and then, you have a stroke."*
Stern: *"That's awful."*
Trump: *"Longest guy you've ever seen."*
Stern: *"Wow."*
Trump; *"Had a stroke and died. And by the way, that happened to Steve Florio at [inaudible] who was a great friend of mine. Went to a dentist. I'm afraid to go to a dentist."*
Stern: *"And he got an infection?"*
Trump: *"It seems that way, yes. It would seem that way. That seems to be the theory."*
Stern: *"Wow, that's awful. Have you been—"*

---

51 Factbase. "Transcript Quote - Remarks: Donald Trump Gives Remarks on MS-13 to Law Enforcement - July 28, 2017." *Factbase*, factba.se/transcript/donald-trump-speech-ms13-law-enforcement-july-28-2017.

Trump: *"That happens, by the way a lot."*
Stern:_"Have you been—"_
Trump: *"Beware of dentist."*[52]

Think of this conversation in the context of a very scared young child. Just ignore that this was a man in his sixties. His language is more of a child of seven or eight years old due to the idiosyncratic nature of his language. He also conveys a generalized irrational fear because Steve Florio, his friend, went to a dentist and died, that if he too went to a dentist, he might die as well. Stern changes the conversation to Tiger Woods and sex which removes the tension quickly arousing Trump's other faculties. This was probably for the best as Donald was likely to perseverate on morbidity without a quick intervention.

> *"We just got back from Florida. It's been a rough time for Florida. But the first responders and the Coast Guard, and to all of the people—FEMA—all of the people that worked so hard have done an A-plus job.*
>
> *"You know, we had—as you know very well, some of you are from Texas and some of you are from Florida. And you both got hit. In Texas you got hit with the largest amount of water anybody has ever seen. I guess the largest ever recorded. And in Florida you got hit with the strongest winds ever recorded. It actually hit the Keys with a—it was a Category 5. I never even knew a Category 5 existed. And they suffered greatly.*
>
> *"But in both bases, and in other cases such as Alabama, Louisiana, and plenty of others—Puerto Rico; the Virgin Islands was hit brutally, brutally. It got hit dead center with a strong five. And it's almost not standing, but the people are standing. And some incredible things have happened."*[53]

No one does idiosyncratic language quite like the Donald. This speech at the White House Historical Association on September 14, 2017, has the hallmarks

---

[52] Factbase. "Transcript Quote - Interview: Donald Trump on *The Howard Stern Show* - April 12, 2010." *Factbase*, factba.se/transcript/donald-trump-interview-howard-stern-show-april-12-2010.

[53] Canty, Jennifer. "Transcript Quote - Remarks: Donald Trump Speaks at a White House Historical Association Reception - September 14, 2017." *Factbase*, CantyMedia, factba.se/transcript/donald-trump-remarks-white-house-historical-association-september-14-2017.

of Trump's everything is bigger, even the disaster statistics, under his leader-ship. The main quote, *"In Texas you got hit with the largest amount of water any-body has ever seen,"* even Noah from the Old Testament likely was pulling out records to compare with Trump's claims.

There were just too many juicy tidbits to pass by with JUST the water quote. Bases? I think Trump intended to say places as he was referring to Florida and Texas. He often gets his words mixed up, and keeps on going blissfully unaware of the error just like he did here. Then we have his statement of him not knowing there was such a thing as a category five, referring to the magnitude of Hurri-canes. Like many Autistics, Trump is making a sincere truthful statement in an unexpected way. Trump appeared genuinely surprised to learn something new.

Trump cannot stop himself from making careless mistakes no matter how hard he tries, as he has been doing this probably all of his life. I can pull up almost any interview or speech and find at least one if not dozens of the most head-scratching lines made possible by Trump's inability to filter or his idiosyncrasies. Below is a sampling of just a few of his greatest cognitive misfires, or Trumpisms:

"This is an island surrounded by water—big water, ocean water."[54]

Trump describing Puerto Rico on September 29, 2017, at the National Asso-ciation of Manufacturers meeting.

> *"We also stand with the millions of people who have suffered from the massive fires, which are right now raging in California, and the catastrophic hurricanes along the Gulf Coast, in Puerto Rico, the U.S. Virgin Islands. And I will tell you, I left Texas, and I left Florida, and I left Louisiana, and I went to Puerto Rico, and I met with the president of the Virgin Islands."*[55]

Trump is the President of the Virgin Islands, as well as all US territories. Note the sparse use of the word "I" and "left." That is idiosyncratic and total Trumpian.

---

[54] Factbase. "Transcript Quote - Remarks: Donald Trump Addresses the National Association of Manufacturers - September 29, 2017." *Factbase*, factba.se/transcript/donald-trump-remarks-na-tional-association-manufacturers-september-29-2017.

[55] Factbase. "Transcript Quote - Speech: Donald Trump Addresses the Value Voters Summit - Octo-ber 13, 2017." *Factbase*, factba.se/transcript/donald-trump-speech-value-voters-summit-october-13-2017.

This came from the October 13, 2017, Speech Value Voters Summit.

> *"Now, we're getting them out anyway, but we'd like to get them out a lot faster. And when you see these towns and when you see these thugs being thrown into the back of a paddy wagon—you just see them thrown in, rough—I said, please don't be too nice. Like when you guys put somebody in the car and you're protecting their head, you know, the way you put their hand over? Like, don't hit their head and they've just killed somebody—don't hit their head. I said, you can take the hand away, okay?"[56]*

Trump again addressing Long Island police officers on July 28, 2017, essentially telling them it is okay to harm suspects during arrests. Trump does not fully comprehend why saying such a thing is problematic, as he lacks typical judgement skills most develop in their early teens.

While unintentional, funny and surprisingly truthful given his own administration's track record on these issues, this quote about ending Civil Rights was misread off a prepared speech from teleprompter:

> *"…Our sons, the pride of our Nation, on this day have set upon a mighty endeavor, a struggle to preserve our Republic, our religion, and our civilization. Since the founding of our nation, many of our greatest strides—from gaining our independence, to abolition of civil rights, to extending the vote for women—have been led by people of faith and started in prayer."[57]*

Trump's poor grammar, word choice, syntax and frequent errors are more reminiscent of the speaking ability for children aged seven to eight years old, easily fulfilling the requirement of severe communication deficits needed for an Autism Spectrum Disorder.

---

[56] Factbase. "Transcript Quote - Remarks: Donald Trump Gives Remarks on MS-13 to Law Enforcement - July 28, 2017." *Factbase*, factba.se/transcript/donald-trump-speech-ms13-law-enforcement-july-28-2017.

[57] Factbase. "Transcript Quote - Remarks: Donald Trump Addresses the National Prayer Breakfast - February 7, 2019." *Factbase*, factba.se/transcript/donald-trump-remarks-prayer-breakfast-februray-7-2019.

Chapter Four

"Special Friends and Very Special People"

I would bet that Donald Trump would get along smashingly well with Robert Mueller should the two ever sit down for a heart to heart chat over the whole Russia investigation. I really do. Why? Donald Trump has a very strong desire to please others while having very limited ability to effectively "read" those people he interacts with.

When giving the recorded deposition on June 16, 2016, 10:30 A.M., mentioned previously, Donald made great effort to please the speaker asking him to read, tuning out the frequent objections of his lawyer, instead engaging in "teacher pleasing behavior" as we call it in the Special Education world. Trump knows his lawyer really well by this point, and is likely engaging with the person asking the questions for the first time making his behavior quite interesting. Trump did not fully grasp that this was not a social situation and was potentially risky tuning out his attorney and working to please the judge or prosecutor in the recording.

We have seen a consistent pattern to Don's social behavior in many of his interviews and recordings. He starts talking and talking, with very little reciprocity from his audience, even when they are the one conducting the interview. He sees that they are listening and finds that reinforcing. That reinforcement may lead to an action by Trump that demonstrates his appreciation, such as a story, when they are giving him adequate attention.

Trump tells Maria Bartiromo of Fox on April 12, 2017, *"I will tell you. Only because you treated me so good for so long I have to tell you, right?"* Then Trump rewards Maria with the story about Xi, the most delicious piece of chocolate cake and the fifty-nine missiles.[58]

Sharing a story to reward a newfound friend is perfectly fine, as a story is something social and rarely has meaning or significance beyond that. What if Trump were to repeat this behavior as President of the United States? Wouldn't that potentially have far-reaching consequences as he has access to many things that should not be shared or given to a foreign adversary? This is a very common refrain with many children with moderate to severe cognitive disabilities, giving away their stuff. So, what if Trump also gave away American secrets, technology or other things?

Trump has.

When Trump decided on his own to meet two Russian officials Sergei Lavrov and Sergey Kislyak in the Oval Office on May 10, 2017, ignoring all established protocols and safeguards set in place to protect the United States government, the three men became smashingly close friends. While other administration officials and American media were locked out, Russia had been given exclusive access to the story, with at least a reporter and photographer on record in attendance. The White House also had a photographer and likely an interpreter at the meeting. TASS, a state-sponsored Russian News media outlet had a field day trolling the unsuspecting Trump with their exclusive reporting of the event.

Trump was in a jovial mood having "killed" the Russian investigation the day before by firing the "nut job" head of the FBI James Comey, and even bragged about the great pressure being off of him. According to a *NY Times* report on May 19, 2017, by Matt Apuzzo, Maggie Haberman and Matthew Rosenberg based on a document read of the event, Trump said the following:

> *"I just fired the head of the FBI. He was crazy, a real nut job."*
> *"I faced great pressure because of Russia. That's taken off."*
> *"I'm not under investigation."*[59]

If only Trump's misunderstanding of how firing the FBI director wasn't going to end the investigation was the big story of the event. Trump buddying

[58] Factbase. "Transcript Quote - Fox Business: Maria Bartiromo Interviews Donald Trump - April 12, 2017." *Factbase*, factba.se/transcript/donald-trump-interview-fox-business-april-12-2017.

[59] Relman, Eliza. "Bombshell Report Reveals New Details about Trump's Oval Office Meeting with Russians after He Fired Comey." *Business Insider*, Business Insider, 24 Nov. 2017, www.businessinsider. com/bombshell-report-trump-oval-office-meeting-russians-comey-2017-11.

up to the Russians turned over classified intelligence reports he felt interested the Russian Federation as a gift which was much more significant as that poor judgement would reverberate through allied intelligence agencies questioning whether sharing secrets with the US under Trump could continue.

"I get great intel. I have people brief me on great intel every day."[60]

Those reports were given to the US by Israeli intelligence officials who successfully planted a listening device in a Syrian compound in a clandestine operation. To even know where the compound was, likely took years of painstaking work to plant an Israeli agent into ISIS and gain trust within the organization. The device picked up the details of an undetectable suitcase bomb capable of easily taking down a plane by Saudi national Ibrahim al-Asiri, expert bomb master.

What was the cost of Trump's ignorant and cavalier betrayal of Israel's trust? What of the spy? One Israeli intelligence officer had this to say:

"Whatever happened to him, it's a hell of price to pay for a president's mistake."[61]

Likely all US allies took pause at how Trump's lack of critical judgement led to him giving away shared secrets to others. So did our enemies. One of them already had got Donald's attention and was ready for his turn accepting things from a gracious President.

Trump, the dealmaker, who doesn't listen, doesn't read briefings became the first sitting US President to engage North Korea directly after mansplaining who had bigger red buttons and threatening fiery death to the hermit kingdom of North Korea.

I have been fascinated by North Korea as much as I have been with Mr. Trump, so I know a great deal more about the country than a reasonable person would. Such extensive fascinations are part of my shades of Autism after all. Most of my information came from my father, with some gathered from reading news reports. My father who served in the Korean War era in the Army, related the story of traveling alone by jeep northward past the Demilitarized Zone as part of an intelligence gathering mission. Dad parked the jeep facing towards the South if he needed to make a quick retreat. He fortunately was ignored. Dad took pictures from an opposing ridge where

---

[60] Apuzzo, Matt, et al. "Trump Told Russians That Firing 'Nut Job' Comey Eased Pressure From Investigation." *The New York Times*, The New York Times, 19 May 2017, www.nytimes.com/2017/05/19/us/politics/trump-russia-comey.html.

[61] Blum, Howard. "Exclusive: What Trump Really Told Kislyak After Comey Was Canned." *The Hive, Vanity Fair,* 21 Dec. 2017, www.vanityfair.com/news/2017/11/trump-intel-slip.

he could safely view and photograph DPRK troops conducting "drills." The troops were planting.

For years these springtime troop movements had sent the US and allies on edge anticipating a possible invasion from the North. My father's Intel explained what was happening and perhaps formed the basis of the timing of joint South Korea and United States war games exercises, Team Spirit (1976 to 1993), during the planting season, late March. The timing would allow needed training exercise and readiness preparation while the North, relying on its military getting crops in the field were less able to respond with drills of their own least they starve their people.[62]

Those drills were renamed and ongoing until Donald Trump desperate to chalk up a Nobel Prize that his predecessor Obama had achieved was played by Kim, the leader of North Korea.

The objectives of North Korea regarding the United States are pretty clear and straight forward. First, they want a "denuclearized peninsula," meaning the removal of the US troops and hardware. Second, they want the joint drills ended. Third, they want to be acknowledged and treated as equals on the World stage. Fourth, they want an official end to the Korean War. Fifth they want the reunification of the two Koreas. When a man who had "*bone-spurs*" and a "*high draft number*" [63] dodges military service walks into high-level talks with a foreign military adversary without sufficient ability to understand what is going on, he is going to be at significant disadvantage in any negotiation, and it showed.

Trump, just by walking in and shaking Kim's hand with the flags of both countries displayed behind them, gave Kim and the DPRK equal footing, and objective number three on the their big list. This was done with no preconditions, after the North had demonstrated that they were nuclear, able to target the mainland US with a payload and could triangulate a prospective target. That is pretty advanced stuff.

I didn't add being a nuclear power on the list of North Korean objectives purposefully. Being a nuclear power, as they demonstrated in rapid fashion once Trump entered office, served the purpose to advancing objectives one,

---

[62] Johnson, Richard, and North. "A Brief History of the US-ROK Combined Military Exercises." 38 North, 24 Feb. 2017, www.38north.org/2014/02/rcollins022714/.

[63] "Donald Trump's Selective Service Records." *The New York Times*, The New York Times, 26 Dec. 2018, www.nytimes.com/interactive/2018/12/26/us/politics/trumpfeet-copy.html.

two, three, four and five. That ability is the glue that holds all other objectives together. I don't see North Korea giving up their program, as it defines who they are and what they want to be in a way nothing else can.

Trump met Kim on June 12, 2018, in Singapore, announced he was suspending the drills (objective two completed). Trump then declared that North Korea was no longer a threat; the GOP celebrated and even persuaded Abe to officially nominate Trump for the Nobel.[64]

"Prime Minister Abe of Japan gave me the most beautiful copy of a letter that he sent to the people who give out a thing called the Nobel Prize. He said, 'I have nominated you, respectfully, on behalf of Japan. I am asking them to give you the Nobel Peace Prize.' You know why? Because he had rocket ships and he had missiles flying over Japan. They feel safe. I did that."[65]

While the tests and missile launches did indeed stop, there were justifiable and logic reasons for this. The North completed every phase of testing nuclear capability and no longer needed to run such expensive tests. The same is true of their missile technology. Launching missiles is an expensive investment, especially considering how low their GDP is. I personally felt each of the nuclear tests conducted was a good thing in that they had less material for future bombs. That proved wrong when the last test revealed they advanced well beyond the old-school nuclear bombs to a higher form of nuclear detonation technology of their final test. That all happened under Trump as before, most rocket tests "failed" and likely did so due to US interference (a guess on my part).

The majority of aggressive actions over the years by the North has been attention seeking. The US is their main target, and for the most part past Presidents heed the advice of their military chiefs and intelligence officers and limit their engagement. Not so with Trump who claims he is smarter than those around him on a frequent basis. He engaged with fiery and bombastic broadsides that played well into what the North wanted, attention. Likely both Trump and Kim enjoyed the engagement immensely as it isn't nearly as much "fun" yelling at someone for the better part of two decades and they just ignore you.

---

[64] Copp, Tara. "President Trump Has Ordered the Pentagon to Cancel Military Exercises with South Korea - What Happens next?" *Military Times*, Military Times, 13 June 2018, www.militarytimes.com/ news/your-military/2018/06/12/pentagon-assessing-trump-directive-to-cancel-korea-military-exercises/.

[65] Factbase. "Transcript Quote - Remarks: Donald Trump Announces Border National Emergency at The White House - February 15, 2019." Factbase, factba.se/transcript/donald-trump-remarks-border-wall-emergency-february-15-2019.

Things went beyond yelling. The United States launched ICBM tests of its own, with missile interceptions of all displaying how well the Star Wars technology worked, a 55% successful intercept rate. Then Trump authorized the MOAB, the Mother of All Bombs, the largest conventional US bomb to be dropped flattening an Afghan hillside.[66][67]

Trump's military actions had consequences beyond North Korea. Russia and China both dropped their largest conventional bombs too, as well as designed plans to negate Star Wars defenses by either hacking or destroying the satellites that make the system work. Ever wonder why Trump created his big idea of Space Force? Perhaps his briefings on satellites being vulnerable to Russian and Chinese attacks had something to do with it. [68][69][70]

So what does this have to do with Social deficits? Trump gave away US intelligence to Russian spies because he was being "social" and showed lack of judgement about who he was interacting with. Trump doesn't get that not everyone is your friend that is being nice to you. With North Korea, his desire for a Nobel, a social need for recognition and comparison with a predecessor, led to revealing military operational secrets. He additionally gave away two important bargaining chips, things long sought from the North without getting anything sizeable in return. His social inability has put the United States and our allies at risk whenever he meets with foreign actors (and domestic) looking to exploit that weakness.

Trump's inability to read others socially isn't always just a threat to national security. Sometimes he instead just embarrasses the United States and himself on national stages.At the first G20, July 7-8, 2017, in Hamburg, Germany, Trump attended, UK Prime Minister May saved the day when she was aware Donald was sitting facing the wrong direction for a group picture as he missed the verbal signal to turn towards the camera man at the start of the

[66] Cooper, Helene, and Mujib Mashal. "U.S. Drops 'Mother of All Bombs' on ISIS Caves in Afghanistan." The New York Times, The New York Times, 13 Apr. 2017, www.nytimes.com/2017/04/13/world/ asia/moab-mother-of-all-bombs-afghanistan.html.

[67] Pickrell, Ryan. "Can America's Missile Defenses Really Beat ICBMs Fired from Russia, China or North Korea?" The National Interest, The Center for the National Interest, 2 June 2017, nationalinterest.org/ blog/the-buzz/can-americas-missile-defenses-really-beat-icbms-fired-russia-20973.

[68] CNN. "Meet the 'Father of All Bombs.'" YouTube, YouTube, 19 Apr. 2017, www.youtube.com/ watch?v=L_iEXyqItDw.

[69] "PressTV." China Unveils Footage of Own 'Mother of All Bombs', www.presstv.com/Detail/2019/01/ 04/584873/Chinese-Mother-of-All-Bombs.

[70] Gould, Joe. "Think Space Force Is a Joke? Here Are Four Major Space Threats to Take Seriously." Defense News, Defense News, 10 Aug. 2018, www.defensenews.com/space/2018/08/09/think-space-force-is-a-joke-here-are-four-major-space-threats-to-take-seriously/.

first working session. The likely reason he missed the verbal cue was that he didn't bother to put his earpiece in connecting him to an interpreter, however he should have picked up on the social cue when everyone else seated around the square seating arrangement shifted themselves towards something directly behind him and were smiling upward. This I believe was the earliest moment of his Presidency where it was clear that Trump doesn't pick up on social cues such as reading others body language. Social referencing is a very important skill, which Trump seems to have limited ability with.

Trump doesn't always wear an earpiece when "communicating" with foreign dignitaries. When he doesn't, he just goes through the motions, nodding his head and pretending to be listening when he clearly doesn't know the language being spoken. He did this with Abe during a White House visit February 10, 2017. He has been given the needed devices connecting him to an interpreter in two sizes. Most of the time Trump probably listens. Sometimes both the small and headphone types are spotted in pictures lying in front of Trump, or that he has none in his ear when viewed from both angles. It is possible that Trump more or less is faking it when he is unable to communicate, something one cannot do and adequately represent an entire country as President.[71]

Most embarrassing photos are snapped or taken from a paused video as a screenshot of Trump looking or doing something absurdly different from the rest of a social group or his family, are of short duration when viewed in video. For instance, Trump appears with his wife on the White House balcony and is corrected by her to put his hand over his heart for the national anthem very subtly on April 18, 2017, or when she nudges him to stand up when the crowd had been prompted "*if you love America*" by the Piano Guys at his inauguration. Being reliant on prompts and cues to demonstrate an expected social behavior is part of the territory with Autism, but can be learned and mastered as any behavior. [7273]

Perhaps the most ludicrous social mistake Trump has made was his brief looking into the Sun during the solar eclipse on August 21st, 2017, appearing

[71] Novak, Matt. "President Trump's Translation Earpiece Is Just Really Small." *Gizmodo*, Gizmodo, 29 May 2017, gizmodo.com/president-trumps-translation-earpiece-is-just-really-sm-1795615655.

[72] Usborne, Simon. "Hand on Heart, This Star-Spangled Gesture Really Matters in the US." *The Guardian*, Guardian News and Media, 18 Apr. 2017, www.theguardian.com/us-news/shortcuts/2017/ apr/18/stars-and-stripes-gesture-donald-trump-nudge-national-anthem.

[73] Lucy Pasha-Robinson @lucypasha. "Donald Trump Had to Be Reminded to Stand up at His Own Inauguration Concert by Melania." *The Independent*, Independent Digital News and Media, 20 Jan. 2017, www.independent.co.uk/news/world/americas/donald-trump-inauguration-concert-president-elect-melania-reminded-stand-up-a7536476.html.

on the balcony and then squinting looking directly towards the event to the laughter of the press below. We constantly tell children to NOT look at the sun as it can damage your retinas permanently. There even are voices telling Trump to not do it during the video. He does so, starts acting silly to "hide" his mistake, finds the solar glasses in his pocket and puts them on and then looks again. The time he looked up without the glasses was brief, predictable and likely not too damaging to his eyes. His acting silly is a coping strategy many children develop to hide embarrassment.[74]

Being social is part of the human experience. There are rituals such as greeting that Trump has clearly struggled with, adopting such strange and comical jerks and pulls when engaged in a handshake with a foreign leader. The oddest ones in my opinion are his greetings with Angela Merkel. At a press conference when they met in the White House on March 17, 2017, there wasn't a handshake despite multiple requests.

The optics when Trump is sitting is poor to begin with. His legs are typically spread far apart and he leans forward. He tends to put his hands in front of him open with palms flat against each other and based on his expression he generally appears disconnected. If he is instead holding his arms in his self-hug, he is more engaged but still looks odd. This occasion was no different, with his hands touching and slumped posturing making him appear the same size as Merkel. As the cameras were flashing, voices urged the two to shake hand. Merkel speaking in English says, "They want to have a handshake." Trump just sort of sits there moving slightly his head with a blank flat affect expression unaware people are trying to engage him. Judging by his failure to register what was said and going on around him, he failed to show appropriate social approach.

The White House meeting on April 28, 2018, Trump actually kissed Merkel on her left cheek! This isn't part of German custom, rather French, which probably was a bit of a surprise given the lack of rapport that Trump had shown with Merkel in their previous White House encounter. This is an example of over-generalization, the learning of a skill or piece of knowledge and liberally applying it to other situations inappropriately. Macron had visited that week as a failed lobbying effort by the two leaders to persuade Trump from pulling out of the Iran treaty. There were kisses, and Macron is European.

---

74 Reuters, Source: "The Moment Donald Trump Is Warned Not to Look Directly at the Sun – Video." The Guardian, Guardian News and Media, 21 Aug. 2017, www.theguardian.com/us-news/video/2017/aug/21/donald-trump-look-directly-sun-eclipse-video.

Angela is European, therefore I should kiss her on the cheek when greeting. Trump overgeneralizes a lot of things, another sign of a cognitive developmental difference compared with the average population. Trump and Merkel had plenty of handshakes at this meeting and others at several summits.[75]

There eventually was this incredibly awkward moment captured of the two sort of shaking hands, with both again seated in the White House, Trump's right hand extended over and holding Merkel's thumb of her right hand and both looking forward not at each other. Merkel is smiling, and Trump with his flat affect expression likely speaking to whoever they are looking at as his mouth is slightly open. Merkel and Trump have the best collection of strange interactions currently of Forty-Five and foreign leaders.[76]

Likely the most blatant social skill failing at a major summit was the May 25, 2017, NATO summit where Trump grabbed and shoved his way past the gasping Prime Minister of Montenegro then adjusted his suitcoat obliviously while moving forward to a staging area for picture taking. Trump in this instance failed to recognize the social cues of waiting his turn or getting someone's attention and was unaware he had crossed acceptable behavior even after the social offense.[77]

On July 18, 2018, Trump comments to Tucker Carlson, of Fox News, when asked directly about the country Montenegro in relation to NATO obligations made this faulty and contrasting statement about the country whose leader he shoved aside a year earlier:

"By the way, they're very strong people. They're very aggressive people. They may get aggressive. And, congratulations, you are in World War III."[78]

Most of the US traditional "friendships" under the Trump era have become shaky or turned into extreme distrust due to Donald's social deficits as he has been pretty "set in his ways" about his perception of the world and

---

[75] Nelson, Soraya Sarhaddi. "Merkel And Trump Meeting Includes Some Strange Moments, But No Tangible Results." NPR, NPR, 28 Apr. 2018, www.npr.org/sections/parallels/2018/04/28/606369041/merkel-and-trump-meeting-includes-some-strange-moments-but-no-tangible-results.

[76] Bender, Michael C. "Trump Displays Warmth for Merkel at White House Despite Differences." *The Wall Street Journal,* Dow Jones & Company, 27 Apr. 2018, www.wsj.com/articles/merkel-meets-trump-at-white-house-1524870641.

[77] "Watch Trump Shove the Prime Minister of Montenegro out of the Way." *YouTube*, 26 May 2017, youtu.be/-xeCgOhCFiA.

[78] Factbase. "Transcript Quote - Interview: Tucker Carlson Interviews Donald Trump in Helsinki - July 17, 2018." *Factbase*, factba.se/transcript/donald-trump-interview-tucker-carlson-fox-helsinki-july-17-2018.

doing what he feels is best for America. These core beliefs are a huge part of understanding Donald's Autism as they further build a case to support a diagnosis being prime examples of restricted patterns of behavior.

Chapter Five

"Thoughts and Prayers" Parkland High Shooting

We probably have all seen toddlers or other very young children overwhelmed having extreme emotional outbursts in public places. Having young children myself, it can be quite embarrassing and a learning moment for both parent and child when these behaviors are put on full display, especially when passing a toy or sugary treat in the supermarket. A two- or three-year old is not emotionally equipped to handle these moments as the brain hasn't fully matured. We expect an occasional meltdown or two, especially if our little duplicates of ourselves haven't had their naps. An adult exhibiting these behaviors, especially one who is in his seventies and should in theory know better, provides fodder for late-night comedians and comedy writers, while also showing significant evidence of developmental delays connected to the core of what Autism is all about.

Donald meltdowns are generally reported by unnamed White House staffers but not directly documented via video or photographic evidence. When they are, sensational and unforgettable imagery almost always ensue. His verbal explosions on twitter are a daily occurrence and signs that he isn't emotionally capable of handling the stress of the Presidency. With both reports from his office staff former and current, a handful of explosive interviews and his twitter feed, I clearly believe it is accurate to say that Donald Trump has more meltdowns than is typical for his age. The behaviors are just simplistic means to manipulate others.

Donald's inability to project compassion, empathy and sincerity following tragedy is probably the most difficult and painful aspect of his personality for others to understand. It isn't that Donald doesn't care; rather he may not have the capability or capacity to care due to the significance of his emotional disability. He has had many opportunities to act as comforter-in-chief, an unofficial yet vital Presidential role, and has failed in most of his attempts to show the correct emotional responses and interpersonal interactions we have come to expect of a President. Following isn't a comprehensive list, just a sampling of the consistent patterns of failure to show the appropriate behavior and emotional response that Trump has had as President.

After the Parkland High School shooting in Florida where seventeen lost their lives, Trump hosted some of these students for a discussion on school safety at the White House on February 21, 2018. A staffer did a wonderful job of preparing the President with at least three statements he should say that would demonstrate empathy. These notes are true gems in the Special Education world as we sometimes need to role play with children so they can learn these social skill lessons.

The side that was visible in the video was held towards the audience and on "THE WHITE HOUSE" notebook-sized stationery. The list contained the following with words in parentheses guessed based on contextual clues as they were covered by Trump's fingers:

What would you most want me to know about your experience?

What can we do to help you feel safe?

Do you (?) see something (?) effective?

Resources? Ideas?

I hear you.

Donald's hands blocked one to one more talking point grouped under number two's heading with a question mark being visible, meaning they were likely different ways to ask students about safety.[79]

Trump kicked off the listening session effectively going through the motions of what needed to be said to start the meeting. Then he introduced and had Mike Pence and Secretary of Education Betsy Devos speak. Both spoke articulate and in a meaningful sincere way that likely connected to the students and parents in the room.

---

[79] Klein, Betsy. "Trump's Note Card for Parkland Shooting Discussion: 'I Hear You.'" *CNN*, Cable News Network, 22 Feb. 2018, www.cnn.com/2018/02/21/politics/trump-parkland-notecard/index.html.

Trump then speaks, and as he so often does when before a crowd, he says what they want to hear:

"Thank you very much, Betsy. And I just want to say before we really begin—because I want to hear your input—we're going to be very strong on background checks. We're going to be doing very strong background checks. Very strong emphasis on the mental health of somebody. And we are going to do plenty of other things."

"Again, next week, the governors are coming in from most of the states, and we're going to have a very serious talk about what's going on with school safety. Very important. And we're going to cover every aspect of it. There are many ideas that I have."

"There are many ideas that other people have. And we're going to pick out the strongest ideas, the most important ideas, the ideas that are going to work. And we're going to get them done. It's not going to be talk like it has been in the past. It's been going on too long; too many instances. And we're going to get it done."

"So, again, I want to thank you all for being here. And I'd like to hear your story. And I'd also like to, if you have any suggestions for the future based on this horrible experience that you've gone through—I'd love to have those ideas. How about we start with you."

For the next roughly half-hour students and parents shared their stories and pled for action. Trump looked and made eye contact, showing physically he was present. With each grief-filled story related complete, Trump responded with a terse polite and non-specific acknowledgement. Here are all thirteen including two yes responses when the one with the microphone asked to give it to someone else.

"I really appreciate it."
"Thank you."
"Yes. Sure— to give a mic to someone.
"That's great. Thank you very much. Thank you."
"Thank you. I appreciate it."

"Thanks. Very nice."
"Thank you. Thank you very much."
"Thank you."
"Thank you."
"Thank you. Thank you very much."
"Yes."
"Thank you. Appreciate it. Thank you."
"Thank you. Thank you."

Between "thank you" and "I appreciate it," there wasn't much variation in Trump's almost scripted response to each suggestion and shared experience. On cue, Trump utters those two familiar refrains before adding some variety to his response:

> *"Thank you very much. I appreciate that. This is an incredible group of people, and we really do appreciate it. Some of the folks in the back, and some of my friends sitting right back here, I'd like to have you say a few words. We can learn a lot from you.*
>
> *"We want to learn everything we can learn, and we're going to go—starting about two minutes after this meeting, we're going to work, because this is a long-term situation that we have to solve. We'll solve it together. And you've gone through extraordinary pain, and we don't want others to go through the kind of pain that you've gone through. It wouldn't be right. So would you like to say something, please?"*

Another parent, Curtis Kelly, stood up and shared how he lost his son Zaire to gun violence, and felt that most politicians only show up for photo ops. The problems are no longer limited to local areas and have spread nationally requiring national action.

> *"Thank you very much. It's incredible. Very sad. Thank you very much. Does anybody have an idea for a solution to the school shooting, and the school shootings that we've gone through over the years? And we've seen too much of it, and we're going to stop it. We got a lot of different ideas. I could name ten of them right now.*

*Does anybody have an idea as to how to stop it? What is your rec-
ommendation to stop it? Yes."*

Asking if anybody has an idea for a solution to school shootings at this point,
when more than a dozen have been presented, gives the perception that Trump
wasn't listening at all, especially considering the repetitive "thank you" and
"appreciate it" responses to each recounting of the events and solutions offered. Trump might have been listening, who really knows, but his ineffective
communication skills and poor filtering always come off very bad in situations
where strong emotional response is expected. Perhaps Trump meant to say,
"Does anybody else," and he made a careless omission?

Trump has been doing a pretty solid job up to this point, by limiting his
interactions and opportunities to make big social errors. Trump listens for a
couple minutes and at roughly fifty-three minutes in interjects himself more
fully into the discussion for the next five minutes:

> *"Well, thank you, too. And I will say, again, background
> checks are going to be very strong. We need that. And then after
> we do that, when we see there's trouble, we have to nab them.*
>
> *"You know, years ago, we had mental hospitals—mental in-
> stitutions. We had a lot of them, and a lot of them have closed.
> They've closed. Some people thought it was a stigma. Some people
> thought, frankly, it was a—the legislators thought it was too ex-
> pensive."*

Gun violence is often portrayed differently depending on who is committing
the crime, especially in the media that Trump depends on for most of his information. Trump in his simplistic understanding of school shootings has made
an overgeneralization error, that all shooters are mentally ill. If there is any
hint of a person being different in their thinking, especially if they are white,
the standard response is that this tragedy happened because the individual has
a mental illness. Perhaps that is why it was deemed okay when the Trump administration repealed an Obama era rule preventing mentally ill people from
having a gun.[80]

---

[80] Berenson, Tessa. "Donald Trump Made It Easier for Mentally Ill People to Buy Guns." *Time*, Time, 6
Nov. 2017, time.com/5011519/texas-church-shooting-mental-health-donald-trump/.

"Today, if you catch somebody, they don't know what to do with them. He hasn't committed the crime, but he may, very well. And there's no mental institution, there's no place to bring them. And we have that a lot. Even if they caught this person—I'm being nice when I use the word 'person'—they probably wouldn't have known what to do.

"They're not going to put them in jail. And yet—so there's none of that middle ground of having that institution, where you had trained people that could handle it and do something about it and find out how sick he really is. Because he is a sick guy. And he should have been nabbed a number of times, frankly."

Understanding people, who are markedly different, Trump including, in their behavior and thoughts doesn't make them any less human than we ourselves are. This dehumanizing behavior, especially when it comes to rationalizing those who kill being separate to ourselves, is a strong emotional behavior I think most people have, constantly reinforced by the stereotypes reflected in society. Trump's use of "sick" connects to that stereotype.

Trump though is right about something here, without his understanding why. We can't be putting someone in jail without due cause. If they pose a threat to society in general, or may cause self-harm, we can indeed take and hospitalize them in an institution. That threat must be established and proven, and the facilities we have across the US are inadequate for dealing with mental health issues.

"Your concept and your idea about—it's called concealed carry—and it only works where you have people very adept at using firearms, of which you have many, and it would be teachers and coaches. If the coach had a firearm in his locker when he ran at this guy—that coach was very brave. Saved a lot of lives, I suspect. But if he had a firearm, he wouldn't have had to run; he would have shot and that would have been the end of it."

Identifying what everyone in the room already knew, that taking a gun into the school hidden legally is called concealed carry, is Trump's attempt at showing his knowledge to the group, another of countless many pragmatic errors in his logic.

"And this would only be, obviously, for people that are very adept at handling a gun. And it would be—it's called concealed carry, where a teacher would have a concealed gun on them. They'd go for special training. And they would be there, and you would no longer have a gun-free zone. A gun-free zone to a maniac—because they're all cowards—a gun-free zone is, let's go in and let's attack, because bullets aren't coming back at us."'

The good guy with a gun stopped the bad guy with a gun mantra is a popular refrain in the rightwing media. What is telling is that Trump sharing a commonly repeated theme does not "get" how to properly retell it. He again names "concealed carry" and this time uses "maniac" to further marginalize shooters to separate them in an Us versus Them manner, which most I think will find justifiable as a social response.

"And if you do this—and a lot of people are talking about it, and it's certainly a point that we'll discuss—but concealed carry for teachers and for people of talent—of that type of talent. So let's say you had twenty percent of your teaching force, because that's pretty much the number—and you said it—an attack has lasted, on average, about three minutes.

"It takes five to eight minutes for responders, for the police, to come in. So the attack is over. If you had a teacher with—who was adept at firearms, they could very well end the attack very quickly."

Simplistic explanation with idiosyncratic trappings all over the place, Trump clearly has some of the opposing concerns to the argument of arming teachers learned. They must be trained, and have a certain kind of talent. What sort of talent is he talking about? Willing to kill someone who is a threat kind of talent?

As a teacher, I prefer using proactive means to deal with a school shooting BEFORE there is a school shooting, not responding to the crisis as it transpires. This includes knowing and meeting the needs of a diverse student body, reaching out to students who are having trouble and making meaningful social connections, keeping communication channels open, and having a school safety plan. None of that entails being ready to kill a student, which is what is expected in the arming the teachers initiates supported by the NRA, a major influencer of Trump's positions on guns. Those are all factors that I can control as an educator. What I can't control is whether or not a student has access to weapons and ammo to carry out an attack. Arming teachers is a reactive solution, and not one without adding additional problems like accidental shootings as the weapon must always be loaded for it to be of any use.

> *"And the good thing about a suggestion like that—and we're going to be looking at it very strongly, and I think a lot of people are going to be opposed to it; I think a lot of people are going to like it—but the good thing is that you'll have a lot of people with that. You know, you can't have a hundred security guards in Stoneman Douglas. That's a big school. That's a massive school with a lot of acreage to cover, a lot of floor area.*
>
> *"And so that would be, certainly, a situation that is being discussed a lot by a lot of people. You'd have a lot people that'd be armed. They'd be ready. They're professionals. They may be Marines that left the Marines, left the Army, left the Air Force. And they're very adept at doing that. You'd have a lot of them, and they'd be spread evenly throughout the school.*
>
> *"So the other thing—I really believe that if these cowards knew that the school was well-guarded, from the standpoint of having, pretty much, professionals with great training, I think they wouldn't go into the school to start off with. I think it could very solve your problem."*

Trump starts a lot of sentences with conjunctions or pronouns, doesn't he? Most have probably heard in elementary school that you should 'never' start sentences out with a conjunction. We teach that in order to advance language ability where there is an overuse, often incorrect grammatically, of conjunctions initiating a sentence. It is okay to use them as the first word, just not advised, as an inverted way of combining two complete simple sentences, with commas, to form a complex sentence structure. Trump's linguistic errors aren't as entertaining as his pragmatic ones.

How did his comment which began talking about arming teachers morph into former military being spread evenly throughout Stoneman Douglas? It is how Trump logically connects one concept to another, elements of circuitous language patterning characteristic of some on the Spectrum. His other pragmatic error is stating, *"I think they wouldn't go into the school to start off with."* Most US-based school shootings that I am aware of originate with a student connected to the school taking in weapons and initiating the tragedy. They already are going into the school on a daily basis in most cases, so the threat is from within the school community. As one parent pointed out, these shooters often enter with the plan to kill themselves or to die in the process, dispelling the notion more guns deters someone from coming in.

"So we'll be doing the background checks. We'll be doing a lot of different things. But we'll certainly be looking at ideas like that. You know, a lot of people don't understand that airline pilots now, a lot of them carry guns. And I have to say that things have changed a lot. People aren't attacking the way they would routinely attack. And maybe you have the same situation in schools."

Airline pilots having guns is another unusual connection Trump associates with the "conversation" of school shootings he is presently sitting in on. He overgeneralized again, believing as his words suggest planes were routinely attacked and only armed pilots stopped a pattern which doesn't exist. This may indicate Trump struggles separating what happens on TV with what is real, a profound and stunning revelation considering his position.

"So does anybody like that idea here? Does anybody like it? Right? Yes. For Meadow—your beautiful Meadow. We talked about that. And do people feel strongly against it? Anybody? Anybody? Strongly against it?

"All right. I mean, I could—look, we can understand both sides. And certainly, it's controversial. But we'll study that along with many other ideas. Anybody else something to say? Yes, go ahead."

Trump showed he listened earlier when he brings up Meadow. While late, that small connection to a person was the best response Trump managed with an emotional connection. Trump continues the listening session going back into his standard mode of thanking the speaker. Later Nicole Hockley brings up this counterpoint:

"Mr. President, thank you for being open to hearing all forms of solutions. I truly appreciate that. One point on the mental health issue—and I think it's important to note that someone with a mental illness is highly unlikely to ever commit an act of violence. It's a very, very small percentage."

She then correctly identifies that the number two killer of children are suicides, most often with guns, and that is a mental wellness issue instead of a mental illness one. These deaths are preventable. Nicole concludes her points:

"This is about prevention. There are some fabulous solutions being talked about today, which still go to imminent danger. Let's talk about prevention. There is so much that we can do to help people before it reaches that point. And I urge you, please, stay focused on that as well. It is the gun, it's the person behind the gun, and it's about helping people before they ever reach that point."

Near the conclusion of the forum, Trump summarized:

"If you have any suggestions, if you have any feelings as to what we should do—because there are many different ideas—some, I guess, are good. Some aren't good. Some are very stringent, as you understand. And a lot of people think they work. And some are less so.

"But in addition to everything else, and in addition to what we're going to do about background checks—we're going to go very strongly to age, that's age of purchase, and we're also going to go very strongly to the mental health aspect of what's going on. Because here was a case where he cried out—this person was sick, very sick. And people knew he was very sick.

"And I know law enforcement is also—I really learned a lot from this—we're also going to look at the institutions. We're going to look at what to do when you find somebody like this—because again, right now we're not equipped like we were many years ago. So we're going to look at that whole aspect of what's going on."

Trump is very fixed minded, stuck in his thinking due to restricted behavior patterns associated with his disorder. Does what he says in the end and early on in the discussion indicate any change or improvement in his understanding of the issue? No. Trump went in with two ideas, arming teachers and more background checks, and blaming mental illness. He ended with the same exact ideas and blame. [81]

School shootings were rampant setting records during that whole first year of Trump's presidency, yet school safety, or rather kids being gunned down by fellow classmates, was not that pressing of an issue warranting his full attention. Trump could not relate to situations he had no experience with. Besides, Trump was too busy attacking everybody and everything, while "defending" himself for each poor choice he was making, that school children dying wasn't the national emergency it actually is.

---

[81] Factbase. "Transcript Quote - Remarks: Donald Trump Holds a Listening Session With High Schoolers on Guns - February 21, 2018." *Factbase*, factba.se/transcript/donald-trump-remarks-listening-session-parkland-shooting-students-february-21-2018.

Chapter Six

"And I did a great job. I did an extra special."[82]

The Devastation of Puerto Rico

Trump's administration in only two years has likely seen more natural disasters than any previous one in US history. It is like Mother Nature is angry that the administration pulled out of the Paris accord and began pushing for increased coal, oil and gas production or something, which is what Trump actually "did" on June 1, 2017, before four hurricanes hit the US and its territories. While Trump doesn't believe in *"global waming"* it doesn't matter. If one jumps off a cliff saying they don't believe in gravity, the end result still will be plunging into the abyss. The same is true of climate change. No matter how stubborn or obstinate one is in opposing the scientific facts, the change, while gradual is showing some very nasty consequences. [82]

By far the worst US government response in history to a natural disaster has to be Trump's failure in Puerto Rico to show empathy or a sense of urgency in responding to the aftermath and catastrophic destruction of the September 20, 2017, battering of Hurricane Maria then about a week later Hurricane Irma.

---

[82] Trump, Donald J. "In the Beautiful Midwest, Windchill Temperatures Are Reaching Minus 60 Degrees, the Coldest Ever Recorded. In Coming Days, Expected to Get Even Colder. People Can't Last Outside Even for Minutes. What the Hell Is Going on with Global Waming? Please Come Back Fast, We Need You!" Twitter, Twitter, 29 Jan. 2019, twitter.com/realDonaldTrump/status/10900742540 10404864?ref_src=twsrc%5Etfw%7Ctwcamp%5Etweetembed&ref_url=https%3A%2F%2Ffactba.se%2 Fsearch.

Trump said a few things on Twitter during the storm, but was more focused on the "greater tragedy" of "disrespectful" NFL players kneeling quietly in protest about police brutality. In his first public statements, on September 26, he had this to say:

> *"As far as Puerto Rico is concerned, I think just the opposite. We have had tremendous reviews from government officials, as we have in Texas and Louisiana, and as we have in Florida, as you know, from Governor Scott and Greg Abbott. Great governors. And this morning, the governor made incredible statements about how well we're doing.*
>
> *"We understand it's a disaster; it's a disaster that just happened. The grid was in bad shape before the storm. And Puerto Rico didn't get hit by one hurricane, it got hit by two hurricanes, and they were among the biggest we've ever seen—with the second one being even worse. I mean, the second one hit Puerto Rico as a Category 5. I don't believe anybody has ever seen that happen before—hit land with that kind of velocity.*
>
> *"And this isn't like Florida where we can go right up the spine, or like Texas where we go right down the middle and we distribute. This is a thing called the Atlantic Ocean. This is tough stuff. The governor has been so incredible in his statements about the job we're doing. We're doing a great job."[83]*

Trump here is "selling" the idea that everything was going great based on his conversation with the governor. Things were not great as San Juan's Mayor Carmen Yulin Cruz pleads on September 29:

> *"We are dying here. And I cannot fathom the thought that the greatest nation in the world cannot figure out the logistics for a small island of 100 miles by 35 miles. So, mayday, we are in trouble.*
>
> *"FEMA asks for documentation, I think we've given them enough documentation. They had the gall this morning—look at*

---

[83] Factbase. "Transcript Quote - Press Conference: Donald Trump and Mariano Rajoy of Spain - September 26, 2017." *Factbase*, factba.se/transcript/donald-trump-press-conference-rajoy-spain-september-26-2017.

this—they had the gall this morning of asking me: 'What are your priorities, Mayor?'

"'Well, where have you been?'

"And I have been very respectful of the FEMA employees. I have been patient but we have no time for patience anymore. So, I am asking the President of the United States to make sure somebody is in charge that is up to the task of saving lives.

"They were up to the task in Africa when Ebola came over. They were up to the task in Haiti, as they should be. Because when it comes to saving lives we are all part of one community of shared values.

"I will do what I never thought I was going to do. I am begging. I am begging anyone that can hear us to save us from dying. If anybody out there is listening to us, we are dying. And you are killing us with the inefficiency and bureaucracy.

"We will make it with or without you because what stands behind me is all due to the generosity of other people.

"Again, this is what we got last night: four pallets of water, three pallets of meals and 12 pallets of infant food. Which, I gave them to Comerío, where people are drinking out of a creek.

"So I am done being polite. I am done being politically correct. I am mad as hell because my people's lives are at stake. And we are but one nation. We may be small, but we are huge in dignity and zealous for life.

"So I'm asking members of the press to send a mayday call all over the world. We are dying here. And if we don't stop and if we don't get the food and the water into people's hands, what we are going to see is something close to a genocide.

"So, Mr. Trump, I am begging you to take charge and save lives. After all, that is one of the founding principles of the United States of North America. If not, the world will see how we are treated not as second-class citizens but as animals that can be disposed of. Enough is enough."[84]

---

[84] Summers, Juana. "Trump Attacks San Juan Mayor over Response." *CNN*, Cable News Network, 1 Oct. 2017, www.cnn.com/2017/09/30/politics/trump-Tweets-puerto-rico-mayor/index.html.

Trump does NOT like to be criticized, part of his restrictive behaviors associated with Autism, and the mayor in her plea to save the 3.4 million American people in Puerto Rico, triggered the petulant and bitter President who took to Twitter early morning on the 30th sending these eye-popping Tweets after catching the news:

> *"The Mayor of San Juan, who was very complimentary only a few days ago, has now been told by the Democrats that you must be nasty to Trump.*
>
> *"...Such poor leadership ability by the Mayor of San Juan, and others in Puerto Rico, who are not able to get their workers to help. They....*
>
> *"...want everything to be done for them when it should be a community effort. 10,000 Federal workers now on Island doing a fantastic job."*

Russel Honoré, a retired general appointed to oversee the 2005 Hurricane Katrina response by George Bush, had this to say about the Trump Twitter meltdown on CNN with Erin Burnett:

> *"The President has shown again he don't give a damn about poor people. He doesn't give a damn about people of color. And the SOB that rides around in Air Force One is denying services needed by the people of Puerto Rico. I hate to say it that way but there's no other way to say it."*

Texas US Representative Al Green further dogpiled on the President on CNN with Ana Cabrera:

> *"If they were all Anglos, I don't believe the President would have the attitude that he has, because you don't hear that kind of dog whistle, of people not wanting to pull themselves up by their bootstraps, when the people are Anglos. That's something reserved for people of color."*[85]

---

[85] Summers, Juana. "Trump Attacks San Juan Mayor over Response." CNN, Cable News Network, 1 Oct. 2017, www.cnn.com/2017/09/30/politics/trump-Tweets-puerto-rico-mayor/index.html.

Eventually, and unfortunately for Mr. Trump and the rest of America, he stepped foot on the Island, and quickly inserted it in his mouth—big time, on October 3, 2017. Multiple times actually. Remember Trump has an extreme deficit for emotional regulation and pragmatic judgement due to his Autism. His errors though the entire visit demonstrated that spectacularly. First up, with the backdrop of a ship, Trump gives a briefing. He starts talking about the weather:

> *"Well, thank you very much. It was a great trip and a beautiful place. I've been to Puerto Rico many times as I think most of you have known. And I've always loved it. And your weather is second to none, but every once in a while you get hit. And you really got hit—there's no question about it."*

This isn't too bad of a start, but the connection to two hurricanes having hit and the comment about the weather is a little off-putting, demonstrating some poor filtering. He starts congratulating and heaping praise on the assembled administration officials. The praise continues:

> *"If you look at the—every death is a horror. But if you look at a real catastrophe like Katrina, and you look at the tremendous hundreds and hundreds and hundreds of people that died, and you look at what happened here with, really, a storm that was just totally overpowering—nobody has ever seen anything like this. What is your death count, as of this moment—17?"*
>
> *"Sixteen certified."*
>
> *"Sixteen people certified. Sixteen people versus in the thousands. You can be very proud of all of your people, all of our people working together.*
>
> *"Sixteen versus literally thousands of people. You can be very proud. Everybody around this table and everybody watching can really be very proud of what's taken place in Puerto Rico."[86]*

---

[86] Factbase. "Transcript Quote - Remarks: Donald Trump Receives a Briefing on Hurricane Relief in Puerto Rico - October 3, 2017." *Factbase*, factba.se/transcript/donald-trump-remarks-hurricane-briefing-puerto-rico-october-3-2017.

Trump just went OFF the rails on this one, showing incredibly poor filtering here. First, he is comparing death tolls, without understanding that those numbers are generally pretty low for the first month especially in an area that currently has power out in most of the territory. The death toll would later be revised to close to 3,000 killed both directly and indirectly from the storm. Secondly, his use *"real catastrophe"* says to everybody that what has happened in Puerto Rico is no big deal. It was just a storm compared to Katrina. Trump does NOT get the context of how hurtful and insensitive these two statements were to millions of people. That is just how severe Trump's Autism traits are. He is blunt, very literal in his thinking, and lacks filtering often blurting out things that are going to get him, his administration and the US in trouble.

Trump still had a worse Presidential moment than bragging about the death toll before leaving the beleaguered US island. He stopped for a photo op at a church and started throwing around paper towels to the crowd. This was the last chance Trump had to act as comforter in chief during the crisis. He failed. Bigly.[87]

On October 19, 2017, Trump at the White House with the Puerto Rican Governor speaks "proudly" about the recovery effort rating it as a perfect 10 and A-Plus:

> *"But all of the armed forces, what they've done has been—Army, Navy, the Marines, the Air Force—all of the goods dropped in. Helicopters that weren't even meant for this purpose, all of a sudden they're delivering food and services. I would give a 10.*
>
> *"I would say, locally—and I understand locally. A person loses his or her or their house, and then they can't go to work. If you lose your house, it's hard to go and be a policeman for the day. You're trying to have your family live, frankly. This is what happened to so many people. You read that they had no truck drivers in Puerto Rico. Well, they have a lot of truck drivers in Puerto Rico, but many of them lost their houses, so they had to be with their families. So we would have the military driving trucks. They're not supposed to be driving trucks. It's not their—it's not even their aptitude.*

---

[87] Graham, David A. "Trump's Puerto Rico Visit Is a Political Disaster." *The Atlantic*, Atlantic Media Company, 9 Oct. 2017, www.theatlantic.com/politics/archive/2017/10/trump-puerto-rico-visit/541869/.

Some of them didn't really know how to drive trucks, but they
learned very quickly. They're smart."

The military apparently had to learn how to drive trucks and helicopters being used for the first time to drop pallets of supplies by air. While this is a completely absurd statement by Trump, it is consistent with his cognitive lapses and charms of his simplistic story telling due to his autism. Donald is pretty enthusiastic in his retelling of what he learned, likely for the first time. Doesn't that remind you of a five to eight-year old child? Excited about his discoveries? It is actually one of the reasons I love working with these children that Donald frequently reminds me of.

"But we had the military, in many cases, driving trucks be-
cause it's not the people's fault; they lost their house. They were dev-
astated. And I think we did a fantastic job. And we are being given
credit.
"It was very nice that the gentleman who worked for Bill Clin-
ton, when he was President, gave us an A-plus, and that included
Puerto Rico. Gave us an A-plus. And I thought that was really
very nice. And I think—I really believe he's correct. We have done
a really great job." [88]

Trump is pushing back against the media narrative about the delayed and inept response. He really needs to hear that praise. The problem is that when 3,000 Americans die, many from Government neglect, and you didn't say hardly anything when the Hurricane had just passed and instead talked about NASCAR and NFL protests, you don't get to give yourself an A. Almost a year later, that disastrous series of missteps would be revisited with a now revised death toll of 2,975 by researchers from George Washington University. Trump responded to a reporter asking about preparedness lessons from the previous four Hurricanes that hit the year before on September 12, 2018, as another storm headed for the mainland:

---

[88] Factbase. "Transcript Quote - Remarks: Donald Trump, Ricardo Rossello and Brock Long on Puerto Rico Recovery - October 19, 2017." Factbase, factba.se/transcript/donald-trump-remarks-rossello-long-puerto-rico-fema-october-19-2017.

"The job that FEMA and law enforcement and everybody did, working along with the Governor in Puerto Rico, I think was tremendous. I think that Puerto Rico was an incredible, unsung success."[89]

The next day, September 13, Trump took to Twitter, and got really defensive about all those deaths being "added" to make him look bad:

"3000 people did not die in the two hurricanes that hit Puerto Rico. When I left the Island, AFTER the storm had hit, they had anywhere from 6 to 18 deaths. As time went by it did not go up by much. Then, a long time later, they started to report really large numbers, like 3000...

".....This was done by the Democrats in order to make me look as bad as possible when I was successfully raising Billions of Dollars to help rebuild Puerto Rico. If a person died for any reason, like old age, just add them onto the list. Bad politics. I love Puerto Rico!"

The reason people died wasn't old age. If someone needs dialysis or oxygen, and they can no longer get to the hospital or the hospital has no electricity they unfortunately die because the storm prevented their medical care. Only a small portion of the people killed died from falling debris or drowning, while the rest might have been saved had we had a more focused and dedicated President at the helm. There might have been MORE deaths had not former Secretary of State and First Lady Hillary Clinton not spoken out calling for a hospital ship to be deployed on September 24, 2017.

"President Trump, Sec. Mattis, and DOD should send the Navy, including the USNS Comfort, to Puerto Rico now. These are American citizens."[90]

---

[89] Keith, Tamara. "FACT CHECK: 'Puerto Rico Was An Incredible, Unsung Success'?" NPR, NPR, 12 Sept. 2018, www.npr.org/2018/09/12/646997771/fact-check-puerto-rico-was-an-incredible-unsung-success.

[90] Lamothe, Dan. "Clinton Pressed Trump to Deploy Hospital Ship Comfort to Puerto Rico. Now It's Preparing to Go." *The Washington Post*, WP Company, 26 Sept. 2017, www.washingtonpost.com/news/checkpoint/wp/2017/09/26/clinton-pressured-trump-to-deploy-hospital-ship-comfort-to-puerto-rico-now-its-on-the-way/.

The ship was sent.

I strongly believe that Donald isn't as cruel, apathetic or as heartless that the media makes him out to be or sometimes behaves; However, due to his emotional deficits Trump is more likely to be incapable of recognizing and expressing sorrow, remorse, or shared grief with his fellow Americans when the experience isn't directly affecting him in a personal way.

Chapter Seven

"Focus does not mean being narrow-minded or rigid."

Donald's Restiction Patterns of Behavior

The most difficult challenge of working with a person who has Autism is the extreme rigidity and inflexibility they frequently display. I could only imagine the challenge of Trump's cabinet and advisors, as he is as extremely set in his behavior as any person I have observed. People in Special Education burn out quickly, just as the administration has, as evidenced by record turnover rates within this White House.

Rex Tillerson's interview on December 7, 2018, in Houston, Texas, high-lighted how difficult it was working with Trump:

> *"It was challenging for me coming from the disciplined, highly process-oriented ExxonMobil Corporation to go to work for a man who is pretty undisciplined, doesn't—doesn't like to read, doesn't read briefing reports, doesn't—doesn't like to get into the details of a lot of things but rather just kind of says, 'Look, this is what I be-lieve and you can try to convince me otherwise, but most of the time you're not going to do that.'"[91]*

---

[91] "Trump 'Frustrated' over Law Violation Warnings: Tillerson." Reuters, Thomson Reuters, 7 Dec. 2018, www.reuters.com/video/2018/12/07/trump-frustrated-over-law-violation-warn?videoId= 489588576.

Note that Trump is pretty fix-minded suggesting Rex would not be able to convince him otherwise. Individuals with ASD rarely budge when their needs are not being met. For Trump those most essential needs are getting his way, people liking him, winning and being a celebrity. In the many interviews and public appearances I have read prior to the campaign, Trump was very fixated on celebrity. For anyone who knows someone with Autism, this is perfectly understandable. Extreme focus on dinosaurs, trucks, shiny things (like gold toilets), rare diseases, and the news media is the norm, often to the exclusion of other interests, is one of the more obvious quirks associated with ASD.

However, Trump's rigidity added with his extreme social deficits almost makes it impossible for him do the job of the President. Take his phone call readouts published by the White House up till the July 24, 2018, announcement they would "protect" the President by reducing transparency further by ending the practice as examples of how bad Trump is at reading and interacting with people socially.[92]

Eight days into his Presidency, January 28, 2017, Trump was on the phone with Australian PM Turnbull, stumbling his way through the conversation with idiosyncratic speech tendencies, and making illogical connections that confused Turnbull. The whole conversation lasted twenty-five minutes and focused mostly on whether Trump would honor a US agreement to take in around 2,000 displaced Christians from Syria entered in by Obama that Australia would not accept due to a legal technicality involving arriving by boat.

> *"Well, actually I just called for a total ban on Syria and from many different countries from where there is terror, and extreme vetting for everyone else—and somebody told me yesterday that close to 2,000 people are coming who are really probably troublesome. And I am saying, boy that will make us look awfully bad. Here I am calling for a ban where I am not letting anybody in and we take 2,000 people. Really it looks like 2,000 people that Australia does not want and I do not blame you by the way, but the United States has become like a dumping ground. You know Malcom [sic], anybody that has a problem—you remember the Mariel boat lift,*

---

[92] Visser, Nick. "White House Will Stop Publishing Reports Of Trump's Calls With World Leaders: CNN." The Huffington Post, TheHuffingtonPost.com, 25 July 2018, www.huffingtonpost.com/entry/readouts-trump-white-house_us_5b57b675e4b0fd5c73c9daa2.

where Castro let everyone out of prison and Jimmy Carter accepted them with open arms. These were brutal people. Nobody said Castro was stupid, but now what are we talking about is 2,000 people that are actually imprisoned and that would actually come into the United States. I heard about this—I have to say I love Australia; I love the people of Australia. I have so many friends from Australia, but I said—geez that is a big ask, especially in light of the fact that we are so heavily in favor, not in favor, but we have no choice but to stop things. We have to stop. We have allowed so many people into our country that should not be here. We have our San Bernardino's, we have had the World Trade Center come down because of people that should not have been in our country, and now we are supposed to take 2,000. It sends such a bad signal. You have no idea. It is such a bad thing."

In this word salad, Trump's mentioning of his Muslim ban as if Turnbull is hearing it for the first time, shows how poorly Trump's thinking is in respect to understanding social context. The purpose of the call was Turnbull's response to that Executive Order and how it relates to the Syrian refugee agreement between the two countries, a fact Trump apparently did not comprehend. Trump lacking filtering, then calls formerly Cuban asylum seekers under Carter accepted into the US "brutal people," a curious statement considering how vital a demographic the Cuban people are to the Republican establishment. Then Trump makes a logic fallacy and overgeneralization that Syrians who are from the Middle East are connected to the same groups that orchestrated 911 and a 2015 mass shooting in San Bernardino.

Such broad mischaracterizations and grouping of people are an unfortunate characteristic and extreme vulnerability of Trump politically and socially as he is apt to react to messaging by associating with groups that share his views. Trump sees something on TV, makes a connection, overgeneralizes and remains very rigid in that thinking even when it is built on faulty logic.

Trump's need to severely restrict both legal and illegal immigration is very fixed into his political agenda and into his thinking due to his generalized fear of minorities and illogical association to crime. What is MORE rigid than his irrational fear of terrorism is his reputation or how he looks to other people. Later in the conversation he says this:

"Malcom [sic], why is this so important? I do not understand. This is going to kill me. I am the world's greatest person that does not want to let people into the country. And now I am agreeing to take 2,000 people and I agree I can vet them, but that puts me in a bad position. It makes me look so bad and I have only been here a week."

Arguing that honoring a deal will make you look bad is weakness easily exploited by political opponents at home, and foreign governments abroad. Remember that this was just a week into his Presidency and his disabilities, needs and how to manipulate him were pretty much known and understood by everyone who interacted with him. Foreign governments executed actions based on this Presidential call readout exploiting the childlike President wherever they could. Turnbull tried to reassure the upset Trump that these Syrian Christians were not the big scary threat Trump perceived them to be:

Turnbull: *These guys are not in that league. They are economic refugees.*

Trump: *OK, good. Can Australia give me a guarantee that if we have any problems—you know that is what they said about the Boston bombers. They said they were wonderful young men.*

Turnbull: *They were Russians. They were not from any of these countries.*

What a zinger in hindsight that last statement properly identifying the Boston bombers origin is! Turnbull was attempting to dispel a misconception and overgeneralization using an established fact that "breaks" the faulty logic.

Trump: *Yes, I will be seen as a weak and ineffective leader in my first week by these people. This is a killer.*

Turnbull: *You can certainly say that it was not a deal that you would have done, but you are going to stick with it.*

Trump: *I have no choice to say that about it. Malcom [sic], I am going to say that I have no choice but to honor my predecessor's deal. I think it is a horrible deal, a disgusting deal that I would have never made. It is an embarrassment to the United States of America and you can say it just the way I said it. I will say it just that way. As far as I am concerned that is enough Malcom [sic]. I have had it. I have been making these calls all day and this is the most unpleasant call all day. Putin was a pleasant call. This is ridiculous.*[93]

Turnbull picking up on Trump's exhaustion with the subject of taking in refugees suggested talking about either Syria or North Korea, but Donald was stuck in his doldrums and the call soon ended politely.

Extreme stubbornness demonstrated from Trump along with his misguided and incorrect thinking soon led to his removing the US from many bilateral agreements, trade agreements and treaties on the basis that they were "bad agreements" or because of influence from others with their own agendas to either weaken the US or to help self-promote themselves for higher positions. He was like a bull in a China shop, smashing everything fully expecting his efforts would bear fruit.

One such item was his efforts to replace NAFTA, the North American Free Trade Agreement with Canada and Mexico that he long complained about was unfair to America on the campaign trail. Trump bragged to a private group of donors about his dealings with Canadian Prime Minister Justin Trudeau on March 5, 2018, where he accused Canada of taking advantage of the US on trade, making up a claim about a trade deficit with Canada that does not exist. Trump was recorded, something he never seems capable to think about, and the recording leaked to the press. Here is what Trump said:

"Trudeau came to see me. He's a good guy, Justin. He said, 'No, no, we have no trade deficit with you, we have none. Donald, please.' Nice guy, good-looking guy, comes in—'Donald, we have no trade deficit.' He's very proud because everybody else, you know, we're getting killed.

"...So, he's proud. I said, 'Wrong, Justin, you do.' I didn't even know.... I had no idea. I just said, 'You're wrong.' You know why? Because we're so stupid.... And I thought they were smart. I said, 'You're wrong, Justin.' He said, 'Nope,

---

[93] "Full Transcript of Trump's Phone Call with Australian Prime Minister Malcolm Turnbull." The Guardian, Guardian News and Media, 3 Aug. 2017, www.theguardian.com/us-news/2017/aug/04/full-transcript-of-trumps-phone-call-with-australian-prime-minister-malcolm-turnbull.

*we have no trade deficit.' I said, 'Well, in that case, I feel dif-
ferently,' I said, 'but I don't believe it.' I sent one of our guys
out, his guy, my guy, they went out, I said, 'Check, because I
can't believe it.'*

*"'Well, sir, you're actually right. We have no deficit, but
that doesn't include energy and timber. ... And when you do,
we lose $17 billion a year.' It's incredible."*[94]

Alternative facts keep popping up in this administration it seems. Generally speaking, when US diplomats meet with foreign diplomats, one would assume each side has done due diligence in preparing for a meeting. Trump wings it, without taking into any consideration what might come up or need to be discussed from America's point of view. He just makes stuff up, then brags about it while being recorded, and causes breakdowns of diplomacy. It is this sheer incompetency due to his restricted behavior that makes statements such as ones made by John Kelly, Mattis and a member of a secret cabal of Americans in his administration critically important.

John Kelly's statement that his tenure as Chief of Staff should be measured by *"what the president did not do"* is significant with his role as one of the "adults" in the room wherever Trump was. Without Kelly, Trump likely would have withdrawn the US from NATO and pulled US troops from South Korea as he publicly threatened he might do.[95]

James Mattis's resignation letter is deserving of being read in its entirety:

December 20, 2018
Dear Mr. President:

*I have been privileged to serve as our country's 26th Secretary
of Defense which has allowed me to serve alongside our men and
women of the Department in defense of our citizens and our ideals.*

*I am proud of the progress that has been made over the past
two years on some of the key goals articulated in our National Defense Strategy: putting the Department on a more sound budgetary*

---

[94] "Trump Says He Accused Canada of a Trade Deficit Without Knowing If There Really Was One." Fortune, fortune.com/2018/03/15/trump-trudeau-trade-deficit/.

[95] "John F. Kelly Says His Tenure as Trump's Chief of Staff Is Best Measured by What the President Did Not Do." Los Angeles Times, Los Angeles Times, 30 Dec. 2018, www.latimes.com/politics/la-na-pol-john-kelly-exit-interview-20181230-story.html.

footing, improving readiness and lethality in our forces, and reforming the Department's business practices for greater performance. Our troops continue to provide the capabilities needed to prevail in conflict and sustain strong U.S. global influence.

One core belief I have always held is that our strength as a nation is inextricably linked to the strength of our unique and comprehensive system of alliances and partnerships. While the US remains the indispensable nation in the free world, we cannot protect our interests or serve that role effectively without maintaining strong alliances and showing respect to those allies. Like you, I have said from the beginning that the armed forces of the United States should not be the policeman of the world. Instead, we must use all tools of American power to provide for the common defense, including providing effective leadership to our alliances. NATO's 29 democracies demonstrated that strength in their commitment to fighting alongside us following the 9-11 attack on America. The Defeat-ISIS coalition of 74 nations is further proof.

Similarly, I believe we must be resolute and unambiguous in our approach to those countries whose strategic interests are increasingly in tension with ours. It is clear that China and Russia, for example, want to shape a world consistent with their authoritarian model—gaining veto authority over other nations' economic, diplomatic, and security decisions—to promote their own interests at the expense of their neighbors, America and our allies. That is why we must use all the tools of American power to provide for the common defense.

My views on treating allies with respect and also being clear-eyed about both malign actors and strategic competitors are strongly held and informed by over four decades of immersion in these issues. We must do everything possible to advance an international order that is most conducive to our security, prosperity and values, and we are strengthened in this effort by the solidarity of our alliances.

Because you have the right to have a Secretary of Defense whose views are better aligned with yours on these and other subjects, I believe it is right for me to step down from my position. The end date for my tenure is February 28, 2019, a date that should allow sufficient time for a successor to be nominated and confirmed as well as to make sure the Department's interests are properly articulated and protected at upcoming events to include Congressional posture hearings and the NATO Defense Ministerial meeting in February. Further, that a full transition to a new Secretary of Defense occurs well in advance of the transition of Chairman of the Joint Chiefs of Staff in September in order to ensure stability Within the Department.

I pledge my full effort to a smooth transition that ensures the needs and interests of the 2.15 million Service Members and 732,079 DoD civilians receive undistracted attention of the Department at all times so that they can fulfill their critical, round-the-clock mission to protect the American people.

I very much appreciate this opportunity to serve the nation and our men and women in uniform.[96]

James N Mattis

When the Generals leaving the White House want to be evaluated by what they prevented from happening or leave due to having different core beliefs, it is a bad, very bad thing. Mattis's scathing rebuke of Trump's abandonment of alliances in favor of authoritarian regimes caused Trump to meltdown, "firing" Mattis three days later effective January 1, 2019, well short of the date Mattis intended to step down.

A *New York Times* Op-ed on September 5, 2018, from a Senior Administration Official described being part of the resistance, keeping the President's more misguided impulses to attack democratic institutions in check. The *NY Times* rarely publish anonymous articles as precedent. This one was colossal, both for the openness and Trump's epic meltdown decrying treason.

"The dilemma—which he does not fully grasp—is that many of the senior officials in his own administration are working diligently from within to frustrate parts of his agenda and his worst inclinations."

---

[96] Hayes, Christal, and USA Today. "Resignation Letter From Defense Secretary James Mattis." DocumentCloud, www.documentcloud.org/documents/5656065-Resignation-Letter-From-Defense-Secretary-James.html.

Trump truly doesn't grasp a great deal of what is going on around him. He can't. It is part of his disability that his lifetime without intervention and corrective growth has profoundly shaped who he is, lacking completely in being able to read social situations and the hidden language associated with being social.

"The root of the problem, is the president's amorality. Anyone who works with him knows he is not moored to any discernible first principles that guide his decision making."

Trump is still very misunderstood in this regard. It isn't that Trump is amoral. Trump believe it or not, has sets of moral rules that he lives by. They do not make sense to most people as many of the bigger core principles everyone else lives by are not seemingly followed by Donald Trump. His two core moral obligations are family and loyalty, however are. Trump is fiercely loyal to his family and those he perceives are loyal to him. Trump also likely believes he hasn't broken any laws due to his rationalization issues of overgeneralizing rules exceptions onto himself. We'll discuss that later.

"It may be cold comfort in this chaotic era, but Americans should know that there are adults in the room. We fully recognize what is happening. And we are trying to do what's right even when Donald Trump won't."[97]

Has it ever occurred to anyone that Trump might not always know the difference between right and wrong because of how long he has had unchecked delusional thinking? It has to me. Trump is on many levels only cognitively matured, at most, to the thinking of a typical twelve-year-old. That is it. His development in language, social skills and executive functioning has long been stagnant. In some regards Trump's ability is regressed more to that of a five-to-six-year-old or worse, particularly when it comes to emotion regulation and self-regulatory behaviors. Trump's disability in these areas is profound. I believe that Trump does know the difference and willfully chooses most of the time to do what he wants, making an "exception to the rule" pardoning himself each time, while being convinced it is okay.

---

[97] "I Am Part of the Resistance Inside the Trump Administration." The New York Times, The New York Times, 5 Sept. 2018, www.nytimes.com/2018/09/05/opinion/trump-white-house-anonymous-resistance.html.

The common theme from those around him reflects this when we hear terms like temper-tantrum, meltdown, and adults in the room. Yet the resistance never did what was constitutionally required of them when they knew Trump was incapable of doing his job, invoking the Twenty-fifth Amendment. The cabinet failed and so did Congress, generally ceding more power and responsibility to the executive branch and further diminishing their own authority.

Senate Leader Mitch McConnell is one of those who failed, as did Paul Ryan who led the House. Instead of showing true leadership by conducting required oversight, they moved forward and kept their heads down. McConnell acting like a first time father embarrassed during his toddler's month long "shutdown," kept shunting off any responsibility suggesting Nancy and Trump work things out, meaning give that screaming child what he wants so he will stop. Rewarding the intolerable behavior just reinforces it.

Fewer and fewer voices objected from the GOP when Trump acted up, accepting and normalizing whatever Trump was doing. At some point, the Republican Party, the party of conservatism, Lincoln, Reagan and grand ideas became the party of MAGA, America First and Trump.

This all has to do with Trump persisting. He is stubborn and unchanging, as restricted in his thinking as any individual I have seen. He bludgeoned the resistance during the campaign. He bludgeoned the resistance through his election. And he continues to stamp out any individual in his way as any domineering toddler does to anyone that reinforces his or her behavior.

It is also why Nancy Pelosi knew how to effectively do what no one before her had done in Washington—get Trump to behave. Sure, he slammed his fists on a table and stormed out of the room saying, *"bye"* when Nancy and Chuck came by on January 9, 2019, after said she would not be giving him his wall, but eventually he knew he was beat. Being consistent, stating the expectations and ignoring the bad behavior when appropriate is probably too hard for the GOP to do.[98]

Trump's extreme rigidity extends well beyond what he does behaviorally, in so much that there are constant stories in the spin cycle of the American media discussing probable OCD-Obsessive Compulsive Disorder. It is easy to confuse OCD with restricted patterns of behavior connected to Autism. There

---

[98] Fandos, Nicholas, et al. "Trump Storms Out of White House Meeting With Democrats on Shutdown." The New York Times, The New York Times, 9 Jan. 2019, www.nytimes.com/2019/01/09/us/politics/government-shutdown-trump-senate.html.

is a difference. Most individuals with OCD are more aware of their tendencies and want to get rid of them. Those with Autism are generally not aware and may even embrace their compulsions. Trump truly appears to embrace his compulsions and delusional thinking, as well as being oblivious to many of his deficits.[99]

Trump appeared as a frequent guest on the *Howard Stern Show* between 1993 and 2015. In a show dated May 8, 1993, Donald discussed his compulsion with cleanliness after Howard accidentally spit on Trump for a second time during the broadcast while discussing the broader topic of Ivana's book, the divorce and Trump's bankruptcy. Donald explains he washes his hands as many times as possible each day and that he likes cleanliness. Howard, a shock jock asked about AIDS and the women Trump sleeps with. Trump explains how he is careful and hopes he doesn't get AIDS. Then he says this quip regarding his safe sex practices after denying a story he has doctors conduct tests with prospective women he sleeps with:

"I own 25% of Goodyear Tire and Rubber."[100]

Trump's compulsive behavior extends to his diet, which mostly consists of *"hamberders"* and other fast food such as the spread of pizza, fish filet and other greasy food he served to the Clemson football National Champions when they attended the White House during Trump's self-imposed government shutdown which he later bragged about paying for on January 14, 2019.

"If it's American, I like it. It's all-American stuff. So—but it's good stuff. And we have the national champion team, as you know Clemson Tigers. And they a fantastic game against Alabama, and they're all here, they're right outside the room, and I think we're going to let you see them.

"But I'll bet you as much food as we have, we have pizzas, we have 300 hamburgers, many, many french fries, all of our favorite foods. I want to see what's here when we leave, because I don't think it's going to be much.

"Reason we did this is because of the shutdown. We want to make sure that everything is right. So we sent out, we got this, and we have some wonderful people working at the White House, they helped us out with this.

"And I will say the Republicans are really, really sticking together. It's great to see, because we need border security. We have to have it. We have to have it. No doubt

---

[99] Rudy, Lisa Jo. "How Are Autistic Behaviors Different From OCD Behaviors?" Verywell Health, www.verywellhealth.com/autism-vs-obsessive-compulsive-disorder-260344.

[100] Factbase. "Transcript Quote - Interview: Donald Trump on The Howard Stern Interview on E! - May 8, 1993." Factbase, factba.se/transcript/donald-trump-interview-howard-stern-may-8-1993.

about it. Should have happened 30 years ago, 20 years ago, 10 years ago, and it's gonna happen now. It's gonna happen now. Thank you very much everybody."[101]

The whole surreal reality-show episode of Trump hovering over the scene supervising the setting of expensive and classy platters with stacks of hamburgers and other greasy faire gave the correct impression Trump has nothing better to do with his time. It also showed his relationship with everyday food is not all that sophisticated. At least this time Trump wasn't again being spotted eating pizza or KFC with a fork.[102]

The most restrictive behavior of Trump's personality is his unapologetic way of refusing to take criticism. It is likely his most damning trait as that weakness alone has caused deterioration of the US relationship with almost every world leader not named Putin. Each world leader that has said something criticizing Donald has soon found Trump unwilling to listen or worse outright hostile to.

So why has Putin stayed well above the fray that trapped nearly all our US traditional allies? He knew Trump's weaknesses because he has incredible Intel, and knows about each and every Autistic trait I am enumerating here.

Putin has never gone off the script of what Trump needs to hear. He flatters and praises Trump regularly and never ever criticizes him in the least. What Putin has done is classic conditioning, making Donald pretty much willing to say and do things aligned with Putin's goals as the two are the best of "friends."

This makes Trump an unwitting agent of Russia.

---

[101] Canty, Jennifer. "Transcript Quote - Remarks: Donald Trump Speaks Briefly With Reporters Before Meeting Clemson Tigers - January 14, 2019." Factbase, CantyMedia, factba.se/transcript/donald-trump-remarks-mcdonalds-wendys-before-clemson-january-14-2019.

[102] Schilling, Dave. "How Donald Trump Tried to Assimilate into Earth Culture and Failed." The Guardian, Guardian News and Media, 2 Aug. 2016, www.theguardian.com/us-news/2016/aug/02/donald-trump-eats-kfc-knife-fork.

Chapter Eight

"The 'Least' Racist Person that Anybody's Going to Meet"

Announcing his entrance into the 2016 Presidential campaign, Trump's lack of filter led to these two memorable quotes:

"When Mexico sends its people, they're not sending their best. They're not sending you.… They're bringing drugs. They're bringing crime. They're rapists. And some, I assume, are good people."

"I would build a great wall, and nobody builds walls better than me, believe me, and I'll build them very inexpensively, I will build a great, great wall on our southern border. And I will have Mexico pay for that wall."[103]

These two soundbites given in New York City on June 16, 2015, are both remarkable and memorable for their voracity, race-baiting and a lead into the central message behind Trump's nationalist agenda, "Make America Great Again." No politician in my lifetime sought openly to energize a white majority base of voters based on resentment, hatred and bitterness. Trump did that by generalizing a group of people with stark dehumanizing language, pitting his campaign as "Us" versus "Them." That had not been seen in American politics in decades, and it worked.

Is Trump truly a racist? I think it is clear that how Trump views himself, his supporters view him and how everyone else believes he is are all different

---

[103] Staff, Washington Post. "Full Text: Donald Trump Announces a Presidential Bid." The Washington Post, WP Company, 16 June 2015, www.washingtonpost.com/news/post-politics/wp/2015/06/16/full-text-donald-trump-announces-a-presidential-bid/.

and easily validated opinions from each respective group. From a simple behavioral perspective, Trump has a history of making insensitive, deliberate racist remarks and is therefore racist. Donald has said repeatedly that he is the "least racist person." That oft repeated phrase is a standard almost scripted retort, given on at least eleven occasions during interviews and video compiled by factba.se as of this writing.

On February 16, 2017, a Jewish reporter, Jake Turx, began a lead-in to a question about the uptick in anti-Semitism attacks in the United States:

"Despite what some of my colleagues may have been reporting, I haven't seen anybody in my community accuse either yourself or anyone on your staff of being anti-Semitic. We understand that you have Jewish grandchildren—you are their zayde [editor's note: grandfather]. However, what we are concerned about and what we haven't really heard being addressed is an uptick in anti-Semitism and how the government is planning to take care of it. There's been a report out that 48 bomb threats have been made against Jewish centers all across country in the last couple of weeks. There are people committing anti-Semitic acts or threatening to—"

Trump cuts off the reporter before the question has been issued and responds:

"You see, he said he was going to ask a very simple, easy question. And it's not. It's not a simple question, not a fair question. Okay, sit down, I understand the rest of your question. So here's the story, folks. Number one, I am the least anti-Semitic person that you've ever seen in your entire life. Number two, racism. The least racist person.

"In fact, we did relatively well, relative to other people running as a Republican—quiet, quiet, quiet. See, he lied about—he was going to get up and ask a very straight, simple question. So, welcome to the world of the media.

"But let me just tell you something, that I hate the charge. I find it repulsive. I hate even the question because people that know me—and you heard the prime minister, you heard Betanyahu [sic] yesterday—did you hear him?—Bibi—he said, 'I've known Donald Trump for a long time,' and then he said, 'Forget it.' So you should take that, instead of having to get up and ask a very insulting question like that. Just shows you about the press but that's the way the press is."[104]

Oy, vey!

---

[104] Robertson, Campbell, et al. "11 Killed in Synagogue Massacre; Suspect Charged With 29 Counts." The New York Times, The New York Times, 27 Oct. 2018, www.nytimes.com/2018/10/27/us/active-shooter-pittsburgh-synagogue-shooting.html.

The question that had not been asked appears to be why the administration had not responded to the uptick in anti-Semitism issues. Trump took offense believing incorrectly that the question was a personal attack, and his instincts kicked in. Trump explained his justification. He knows Israel's President, and did well in the polls for the demographic compared to other Republicans.

Trump in general cannot view himself at all in a negative light, due to his strict aversion to any criticism, another example of restricted behaviors. Trump has exclusion principles that come into play, just as he does for any rule. Trump's behavior is excluded from being racist because he has friends such as Tiger Woods and Kayne West, a daughter and Son-in-law who are Jewish so what he says and does clearly cannot be racist. However, if others who are not him say something mildly offensive they are violating the rule and he will let everyone know they are violating the rule.

Trump's dichotomous belief system allowing him to attack others for similar behaviors that he demonstrates, generally to a worse degree, is further proof of pervasive developmental delays. As President, his divergent nature has consequences. The uptick in hate crimes, not only those anti-Semitic ones draws a direct correlation to his normalization of such behavior inspiring domestic terrorists to rise up and take action. The Tree of Life Synagogue shooting in Pittsburgh, Pennsylvania, on October 27, 2018, was a byproduct of Trump's failure to stem the tide of hate he himself has given rise to, claiming the lives of eleven and marking the deadliest mass shooting of Jewish people in United States history.

I will point out that Trump in his affirmation that he is the least racist person simply because he has friends who are Jewish when he continues to display racist tendencies, is consistent with another "least racist individual," Adolf Hitler. The man who would go on to kill six million Jews found joy in his friendship with a young Jewish girl, Rosa Bernile Nienau who had a shared birthday. After meeting in 1935, the two corresponded seventeen times until Nazi leadership ordered the young girl and her mother to stop writing in 1938. So in a sense, Trump is only as racist as Adolph Hitler was.[105]

This again brings up the question of morality in respect to Trump. There is a certain sense amongst people I have discussed my views of Trump's dis-

---

[105] "Remarkable Tale of Hitler's Young Jewish Friend." BBC News, BBC, 13 Nov. 2018, www.bbc.com/news/world-europe-46192941.

ability that Trump is amoral and has no conscious. This is supported by his racism, bigotry, exceptionalism to rules and complete lack of empathy. I have read the reports saying that Trump has Narcissistic Personality Disorder. Indeed, Trump's behavior is aligned to NPD, but that clearly is not the full explanation of who Trump is, nor does it answer why Trump doesn't function properly as Autism does. Trump clearly lacks empathy, the ability to see and share experiences collectively from other's points of view. This isn't due to his personality, rather his emotional deficit connected to his disability of Autism Spectrum Disorder. [106]

Feuds with the NFL and NBA

NFL superstar Quarterback Colin Kaepernick's decision to take a knee as the National Anthem played in peaceful protest connected to the Black Lives Matter movement during the 2016 football campaign would have largely been a small side note in history books had it not been for Donald Trump picking up the issue, possibly at the insistence of White House Advisor Steve Bannon in 2017.

Trump connected the issue of protesting the inordinate amount of police brutality and extrajudicial killings of African-American males by law enforcement incorrectly to disrespecting the country and the military. While it is difficult to know whether Trump was repeating the talking points of those he saw on TV or the talking heads were repeating what he said and tweeted, the divisive nature of what he was doing was evidently playing well to his base of supporters.

In Alabama in front of an enthusiastic crowd, on September 22, 2017, Trump unleashed this fiery attack encouraging the NFL to fire players:

> *"Wouldn't you love to see one of these NFL owners when somebody disrespects our flag to say get that son of a bitch off the field right now, out, he's fired, he's fired. You know, some owner is going to do that.*
>
> *"He's going to say that guy that disrespects our flag, he's fired. And that owner, they don't know it, they don't know it, they're friends of mine, many of them, they don't know it, they'll be the*

---

106 "Does Trump Suffer from Narcissistic Personality Disorder?" Psychology Today, Sussex Publishers, www.psychologytoday.com/us/blog/the-human-beast/201608/does-trump-suffer-narcissistic-personality-disorder.

most popular person for a week, they'll be the most popular person in this country because that's a total disrespect of our heritage, that's a total disrespect of everything that we stand for, OK? Everything that we stand for.

"And I know we have freedoms and we have freedom of choice and many, many different freedoms. But you know what? It's still totally disrespectful. And, you know, when the NFL ratings are down massively, massively...The NFL ratings are down massively."[107]

At a joint press conference with Rajoy of Spain, Trump on September 26, 2017, was asked if he was preoccupied with the NFL instead of dealing with the deadly aftermath of Hurricane Maria that struck on September 20.

"There's some concern that you were preoccupied with the NFL instead of dealing with Puerto Rico. Why isn't that a fair assessment?"

"Well, I wasn't preoccupied with the NFL. I was ashamed of what was taking place, because to me that was a very important moment. I don't think you can disrespect our country, our flag, our national anthem. To me, the NFL situation is a very important situation. I've heard that before about was I preoccupied. Not at all. Not at all. I have plenty of time on my hands. All I do is work.

"And to be honest with you, that's an important function of working. It's called respect for our country. Many people have died—many, many people. Many people are so horribly injured. I was at Walter Reed Hospital recently, and I saw so many great young people, and they're missing legs and they're missing arms.

"And they've been so badly injured. And they were fighting for our country. They were fighting for our flag. They were fighting for our national anthem. And for people to disrespect that by kneeling during the playing of our national anthem I think is disgraceful."[108]

---

[107] Factbase. "Transcript Quote - Speech: Donald Trump Holds a Political Rally in Huntsville, Alabama - September 22, 2017." Factbase, factba.se/transcript/donald-trump-speech-luther-strange-rally-huntsville-alabama-september-22-2017.

[108] Factbase. "Transcript Quote - Press Conference: Donald Trump and Mariano Rajoy of Spain - September 26, 2017." Factbase, factba.se/transcript/donald-trump-press-conference-rajoy-spain-sep-

Trump eventually got around to visiting Puerto Rico on October 3 to throw paper towels to the crowd and brag about the low death toll. With how spectacularly bad Trump performed once he "focused" on Puerto Rico, maybe it was a good thing he invested his energies on attacking black athletes instead of saying insensitive comments and showing zero ability to show empathy in a devastating and fully non-Presidential way.

October 7, 2017, Trump stages an expensive political message by sending his Vice President to the Colt Forty-niners game with the instructions to bail if any players protested, with the press pool waiting at the exits. When the protests happened, Pence did that; however Trump couldn't help but blurt out his entire charade on Twitter:[109]

> *"I asked @VP Pence to leave stadium if any players kneeled, disrespecting our country. I am proud of him and @SecondLady Karen."*
> *11:16 A.M. 8 Oct 2017[110]*

Off and on throughout the 2017 season, Trump revisited this racist theme of black players taking a knee were disrespecting the country. With his broadsides against the athletes, not just the NFL but also NBA stars Lebron James and Stephon Marbury, some of the most admired idols of the African-American community, a greater awareness and resistance arose against Trump's blatant racism. Whereas two players were Trump's target for kneeling at first, many teams, high school and professional soon took a knee to assert their First Amendment rights. That didn't lessen the attacks by Trump, only intensified his hatred as he took what they were doing as a personal attack and failed to understand what the issue of race relations was all about.

Trump is very tenacious, and that tenacity eventually wears down resistance to him often getting whatever he demands. It is one of the few elements

---

tember-26-2017.

[109] Landler, Mark, et al. "Trump Tells Pence to Leave N.F.L. Game as Players Kneel During Anthem." The New York Times, The New York Times, 8 Oct. 2017, www.nytimes.com/2017/10/08/us/politics/pence-anthem-colts.html.

[110] Trump, Donald J. "I Asked @VP Pence to Leave Stadium If Any Players Kneeled, Disrespecting Our Country. I Am Proud of Him and @SecondLady Karen." Twitter, Twitter, 8 Oct. 2017, twitter.com/realDonaldTrump/status/917091286607433728?ref_src=twsrc%5Etfw%7Ctwcamp%5Etweetembed%7Ctwterm%5E917091286607433728&ref_url=https%3A%2F%2Fwww.cnn.com%2F2017%2F10%2F08%2Fpolitics%2Fvice-president-mike-pence-nfl-protest%2Findex.html.

I see in Trump's personality as a positive trait and a "great" personal strength allowing him to persuade others to do what he wants. During a May 24, 2018, Fox and Friends Interview with Brian Kilmeade, Trump is given the news that the NFL has finally bent to his will taking away players Constitutional right to protest during the National Anthem, instead making them stay inside the locker room. Here is how Don responds:

> *"Well I think that's good. I don't think people should be staying in locker rooms. But still I think it's good. You have to stand proudly for the national anthem or you shouldn't be playing, you shouldn't be there. Maybe you shouldn't be in the country. You have to stand proudly for the national anthem and the NFL owners did the right thing and that's what they've done."[111]*

Suggesting getting kicked out of the country for exercising one's Constitutional rights was just another one of those moments Trump made the National Anthem protests Us versus Them fight. By the time the preseason swung around, the NFL abandoned the policy that had given Donald a partial victory against the players he had fought so hard against. Trump waylaid the NFL again on Twitter Aug. 10, 2018, in these two Tweets at 6:18 and 6:32 A.M.:

> *The NFL players are at it again—taking a knee when they should be standing proudly for the National Anthem. Numerous players, from different teams, wanted to show their "outrage" at something that most of them are unable to define. They make a fortune doing what they love*
>
> *.....Be happy, be cool! A football game, that fans are paying soooo much money to watch and enjoy, is no place to protest. Most of that money goes to the players anyway. Find another way to protest. Stand proudly for your National Anthem or be Suspended Without Pay!*

---

111 Canty, Jennifer. "Transcript Quote - Interview: Brian Kilmeade Interviews Donald Trump on Fox & Friends - May 24, 2018." Factbase, CantyMedia, factba.se/transcript/donald-trump-interview-brian-kilmeade-fox-friends-may-24-2018.

At the end of the 2018-2019 football season Trump had this to say about the Super Bowl and "our" unity when no one kneeled at the beginning of the game:

> *And when our workers win, who really wins? Our country wins because we're all in this together. We're one team, one people, and one family. And we're saluting one great American flag, and everybody stood up yesterday. There was nobody kneeling at the beginning of the Super Bowl. We've made a lot of improvement, haven't we? That's a big improvement. And on top of that, it was a good game. So a lot of good things happened. But there was no kneeling before that Super Bowl."[112]*

I find it striking how often Trump gets or takes credit for fixing something that he himself broke. The National Anthem protests starting with two men kneeling developed into a crescendo of hundreds of thousands, perhaps millions of men women and children taking a knee in solidarity to protest racism that spouts openly from the President. Eventually, no one is currently protesting, so Trump takes credit for fixing the problem he created.

There isn't a single American ethnic group that has been spared it seems from Trump blurting out something racist about its people. Trump attacks on Elizabeth Warren calling her derogatorily Pocahontas weren't that bad, as both women were powerful leaders, till his 5:52 P.M. EST, January 13, 2019, Tweet hit the internet shortly after Elizabeth's campaign ad hit:

> *"If Elizabeth Warren, often referred to by me as Pocahontas, did this commercial from Bighorn or Wounded Knee instead of her kitchen, with her husband dressed in full Indian garb, it would have been a smash!"[113]*

---

[112] Factbase. "Transcript Quote - Speech: Donald Trump Delivers a Speech on Tax Reform in Ohio - February 5, 2018." Factbase, factba.se/transcript/donald-trump-speech-tax-reform-ohio-february-5-2018.

[113] Trump, Donald J. "If Elizabeth Warren, Often Referred to by Me as Pocahontas, Did This Commercial from Bighorn or Wounded Knee Instead of Her Kitchen, with Her Husband Dressed in Full Indian Garb, It Would Have Been a Smash! Pic.twitter.com/D5KWr8EPan." Twitter, Twitter, 14 Jan. 2019, twitter.com/realDonaldTrump/status/1084644517238714369?ref_src=twsrc%5Etfw%7Ctwcamp%5Etweetembed&ref_url=https%3A%2F%2Ffactba.se%2Fsearch.

Invoking powerful memories of the brutality of two US military massacres of Native Americans, Trump mocks a political opponent. When this came out I could think of only one thing more offensive that Trump could have said. He went there at 2:54 P.M. EST, February 9, 2019:

> *"Today Elizabeth Warren, sometimes referred to by me as Pocahontas, joined the race for President. Will she run as our first Native American presidential candidate, or has she decided that after 32 years, this is not playing so well anymore? See you on the campaign TRAIL, Liz!"*[114]

Trail of tears, the forced government removal of many tribes in the South Eastern United States, is about as low as one can go attacking America's indigenous people.

During the campaign candidate Trump's Twitter account tweeted via Dan Scavino, a now deleted image of a piles of hundred dollar bills, Hillary Clinton and a six-sided star saying "most corrupt candidate ever." When it was pointed out the connection of money and the Star of David, someone changed the offending star into a circle.

Trump defended the offensive Tweet for several minutes, blaming CNN, talking about how offensive it was that people took offense to a star with money in Cincinnati, Ohio, July 6, 2016. He argued strongly that taking down the star was wrong. He would rather have defended it. His defense of it was likely MORE offensive than the image as he free-wheeled his attack into Hillary, the media, Bernie who he felt was also wronged by Hillary, and then back to those who criticized him. [115]

The Central Park Five

In Trump's Op-ed on May 1, 1989, he took out in the *NY Times*, costing $85,000, against the Central Park Five, one Latino and four Black kids accused of raping a white woman, suggested to "bring back the death penalty." The language is

---

[114] Trump, Donald J. "Today Elizabeth Warren, Sometimes Referred to by Me as Pocahontas, Joined the Race for President. Will She Run as Our First Native American Presidential Candidate, or Has She Decided That after 32 Years, This Is Not Playing so Well Anymore? See You on the Campaign TRAIL, Liz!" Twitter, Twitter, 9 Feb. 2019, twitter.com/realDonaldTrump/status/1094368870415110145?ref_src=twsrc%5Etfw%7Ctwcamp%5Etweetembed&ref_url=https%3A%2F%2Ffactba.se%2Fsearch.

[115] Factbase. "Transcript Quote - Speech: Donald Trump in Cincinnati, OH - July 6, 2016." Factbase, factba.se/transcript/donald-trump-speech-cincinnati-oh-july-6-2016.

clearly not Trump's words, being too high of a vocabulary, no repetitive phrasing or idiosyncratic language as well as falling on a very high tenth-grade level, perfectly appropriate to reach his intended audience, the readers of the *Times*.

The five "other" victims, who were coerced into confessions by the police, were exonerated through DNA testing and confession of another man who caused the actual crime in 2002 vacating their convictions did little to change Trump's fixed opinion of the group. In his restricted view, he saw them as rapists therefore they would always be rapists. A Ken Burns 2012 documentary about the wrongful conviction of Central Park Five raised the ire of Trump leading to this exchange on Twitter:

> *"The Central Park Five documentary was a one sided piece of garbage that didn't explain the horrific crimes of these young men while in park"*
>
> -Donald J. Trump
> April 24, 2013 1:34 A.M.

> *"@realDonaldTrump DNA EVIDENCE PROVED THEY WERE INNOCENT. THEY COMMITTED NO CRIME. I'll never get an answer. I hope this isn't a real person."*
>
> -Rebecca Erin
> April 24, 2013 1:37 A.M.

> *"@RebeccaErin_ They were viciously attacking other people in the Park-nice guys?"*
>
> -Donald J. Trump
> April 24, 2013 2:47 A.M.

The city later settled for wrongful imprisonment paying out forty-one million. Trump writes in the *New York Daily News*, published on June 21, 2014:

> *"My opinion on the settlement of the Central Park Jogger case is that it's a disgrace. A detective close to the case, and who has followed it since 1989, calls it 'the heist of the century.'*
>
> *"Settling doesn't mean innocence, but it indicates incompetence on several levels. This case has not been dormant, and many people*

have asked why it took so long to settle? It is politics at its lowest and worst form.

"What about the other people who were brutalized that night, in addition to the jogger?

"One thing we know is that the amount of time, energy and money that has been spent on this case is unacceptable. The justice system has a lot to answer for, as does the City of New York regarding this very mishandled disaster. Information was being leaked to newspapers by someone on the case from the beginning, and the blunders were frequent and obvious.

"As a long-time resident of New York City, I think it is ridiculous for this case to be settled—and I hope that has not yet taken place.

"Forty million dollars is a lot of money for the taxpayers of New York to pay when we are already the highest taxed city and state in the country. The recipients must be laughing out loud at the stupidity of the city.

"Speak to the detectives on the case and try listening to the facts. These young men do not exactly have the pasts of angels.

"What about all the people who were so desperately hurt and affected? I hope it's not too late to continue to fight and that this unfortunate event will not have a repeat episode any time soon—or ever.

"As citizens and taxpayers, we deserve better than this."

This OpEd has more "signature" Trump than the original in 1989, as whoever was dictated to by Donald kept more of what he said in the final message. [116] [117]

In a CNN interview the first week of October 2106 with Miguel Marquez Trump said this:

"They admitted they were guilty. The police doing the original investigation say they were guilty. The fact that that case was settled with so much evidence against them is outrageous. And the

---

[116] Trump, Donald. "Donald Trump: Central Park Five Settlement Is a 'Disgrace.'" Nydailynews.com, New York Daily News, 9 Jan. 2019, www.nydailynews.com/new-york/nyc-crime/donald-trump-central-park-settlement-disgrace-article-1.1838467.

[117] Lange, Jeva. "Donald Trump's 30-Year Crusade against the Central Park Five." Image, The Week, 7 Oct. 2016, theweek.com/articles/653840/donald-trumps-30year-crusade-against-central-park-five.

woman, so badly injured, will never be the same."[118]

Such rigidity is a hallmark of Trump's restricted behaviors. He believes intently with his own "alternative facts" and is not going to be convinced otherwise that he is wrong. Which brings up the question, should we start calling him Individual 1 as it only seems fair considering his own history of public lambasting minorities without just cause as criminals based on his own personal belief?

---

[118] Holmes, Steven A. "Member of 'Central Park 5' Blasts Trump." CNN, Cable News Network, 7 Oct. 2016, www.cnn.com/2016/10/06/politics/reality-check-donald-trump-central-park-5/index.html.

Chapter Nine

"This Is the Biggest Liar I've Ever Seen" MAGA

Trump's "biggest" whopper, the one that catapulted him into the spotlight as a Presidential candidate, then into the White House, was that America was truly horrible without his leadership. MAGA, Make America Great Again, is more than a slogan. It was an outreach resonating with many white Americans that felt displaced by minorities and foreign competition. The Wall represented a barrier to keep out the undesirable, and provide job security for a great deal of Trump's base that was heavy white, lower overall levels of education and male than any previous Presidential winner.

MAGA and America First have a deeper history paralleling with 1930s post-World War I Germany where Adolf Hitler used the same slogans substituting Germany for America in his propaganda. Hitler sought to convince everyday Germans that the Jews, historically and stereotypically connected to the banking system at the time, were to blame for the suffering of country. Most of the World was in a deep Depression as economies had hit a particularly hard down slide with protectionist policies and lack of liquidity in the financial markets. Germany, forced to pay exorbitant reparations as part of the 'unfair' Treaty of Versailles to the Allies following World War I, suffered most with the complete collapse of their currency and trust of the government.

Hitler attended a small organization, the German Workers Party in 1919 after the Great War having been sent to spy on the left-wing socialist group for the German Army. He ended up in a debate, impressed the leader, Anton

Drexler, an anti-Semite and nationalist like Adolf. Hitler joined as the fifty-fourth member and brought in similarly minded individuals through his contacts in the military and development of propaganda. Hitler quickly became the lead speaker, propaganda developer and active recruiter.

Hitler designed the parties flag with the swastika, likely taking a native-American peace symbol, reversing its directional orientation, then placing it on a red and black flag, as well as changed the name of the German Workers Party into the National Socialist German Workers Party April of 1920. He insisted on the "national" part of the name, as it identified with his Germany first messaging needed to carry out his social campaign against non-white racial groups. He reluctantly kept "socialist" in the name as he needed to still appeal to a broad base, despite his ultra-right-wing philosophies such as hatred towards social and sexual equality espoused by the left. This redefinition of Socialism as Nationalist Socialism was effective propaganda as he was still able to appeal to workers while denigrating those that were not racially pure. The nickname for the political organization was Nazi, short for nationalist, a term that will forever be connected with the crimes against humanity that would eventually happen during the Second World War, known simply as the Holocaust.[119]

Hitler replaced Drexler as leader of the party in 1921, and formed the Stormtroopers, a private army. Like Trump, Hitler incited others to violence. In September 1921, he spent three months in prison for mob violence against a political opponent. Remember how Trump issued this praise about Greg Gianforte, a Republican candidate that picked up and body-slammed a reporter on October 18, 2018, at a rally in Missoula, Montana?

> *"He's so smart. You know, we've had people—you're on live television all over the place, and we've had people get up speak for 20, 25 minutes. And these guys are going crazy, that's not the deal. But Greg is smart. And by the way, never wrestle him. You understand that? Never. Any guy that can do a body slam, he's my kind of... He was my guy.*
>
> *"I shouldn't say this, because—there's nothing to be embarrassed about. So I was in Rome with a lot of the leaders from other countries talking about all sorts of things, and I heard about it. And*

119"The Nazi Party: Background & Overview." Background & Overview of the Nazi Party (NSDAP), www.jewishvirtuallibrary.org/background-and-overview-of-the-nazi-party-nsdap.

*we endorsed Greg very early, but I had heard that he body-slammed
a reporter. And he was way up. And he was way up. And I said,
oh, this was like the day of the election, or just before, and I said,
oh, this is terrible, he's going to lose the election."[120]*

Hitler like Trump began early cultivating his rise of power, stoking far-right nationalist ideals and extremist views formed alliances based on loyalty, failed in a bold coup attempt, known as the Beer Hall Putsch, on November 8, 1923 and wound up in prison in 1924 for nine months. Hitler wrote a book, *Mein Kampf*, meaning *"My Struggle,"* which was a best-seller at five million copies sold. For a Trump perspective, *The Art of the Deal* has sold roughly one-fifth of Hitler's book.[121] With what is known about Trump, we will probably find an uncovered landfill of tens of thousands of his book purchased by himself through his charities buried just like 1982 Atari's *E.T.: The Extraterrestrial*, meaning that much fewer actually read that instant throw-away "written" by Trump.[122]

Hitler's tome argued similar to Trump that there was an existential threat to the white man, the Aryan race.

*"Every manifestation of human culture, every product of art,
science and technical skill, which we see before our eyes today, is almost exclusively the product of Aryan creative power."[123]*

Trump exercises a similar trope against Central Americans, while "appealing" to his base of marginalized white men while "including" African-Americans in this campaign speech about job security at West Bend, Wisconsin, on August 16, 2016:

---

[120] Factbase. "Transcript Quote - Speech: Donald Trump Holds a Political Rally in Missoula, Montana - October 18, 2018." Factbase, factba.se/transcript/donald-trump-speech-maga-rally-missoula-mt-october-18-2018.

[121] Price, Greg. "Bob Woodward's Book Sold Almost as Many Copies in One Week as Donald Trump's 'Art of the Deal' Has in 30 Years." Newsweek, 19 Sept. 2018, www.newsweek.com/bob-woodward-outsold-trump-art-deal-1126603.

[122] Good, Owen S. "E.T. Cartridges Found in Infamous Atari Landfill." Polygon, Polygon, 26 Apr. 2014, www.polygon.com/2014/4/26/5656282/atari-et-landfill-new-mexico-found-cartridges.

[123] "The Nazi Party: Background & Overview." Background & Overview of the Nazi Party (NSDAP), www.jewishvirtuallibrary.org/background-and-overview-of-the-nazi-party-nsdap.

"First, on immigration. No community in this country has been hurt worse by Hillary Clinton's immigration and all of her policies than the African-American community. And she considers them a guaranteed vote. Now she is proposing to print instant work permits for millions of illegal immigrants to come in and take everybody's job, including low-income African-Americans. Not right, not going to happen. I will secure our border, protect our workers and improve our jobs and wages in your community. We're going to improve our wages. We're going to improve our jobs. And we're not going to let companies leave our country so quickly and so easily for other lands and then take their products and sell it to us. Not going to happen."[124]

Trump of course has used exceedingly more demeaning and caustic language against Central Americans since taking office, so this early example of his nationalist agenda against minorities had to look and sound differently compared to what he could say as President. Like Hitler, he still needed to appeal to minorities and other groups he intends to harm with his policies later, to take power. As President he could use the harsher rhetoric aimed at *"shithole"* countries and infestations to frenzy his most loyal and radicalized base on the far-right.

Hitler's ambitions after failing to take over Germany by force in his coup transformed into taking over the country by coercion and political election when he left prison. His party competed and grew in membership before he himself would run. He didn't need Russian hackers and voter suppression tactics to gain control, as his propaganda was sound. Hitler, like Trump, gave speeches with empty promises (manufacturing is coming back, coal will be king) depending on the audience. To farmers Hitler promised tax cuts and to industrialists, anti-regulation. Hitler and Trump both succeeded in their ploy winning added support with each speech. Hitler lost in 1931 but wielded significant power with his current private militia of 400,000 men, compared to the limited under treaty 100,000 German national army. When four of his soldiers brutally murdered a man with a pool cue in front of his mother, Hitler sided with his men promising support in a letter he would see that they could be released.

---

124 Factbase. "Transcript Quote - Speech: Donald Trump in West Bend, WI - August 16, 2016." Factbase, factba.se/transcript/donald-trump-speech-west-bend-wi-august-16-2016.

Hitler finished second in the 1933 popular vote, just as Trump had finished second to Hillary in 2016 for the US popular vote, granting him power as second to the elderly eighty-four-year-old President Paul von Hindenburg, with the title of Chancellor in 1932. Hitler used that position to launch his political agenda to align with his personal one, pounding opposition within his party and without through intimidation and propaganda. Hitler in 1933 controlled the full government and knocked out remaining political opposition setting the stage for his military ambitions and worse alongside his Nazi party. Hitler pulled out of the League of Nations October of 1933, the equivalent to the United Nations at the time, which Trump frequently attacks.

Hitler became the only head of state after a series of assassinations of rivals within his Stormtroopers and government, and a law enacted by his cabinet abolishing the office of the President. The former President died the next day after losing his position in August of 1934. Hitler was fully in charge, and able to carry out his agenda via propaganda, and force. The business of extermination began around 1939 with the help of desensitized and compliant co-conspirators, of Jews, gays, Gypsies, and other minority groups. It is estimated that roughly two-thirds of the European Jewish population were removed in Hitler's "Final Solution."[125]

Does all this sound familiar? It is why people often draw comparisons between Nationalist Trump and Nationalist Hitler.

Trump has done exactly what Hitler did during the early thirties in stoking racist and xenophobic fear through his campaign speeches and immigration policy appealing to a surprisingly fragile and dangerous demographic.

Trump ALSO has stifled most of his political foes in the same manner, though with significantly less sophistication than Hitler did on his own personal interactions. His red hat campaign, with Make America Great Again slogan emblazoned in white, is a symbol of hate and intolerance against the Muslims he openly persecutes with his promised Muslim ban and the Central American refugees seeking refuge from violence he maligns and dehumanizes calling them invaders, rapists and murderers.

While a great deal of what Trump has done on this front is likely not fully attributed to Donald, no one, not his "better" advisors nor his family have kept him from yielding to his racist impulses, making life under "Heir Dtrumpf"

---

[125] "The Nazi Party: Background & Overview." Background & Overview of the Nazi Party (NSDAP), www.jewishvirtuallibrary.org/background-and-overview-of-the-nazi-party-nsdap.

much different for those "targeted" outside of Trump's base than from within. It is essentially two different Americas. While Hitler rarely pulled the trigger to personally kill anyone, he was the cause of millions being killed influenced by his doctrines. Trump is no different in this regard. If a white nationalist is inspired by Trump, but is tired of waiting for action says this before committing the largest mass killing of Jewish people in America, the President is to blame:

> *"HIAS likes to bring invaders in that kill our people. I can't sit by and watch my people get slaughtered. Screw your optics, I'm going in."*

Since mid-2016, when Trump's campaign was in full swing, a corresponding increase in far-rightwing violence, fueled by identity politics, made popular in the campaign with advisor Steve Bannon directing much of the propaganda, was going on. The Tree of Life shooter had been radicalized with help from Trump's anti-immigrant attacks. HIAS, the Hebrew Immigrant Aid Society, a Jewish group that helps immigrants of any faith to assimilate in American culture, as well as billionaire philanthropist George Soros had been tied to the migrant caravans the President had been so fervently maligning. The shooter's use of "invaders," a word frequently used by Trump and his media, is a clear connection of why this tragedy happened. [126]

The Rundberg neighborhood of Austin, Texas, where I worked from 2016-2017 at IDEA public schools, was similarly under attack directly due from Trump and his ICE "stormtroopers." The IDEA Rundberg campus and two companion campuses in the city cater to a mostly immigrant base of students, some with limited English proficiency. Austin, Texas, is one of those *"sanctuary cities"* Trump marginalized frequently in his rallies to his mostly white base supporters, which made what ICE did very personal during February and March of 2017.

> *"...We've ordered a crackdown on sanctuary cities that refuse*

---

[126] "How Robert Bowers Went from Conservative to White Nationalist." Gazette, www.postgazette.com/news/crime-courts/2018/11/10/Robert-Bowers-extremism-Tree-of-Life-massacre-shooting-pittsburgh-Gab-Warroom/stories/201811080165.

to comply with federal law and that harbor criminal aliens, and we have ordered an end to the policy of catch and release on the border. No more release. No matter who you are, release. We have begun a nationwide effort to remove criminal aliens, gang members, drug dealers and others who pose a threat to public safety. We are saving American lives every single day...."

-Donald Trump
February 16, 2017[127]

What happened in the neighborhood was dangerous and unconstitutional. ICE soldiers terrorized the community, arresting *"fifty-one foreign nationals"* according to initial reports on local channels between the dates of February 9-12, 2017. The total was later revealed to be One hundred thirty-two people, sixty of which had no criminal convictions. ICE has no authority for the arrest and detainment of non-criminals.[128]

"One consequence of this is the fear and panic among many of our neighbors who do not pose threats to our community," Adler wrote. "Some family members are disappearing with their whereabouts unknown. Some parents, fearful of apprehension, aren't sure of what will happen to their U.S.-born citizen children, not to mention the home they've owned for years and into which they've placed all their family savings."[129] Austin Mayor Steve Adler March 9, 2017

At our campus, we had families go in and out of hiding, fearing for their safety. Others disappeared. Plenty of students came to school terrorized having seen the raids in the complexes where they lived and no one seemed to feel safe or secure. Some lamented having their relatives arrested. We kept

---

[127] Factbase. "Transcript Quote - Press Conference: Donald Trump at The White House - February 16, 2017." Factbase, factba.se/transcript/donald-trump-press-conference-washington-dc-february-16-2017.

[128] Hall, Katie. "State Rep Slams Feds after New Data Says Twice as Many People Netted in ICE Raids." Statesman, Austin American-Statesman, 22 Sept. 2018, www.statesman.com/NEWS/20180125/State-rep-slams-feds-after-new-data-says-twice-as-many-people-netted-in-ICE-raids.

[129] Flores, Nancy, et al. "Austin No. 1 in U.S. - for Noncriminals Arrested in ICE Raids." Statesman, Austin American-Statesman, 25 Sept. 2018, www.statesman.com/news/20170309/austin-no-1-in-us—for-noncriminals-arrested-in-ice-raids.

the best normalcy and safe place that we could offer while these precious children were at the school.

I am more observant than most people. It is part of my own autism which I cherish. During this critically challenging time for our students ICE did things that did not get reported to the news by campus officials knowing if something was said, ICE would likely increase their activities. One was witnessed by me. At carpool a low-flying black-and-white glass-bottom helicopter did a flyby surveil of our families cars, circled around and did it a second time. There was no other reason in the flight pattern for this behavior. The target was clearly the families at the school. As I was too busy making sure each child was safely tucked in their car, I did not get out and record a video, something I regret to this day. Only two of us, the second being a parent, looked up at the helicopter perhaps only 150 meters hovering above slowly moving well above the cars full of families. I was livid as I knew they were using this expensive flyover as an intimidation effort, but relieved that only two of us saw what ICE had done.

The Rundberg campus had it easy compared to what other staff at the Allen campus encountered. ICE troopers on foot once came up to the fence on the campus and began "cat-calling" children by first and last names, terrorizing hundreds of children in the process. These in-uniform "child-snatchers" left when campus staff approached and threatened to call authorities, knowing that the harassment they were engaged in wasn't legal and they better leave before being arrested or attracting more negative attention.

Trump wasn't only limiting his executive power to terrorize immigrants in sanctuary cities. He was intent on shutting down all forms of immigration from *"shithole"* countries. He attacked "chain immigration" while using it to get his in-laws here, as un-American.

> *"We have so many other things. You have chain migration, where a bad person comes in, brings 22 or 23 or 35 of his family members—because he has his mother, his grandmother, his sister, his cousin, his uncle—they're all in."*[130]
>
> *-Donald Trump*
> *February 15, 2019*

---

[130] "Remarks by President Trump on the National Security and Humanitarian Crisis on Our Southern Border." The White House, The United States Government, www.whitehouse.gov/briefings-statements/remarks-president-trump-national-security-humanitarian-crisis-southern-border/.

I have often wondered if Donald Trump's grandfather, Freidrich Trump, the owner of a Bennet, Canada, brothel where the family real estate fortune started, had been subject to this sort of logic that he was a bad person whoring out women for cash, that Trump's forefather would never have been let into the US.[131]

Chain immigration has another kinder name, family-based immigration a hallmark of how in this great nation, including Trump's own family, immigrants have entered the country, put down roots and raised a family. Nothing could be crueler than separating a person permanently from their family, so naturally as with many of Trump's policies, the Zero Tolerance policy was subsequently adopted and immediately enforced for the misdemeanor crime of entering the country "illegally."

The Zero Tolerance scheme, the forced separation of children including infants from their parents seeking legal asylum claims within the United States and/or those with children who were otherwise detained officially began on April 6, 2018, when Jeff Sessions announced the Nationalist policy to keep out the riff-raff Trump has long demonized as monsters invading our country. According to the Human Rights Watch, an organization that tracks oppressive governments abusing the dignity and rights of people around the world, the US had implemented some of the procedures prior to the announcement as early as October 17, 2017. After the announcement all families entering including at legal ports of entry were subjected to this cruel and unusual government sponsored abuse.[132]

Trump's gestapo claimed falsely that other administrations were to blame. The courts didn't allow detainment of children, and the government was therefore obligated to separate the children while incarcerating the parents. Other administrations rarely prosecuted families, and none children as the Trump administration set out to do as a deterrent to stop future migrant caravans from forming and traveling to the US.

Diaper clad babies were forced before judges, in one case a one-year-old asking the judge for "agua" when asked a required question of the judge.

---

[131] Bloomberg.com, Bloomberg, www.bloomberg.com/features/2016-trump-family-fortune/.

[132] "Q&A: Trump Administration's 'Zero-Tolerance' Immigration Policy." Human Rights Watch, 16 Aug. 2018, www.hrw.org/news/2018/08/16/qa-trump-administrations-zero-tolerance-immigration-policy.

"I'm embarrassed to ask it, because I don't know who you would explain it to, unless you think that a one-year-old could learn immigration law."[133]

-Judge John W. Richardson
July 8, 2019

This serious violation of International law and US Federal law brought swift condemnation, and many court challenges which were piled up as steady judicial defeats against the administration. The crisis inducing policy was ended by Trump on June 20, 2017, replaced with housing "criminal" families together in detention centers. Trump Tweets his desire to suspend the Constitutional rights of Due Process on June 24, 2018, at 8:02 A.M.:

"We cannot allow all of these people to invade our Country. When somebody comes in, we must immediately, with no Judges or Court Cases, bring them back from where they came. Our system is a mockery to good immigration policy and Law and Order. Most children come without parents..."[134]

Then on June 27, 2018, Trump's administration was handed another court defeat by President George W. Bush appointee Dana Sabraw, ordering the reunification of children separated and "lost" under Trump's watch:

"The government readily keeps track of personal property of detainees in criminal and immigration proceedings. Money, important documents, and automobiles, to name a few, are routinely catalogued, stored, tracked and produced upon a detainee's release, at all levels—state and federal, citizen and alien. Yet, the government has no system in place to keep track of, provide effective communication with, and promptly produce alien children. The unfortunate reality is that under the present system migrant chil-

---

[133] Galvan, Astrid. "Kids as Young as 1 in US Court, Awaiting Reunion with Family." AP NEWS, Associated Press, 8 July 2018, www.apnews.com/4cb60fc06ca34160bf7445fdc1f47eed.

[134] Hegarty, Aaron. "Timeline: Immigrant Children Separated from Families at the Border." USA Today, Gannett Satellite Information Network, 25 July 2018, www.usatoday.com/story/news/2018/06/27/immigrant-children-family-separation-border-timeline/734014002/.

dren are not accounted for with the same efficiency and accuracy as property. Certainly, that cannot satisfy the requirements of due process."[135]

-DS District Court Judge Dana Sabraw
June 27, 2018

Several thousand children who were "detained" by the government had to be returned to their parents, some who had been deported without required due process, possibly will never able to see or hear from their children again, due to lack of record keeping on the governments part. The administration then moved to "eliminate" asylum rules via executive order on November 9, 2017, broader definition to end the legal practice most of the refugees had used to enter the States legally near the end of the year. Again the Trump administration was blocked by Judges on November 20, 2017, and on December 19, 2018:

"Whatever the scope of the president's authority, he may not rewrite the immigration laws to impose a condition that Congress has expressly forbidden."[136]

-US District Judge Jon Tigar

"Many of these policies are inconsistent with the intent of Congress as articulated in the (Immigration and Nationality Act), and because it is the will of Congress—not the whims of the Executive—that determines the standard for expedited removal, the Court finds that those policies are unlawful."[137]

-US District Judge Emmet Sullivan

---

[135] Stanglin, Doug. "Immigrant Children: Federal Judge Orders Families Separated at Border Be Reunited within 30 Days." USA Today, Gannett Satellite Information Network, 27 June 2018, www.usatoday.com/story/news/politics/2018/06/27/judge-orders-families-separated-border-reunited-within-30-days/737194002/.

[136] Laughland, Oliver. "'He May Not Rewrite Immigration Laws': Trump's Asylum Ban Blocked by Federal Judge." The Guardian, Guardian News and Media, 20 Nov. 2018, www.theguardian.com/us-news/2018/nov/20/trump-asylum-ban-blocked-federal-judge-us-mexico-border.

[137] Gomez, Alan. "Federal Judge Blocks Another Attempt by Trump to Limit Asylum." USA Today, Gannett Satellite Information Network, 20 Dec. 2018, www.usatoday.com/story/news/world/2018/12/19/second-judge-blocks-attempt-trump-limit-asylum-migrant-caravan-immigration-border/2066608002/.

Chapter Ten

"Grab Them by the Pussy"

Trump's 2005 Access Hollywood Tape with Billy Bush was released weeks before the 2016 General Election on October 7, 2016, via *The Washington Post*. Its recorded contents were dismissed as boys being boys or locker room talk, forgetting that Trump was married to his third wife or that even though he behaved childlike he was fifty-nine, old enough to use better judgement. Trump's poor filtering and eagerness to please others lead to the following exchange:

> **Trump**: *I moved on her, actually. You know, she was down on Palm Beach. I moved on her, and I failed. I'll admit it.*
> **Unknown**: *Whoa.*
> **Trump**: *I did try and fuck her. She was married.*
> **Unknown**: *That's huge news.*
> **Trump**: *No, no, Nancy. No, this was [unintelligible]—and I moved on her very heavily. In fact, I took her out furniture shopping.*
> *She wanted to get some furniture. I said, "I'll show you where they have some nice furniture." I took her out furniture—*
> *I moved on her like a bitch. But I couldn't get there. And she was married. Then all of a sudden I see her, she's now got the big phony tits and everything. She's totally changed her look.*

> *Billy Bush: Sheesh, your girl's hot as shit. In the purple.*
> *Trump: Whoa! Whoa!*
> *Bush: Yes! The Donald has scored. Whoa, my man!*
> *Trump: Look at you, you are a pussy.*
> *Trump: All right, you and I will walk out.*
> *[Silence]*
> *Trump: Maybe it's a different one.*
> *Bush: It better not be the publicist. No, it's, it's her, it's—*
> *Trump: Yeah, that's her. With the gold. I better use some Tic Tacs just in case I start kissing her. You know, I'm automatically attracted to beautiful—I just start kissing them. It's like a magnet. Just kiss. I don't even wait. And when you're a star, they let you do it. You can do anything.*
> *Bush: Whatever you want.*
> *Trump: Grab 'em by the pussy. You can do anything.*
> *Bush: Uh, yeah, those legs, all I can see is the legs.*
> *Trump: Oh, it looks good.*
> *Bush: Come on shorty.*
> *Trump: Ooh, nice legs, huh?*
> *Bush: Oof, get out of the way, honey. Oh, that's good legs. Go ahead.*
> *Trump: It's always good if you don't fall out of the bus. Like Ford, Gerald Ford, remember?*
> *Bush: Down below, pull the handle.[138]*

Let's pause and think for a moment. Does everything Trump said on that recording match up with what is known about the Donald?

It does.

Donald also reveals a pattern to his rule breaking, finding an exception that personally excludes him from having to follow the rules everyone else does. In his own explanation, Donald is excluded from the rule about how to socialize with women appropriately, by creating the exception to that rule—Women will allow celebrities to do whatever they want with them.

Donald has no social inhibitions when it comes to flirting, groping objectifying or assaulting women based on his comments over the years, having

---

138 "Transcript: Donald Trump's Taped Comments About Women." The New York Times, The New York Times, 21 Dec. 2017, www.nytimes.com/2016/10/08/us/donald-trump-tape-transcript.html.

failed in marriage a couple of times and the long list of his accusers. Additionally, lacking social inhibition is wholly consistent with the Autism Spectrum, as many individuals on the spectrum will say or do the first thing that pops into their head because they lack self-regulation, the ability to fully control their behavior.

Speaking of no social inhibitions, Donald on the April 11, 2005, *Howard Stern Show* described how he would "get away with" walking backstage at his beauty pageants.

> ***Trump:*** *"Well, I'll tell you the funniest is that I'll go backstage before a show. And everyone is getting dressed and ready, and everything else and then there are no men or anywhere, and I'm allowed to go in because I'm the owner of the pageant and therefore I'm inspecting it. You know, I'm inspecting it. You know I'm inspecting it, I wanna make sure that everything is—"*
> ***Stern:*** *"You're like a doctor, you need to be there."*
> ***Trump:*** *"Yeah, the dress... 'Is everyone okay? Is everybody okay,' and you see this incredible looking women. And so I sort of get away with things like that, but..."[139]*

Donald understood social rules forbade men from entering a place where women were getting dressed. He wanted to go in, see the women naked, so he created an exception that would allow him to, by his owning the pageant. While this isn't how things work in the real world, Donald's penchant for making exceptions to excuse or justify his own bad behavior, then having zero consequences reinforcing him, explains how Trump still views himself, as innocent and law-abiding despite what he has done. This wasn't limited just to his adult pageants. Trump took the liberty of walking in on his teen contestants as well, such as the 1997 pageant at South Padre Island with girls as young as fifteen a behavior that one would think would land him on the registered sex offenders list. [140]

---

[139] Factbase. "Transcript Quote - Interview: Donald Trump on The Howard Stern Show - April 11, 2005." Factbase, factba.se/transcript/donald-trump-interview-howard-stern-show-april-11-2005.

[140] Barbash, Fred. "Former Miss Arizona: Trump 'Just Came Strolling Right in' on Naked Contestants." The Washington Post, WP Company, 12 Oct. 2016, www.washingtonpost.com/news/morning-mix/wp/2016/10/12/former-miss-arizona-trump-just-came-strolling-right-in-on-naked-contestants/.

Trump's most creepy moment captured on tape happened when he was forty-six speaking to an unseen female child, as seen on Entertainment Tonight's Christmas piece in 1992 filmed in Trump Tower. Trump (not viewed in the clip) is speaking to an unseen individual, answers a question then Trump asks a simple question to an unseen girl then blurts out without filtering the unthinkable. Here is the exchange:

"Soon, Thursday Night. You going to go up the escalator?"

"Yeah"

"I am going to dating her in ten years. Can you believe it?"

Seconds later in the clip a girl in a pink coat with blonde hair enters the video on the escalator, back turned at first then turning around towards the camera, shifting from one side of the escalator to the other. Judging by others on the escalator as a reference point, her height is less than five feet tall, and appears very young. Judging by her size and movement she can't be any older than twelve.[141]

Trump's behavior in the clip is inexcusable, yet he was never held to account for what he said. Yes, it is consistent with lack of filtering from Autism, but there are many accounts out there about Trump's sexual comments or behavior where no recording exists that have greater believability and criminal context in light of stuff like this, or say his attraction to a twelve-year-old Paris Hilton admitted unfiltered on the *Howard Stern Show* after her sex tape "leak" January 4, 2004:

> ***Trump****: "Now, somebody who a lot of people don't give credit to but in actuality is really beautiful is Paris Hilton. I've known Paris Hilton from the time she's twelve, her parents are friends of mine, and the first time I saw her she walked into the room and I said, 'Who the hell is that?'"*
>
> ***Stern****: "You wanna bang her?"*
>
> ***Trump****: "At twelve I wasn't interested. I've never been into that. That's sort of always stuck around that twenty-five category."*
>
> ***Stern*** *:"But even at twelve you were kind of what, she's hot?"*
>
> ***Trump****: "Well at twelve she was beautiful. But honestly you know, Paris gets knocked in this and that but she's very beautiful. She gone flawless. She's she's dumb like a fox."[142]*

---

141 News, CBS. "Trump Makes Questionable Comments about Young Girls in 1992 Video." YouTube, YouTube, 12 Oct. 2016, www.youtube.com/watch?v=yRAPLodRnd4.

142 Factbase. "Transcript Quote - Interview: Donald Trump on The Howard Stern Show - January 7,

"Dumb like a fox" isn't the social idiom we use. The correct idiom is "crazy like a fox." Trump then explains that the sex tape, which he says wife Melania showed him, was *"just yeah."* I guess since his wife showed him the tape its fine, right? These sort of sugar coats, to make something sweet instead of bitter, indicate that Trump feels a little guilt if he was watching a porn with his wife not knowing, perhaps as if he feels that would be cheating.

Trump did identify, a little too late, that saying he has sexually attracted to a child was socially inappropriate, as evidenced by his then bringing up his twenty-five-year-old rule. This back-tracking works well in casual conversation but not when you are being recorded! I say this as I too had times where I didn't think and blurted out something inane that could have multiple contextual meanings. I had a whole group of elementary boys snickering over my error at the end of recess in line who were not ready to go into the building, blurting very loudly with forcefulness the command, *"Boys, stop bouncing your balls and hold them in your hand."*

Ugh, that was NOT what I meant to say. It happens. Had I used the word "equipment" it still would not work, though only three or four of the boys would have guffawed. I then went over the procedure and expectations of when the whistle was blown, to hold all playground *"supplies"* and be ready to enter the building silently. I rarely make this sort of mistake, as I created a strategy of pausing before I speak, something Trump may want to consider.

Trump's interest in the female form wasn't just limited to women, preteens and teens. His conversations about his daughter Ivanka often were inappropriate due to his lack of filter, and need for constant attention. His March 6, 2006, appearance on *The View* was one of many cringe-worthy moments:

> *"I don't think Ivanka would do that, although she does have*
> *a very nice figure. I've said if Ivanka weren't my daughter, perhaps*
> *I'd be dating her.*
> *"Isn't that terrible? How terrible? Is that terrible?"[143]*

Yes, it is terrible and Trump knew he should not say it but did. He could not help it. Trump has no filter, and will continue to say and do these sorts of

---

2004." Factbase, factba.se/transcript/donald-trump-interview-howard-stern-show-january-7-2004.

[143] Aulari, Baudolino. "Trump: If Ivanka Weren't My Daughter, I'd Be Dating Her." YouTube, YouTube, 8 Aug. 2015, www.youtube.com/watch?v=diMp241gAcw.

things as he might not be capable of changing his behavior with it going unchecked for so long.

Trump has said socially worse things on tape about his girl, like during a taped appearance alongside his daughter on *The Wendy Williams Show* in 2013. What do Ivanka and her father have in common? Ivanka gave a polite answer of golf and real-estate. Trump, lacking filter, answers this way while pointing to his daughter who was cringing in embarrassment:

"Well, I was going to say sex, but I can't relate that to her."[144]

His *"I can't relate that to her"* implies that he has never had sex with his daughter, not that he can't say that to Ivanka (because he just did in front of a nationally televised audience and those who were attending live). What likely went through Don's head was that since Ivanka was married, she has sex. I have sex. It is both something we enjoy doing so it is a shared interest. Sex happened to be the first thing that popped into his mind, not golf or real-estate. People chalked this up to a crude joke when the problem was limited cognitive filtering and poor self-control due to Autism.

Daughter Tiffany was only a baby when Trump, appearing on a 1994 interview for *Lifestyles of the Rich and Famous* with Robin Leach, said this:

> *"Well, I think she's got a lot of Marla, she's a really beautiful baby. She's got Marla's legs. We don't know whether or not she's got this part yet, but time will tell."*[145]

Trump indicated with his hands that he was referencing breasts, clearly had poor reasoning in that moment.

Donald appears to have good relationships with all of his children including his two daughters. They love him and I presume he has been nothing but a caring father in their view. While there are statements and even one picture with he and teen daughter Ivanka in an embrace better suited for a wedding announcement than a father-daughter embrace, none in the family

---

[144] MailOline, Hannah Al-Othman For. "Trump Jokes He Has 'Sex' in Common with Daughter Ivanka in Bizarre Wendy Williams Interview." Daily Mail Online, Associated Newspapers, 26 Oct. 2016, www.dailymail.co.uk/news/article-3870754/The-thing-common-sex-Bizarre-interview-Donald-Ivanka-Trump-resurfaces-three-years-later.html.

[145] Moran, Lee. "That Time Trump Speculated About His 1-Year-Old Daughter's Breasts On TV." The Huffington Post, TheHuffingtonPost.com, 25 Aug. 2018, www.huffingtonpost.com/entry/donald-trump-daughter-breasts-robin-leach_us_5b8111fde4b07295151325bd.

have indicated any sort of sexual abuse. Donald has even has maintained positive relationships with his first two wives over the decades.

The conversation of the May 8, 1993, *Howard Stern Show* focused on Ivana, Trump's first wife, and how she got twenty-five million in a settlement and then wrote a book about *"Ronald"* to get around prenuptial agreements. Howard remarked about Ivana's transformation to keep Donald's attention which I assume means plastic surgery:

> *"Well, I don't want—I don't want to talk about what she did or whatever but—And she's a good woman and I'll always love her."*
>
> *"She's not a good woman, Donald. I'm going to tell you something. Any woman, if you give her $25 million—You don't have to say she's a good woman. She's not a good woman. She's the mother of your children. That's true."*
>
> *"True."*
>
> *"But that's it. That's as far as it goes."*
>
> *"Yeah. But she's the mother of my children."*

Trump still has a strong relationship with Ivana calling her periodically despite the book. With how quickly Trump has turned on others for similar betrayals, I find his continued warmth for Ivana a positive in an otherwise challenged list of damaged relationships.

The conversation then turns to looking and comparing other women connected romantically to Trump, such as wife number two Marla Maples and lingerie model Fredrique.

> *"Well she's a really good friend and she's a great woman and she's going to be very successful as time goes by in terms of other things. But right now she's one of the most successful models she works for Victoria's Secret."*

Howard already knew Fredrique works for Victoria's Secret, so Trump not realizing that he knew the context of the picture he was showing him, clearly shows that Trump has had these deficits that this book is based on for at least twenty-five years. The rest of the pictures Howard showed to Trump, all rumored to be connected to him, and Trump's openly honest reactions to Stern's queries was full of interesting tidbits. Trump viewed many of the women as "good friends." One woman, Kim Alley, clearly used and embarrassed Trump with a kiss and tell, and Donald's childlike innocence that he "didn't even know" meaning she would use his celebrity to advance herself seemed to sting the vulnerable Mr. Donald.

Howard then lines up all these pictures for Donald to organize in order of attractiveness. Trump puts the woman he replaced Ivana with, Marla Maples at the top, then another woman he slept with and the women he hadn't slept with but identified as "friends" at the bottom. He had Kim Alley booted hilariously from the line-up. Then Howard showed a pick of model "Howina" (Howard as a girl) and asked Trump what he thought of this woman as a potential girlfriend. Trump was not impressed and gave a blunt response:

"That's not a good body, I'll tell you."

The conversation then returns to Trump's compulsion for hand washing discussed in a previous chapter of this book, and drinking through a straw to prevent germs, wrapping up the conversation neatly for the segment. Howard asks Don how he would react if he were in a public bathroom and someone wanted to shake his hand:

"I may be a bad guy. When you say excuse me, you were just holding the urinal."[146]

"Fat," "ugly," and other childish insults over the years have crawled out of Trump's brain on Twitter, interviews and on video. So has his objectifying women, comparing their physical traits and other demeaning remarks appeared both past and present as he moved to a bigger stage. The allegations of sexual misconduct against Donald exploded when he decided to announce his candidacy for President. He had a plan to combat this.

Donald had managed to keep some of his reputation protected from some of the most salacious accusations over the years by recruiting others to squelch stories such as David Pecker of *The National Enquirer.* We know from the guilty

---

[146] Factbase. "Transcript Quote - Interview: Donald Trump on The Howard Stern Interview on E! - May 8, 1993." Factbase, factba.se/transcript/donald-trump-interview-howard-stern-may-8-1993.

plea by Trump's almost decade-long personal lawyer and fixer Michael Cohen that an illegal conspiracy involving a "catch-and-kill" scheme was hatched to increase Trump's likelihood of getting elected.

Trump likely had been doing this sort of thing for decades, as it was legal to do as a private citizen but not for a Presidential candidate due to added Federal Laws overseeing elections. Cohen arranged for Pecker to buy up any negative Trump stories with a non-disclosure and exclusive publishing rights given to those who brought the stories to the company. At least two stories involving Trump having sexual relationships while his wife Melania was postpartum after birthing son Barron were snagged in this manner. These were Playmate Karen McDougal's and adult film star Stephanie Clifford's (Stormy Daniels') accounts of the affairs they had with the future President.

The National Enquirer paid the women, after contracts were signed and then held onto their stories, then would reach out to Cohen for reimbursement. Cohen then made a shell company making false statements to a banking official to open an account to transfer what later turned out to be campaign donations, to *The National Enquirer.*

The Trump administration's stance over the story, like everything having to do with crimes connected to the President surfacing, is that the crimes are in no way related to the President, only to the individual that just pled guilty. The President isn't directly named in the court filing, rather identified in court filings as Individual 1. [147]

Cohen's lawyer then released part of an audio recording taken in September 2016:

> ***Cohen:*** *"I need to open up a company for the transfer for all that info regarding our friend David, you know, so that I'm going to do that right away.*
> */A section of the conversation is missing or redacted/*
> ***Cohen:*** *"When it comes time for the financing, which will be—"*
> ***Trump:*** *"What financing?"*
> ***Cohen:*** *"We'll have to pay."*
> ***Trump:*** *"Pay with cash."*

---

[147] Stewart, Emily. "Read Michael Cohen's Plea Deal." Vox, Vox, 21 Aug. 2018, www.vox.com/2018/8/21/17765496/michael-cohen-plea-deal-sdny-criminal-prison.

Cohen: "*No, no, no—I got—no no no—*"[148]

When Cohen's office and home were raided by federal agents they recovered this tape along with other evidence not yet in the public domain. His lawyer is entitled to copies of the evidence against his client, and as Michael had already entered in a plea deal with cooperation agreement, the audio presumably has more details than the Mueller Investigation team wanted released.

Michael Cohen went on to plead guilty on August 21, 2018, in the Southern District of New York, who had received the criminal complaint from the Mueller investigation, for these crimes and several unrelated (non-Trump) tax crimes, for eight total charges. Cohen admitted in court to committing some of the crimes in coordination with and at the direction of a candidate for federal office.[149]

---

[148] HuffPost. "Trump And Cohen Recording Released." YouTube, YouTube, 25 July 2018, www.youtube. com/watch?v=faYUae7H8qU.

[149] Stewart, Emily. "Read Michael Cohen's Plea Deal." Vox, Vox, 21 Aug. 2018, www.vox.com/2018/8/ 21/17765496/michael-cohen-plea-deal-sdny-criminal-prison.

Chapter Eleven

"This Russia Thing Is a Made-Up Story"[150]

"**B**ut it would be interesting to see—I will tell you this—Russia, if you're listening, I hope you're able to find the 30,000 e-mails that are missing. I think you will probably be rewarded mightily by our press. Let's see if that happens."

-Donald Trump, July 27, 2016

And so began the "biggest" political crime in American History, with Trump now centering himself at the middle of it. Trump had been speaking about how bad it was that someone, maybe Russia, would hack into a major political party, then said the unthinkable, by asking that foreign power to do something he wanted—to get Hillary's emails.

The connections why he did this are very clear in his pattered, often repeated behavior. Trump wants something done, something he knows is fundamentally wrong, but is able to make an exception to that rule that would otherwise forbade him, allowing him to act without guilt.

Let's step back for a moment, as what Trump did, asking a foreign power to spy on his Democrat opponent on his behalf, was something seemingly impulsive and in line with everything we know about Trump's inability to self-regulate his own behavior. Has he done this before, and if so why?

Yes.

Donald Trump watches a lot of TV where he gets most, if not all his information. He has an intense fascination for certain media, namely Fox News and other outlets that push a great deal of conspiracy theories and other unsupported stories in their "reporting." This intense fixation is part of his restricted patterns of behavior that are associated with his disability of Autism. He is obsessed with those conspiracy topics so much in fact, that he has before attempted to recruit others to break in to Columbia University to "discover" if one of those theories was true or not.

Yes, Donald knows it is wrong to break into Columbia. He makes an exception to the rule of breaking in on the basis that if he is able to get the records to prove the theory that Obama was born outside of the United States in Kenya, it would be fine. Trump failed in his attempt to recruit political activist and Project Veritas founder James O'Keefe in 2013, according to James account in the book *American Pravda: My Fight for Truth in the Era of Fake News.*[150]

Trump's attempted recruitment may have failed with O'Keefe, but with the Russians, Trump asked and they obliged launching an infiltration getting into the Podesta server on the same date, July 27, 2016, as Trump's request, according to the Indictment of seven Russians filed July 13, 2017, by the Office of the Special Counsel, page 7, section 22:

> *"The Conspirators spearphished individuals affiliated with the Clinton Campaign throughout the summer of 2016. For example, on or about July 27, 2016, the Conspirators Case 1:18-cr-00215-ABJ Document 1 Filed 07/13/18 Page 7 of 29 8 attempted after hours to spearphish for the first time email accounts at a domain hosted by a thirdparty provider and used by Clinton's personal office. At or around the same time, they also targeted seventy-six email addresses at the domain for the Clinton Campaign."[151]*

There is virtually no difference in how the Columbia conspiracy and the Russ-

---

[150] Athey, Amber. "What Trump Asked James O'Keefe To Find Out About Obama." Trump Allegedly Asked O'Keefe To Get Obama's Sealed Columbia Records, The Daily Caller, 11 Jan. 2018, dailycaller.com/2018/01/11/trump-allegedly-asked-okeefe-to-get-obamas-sealed-columbia-records/.

[151] United States, Congress, UNITED STATES DISTRICT COURT FOR THE DISTRICT OF COLUMBIA. "Case 1:18-Cr-00215-ABJ." Case 1:18-Cr-00215-ABJ, UNITED STATES DISTRICT COURT FOR THE DISTRICT OF COLUMBIA, 2018, pp. 1–29.

ian conspiracy began, with Trump making a suggestion to someone, andseeing if they did what he asked. Whereas O'Keefe walked away, Russia saw a clear opportunity with such an open invitation to help out Trump in his efforts to secure the White House that they were more than willing to support his bid by fulfilling his request.

As most of the more salacious details involving the Trump Campaign and Russian Conspiracy to subvert the 2016 election have to do with his co-conspirators that willingly acted on his behalf, and this book centers on how Trump's behavior relates to his disability, we will instead focus on how Donald's manipulation led others to commit crime on his behalf. Let's start with individuals who Trump was unable to manipulate.

December 7, 2018, Rex Tillerson, former Secretary of the State, spoke very candidly about Trump and his way of how he wants to get things done often didn't jive with the law:

> *"Our differences were always on tactics. When the president would say, 'Here's what I want to do and here's how I want to do it,' and I would have to say to him, 'Mr. President, I understand what you want to do, but you can't do it that way. It violates the law. It violates a treaty."*
>
> *"I didn't know how to conduct my affairs with him any other way than a straight-forward fashion, and I think he grew tired of me being the guy every day that told him you can't do that. And uh, let's talk about what we can do."* [152]

Tillerson is a stand-up great guy that came into the administration having never met the President. Trump began publicly undercutting him as he did others who didn't do what he wanted, and eventually fired Tillerson. The reason for the rift—Tillerson didn't give Trump what he had asked for.

Former FBI director James Comey, also eventually fired by Trump, counseled then President Elect Trump about Russian interference into the 2016 General Election. Like many who encounter Trump, Comey sensed something was different about the man he was meeting. His memos detailed that

---

[152] "Trump 'Frustrated' over Law Violation Warnings: Tillerson." Reuters, Thomson Reuters, 7 Dec. 2018, www.reuters.com/video/2018/12/07/trump-frustrated-over-law-violation-warn?videoId= 489588576.

first encounter:

> *"I said, the Russians allegedly had tapes involving him and prostitutes at the Presidential Suite at the Ritz Carlton in Moscow from about 2013. He interjected, 'There were no prostitutes; there were never prostitutes.' He then said something about him being the kind of guy who didn't need to 'go there' and laughed (which I understood to be communicating that he didn't need to pay for sex). He said '2013' to himself, as if trying to remember that period of time, but didn't add anything. He said he always assumed that hotel rooms he stayed in when he travels are wired in some way. I replied that I do as well."[153]*

Trump is very naive and simple at times. He takes risks without thinking about the consequences based on his candid conversations on the *Howard Stern Show*, including his using a condom to prevent AIDS. He has slept with plenty of women over the years and is viewed as a rich playboy. That a story with prostitutes bothers him and makes him uncomfortable is a signal that Trump is too trusting.

Using Trump's possible distorted thinking discussed in earlier chapters as a basis for his making faulty justifications for his behavior, it is possible Donald did not pay these women, therefore in his mind were not prostitutes. The event is consistent with what is known about Trump in regards to attractive women. It is also seemingly consistent with how one would assume Russia would respond given a chance to blackmail a target.

The timing mentioned was connected to the Ms. Universe Pageant Trump took to Moscow, and formed the basis of one of the more salacious details of the Steele Dossier, dated June 20, 2016, paid initially for by a GOP primary challenger to Trump, then later sold to the Clinton campaign. In that document Trump is said to have directed a pair of women to pee on the bed that Obama has previously stayed in. [154]

Comey then explains policy of keeping these sort of things close and ad-

---

[153] Day, Chad, and Associated Press. "Ex-FBI Director James Comey's Memos." DocumentCloud, www.documentcloud.org/documents/4442900-Ex-FBI-Director-James-Comey-s-memos.html.

[154] Schoofs, Mark. "Trump Intelligence Allegations." DocumentCloud, www.documentcloud.org/documents/3259984-Trump-Intelligence-Allegations.html.

vising Trump that this story may come out in the media, as they already were known to have the details.

> *"I said I wasn't saying this was true, only that I wanted him to know that it had been reported and that the reports were in many hands. I said media like CNN had them and were looking for a news hook. I said it was important that we not give them the excuse to write that the FBI has the material or /redacted/ and that we were keeping it very close-hold. He said he couldn't believe they hadn't gone with it. I said it was inflammatory stuff that they would get killed for reporting straight up from the source reports.*
>
> *"He then started talking about all the women who had falsely accused him of grabbing or touching them (with particular mention of a 'stripper' who said he grabbed her) and gave me the sense that he was defending himself to me. I responded that we were not investigating him and the stuff might be totally made up but it was being said out of Russia and our job was to protect the President from efforts to coerce him. I said we try to understand what the Russian are doing and what they might do. I added that I also wanted him to know this in case it came out in the media."[155]*

So why then did Trump and Putin get along so well? The Russians know what I am saying, that Donald Trump has compulsive behaviors and probably deducted he was autistic based on their own observations. The PP tape likely exists. So does perhaps a couple dozen other videos or recordings of the unsuspecting Trump. If Putin pulled any of that out on Donald in one of their meetings, believe me, Trump would not be acting consistently in a warm and cordial way each and every interaction he has had with Vladimir. They are the best of friends and Trump's sincere demeanor shows that Trump trusts that relationship.

Donald Trump is a Russian Asset. He just doesn't know it.

---

[155] Day, Chad, and Associated Press. "Ex-FBI Director James Comey's Memos." DocumentCloud, www.documentcloud.org/documents/4442900-Ex-FBI-Director-James-Comey-s-memos.html.

Chapter Twelve

"Do I Have Social Skills? I Don't Know"

One shouldn't need to tell an adult that maybe their new pal Vladimir Putin doesn't have his best interest in mind, or that he shouldn't trust what Putin says before the two were scheduled to sit down in Helsinki. After all, Putin has always had at minimum an adversarial relationship with his American counterpart always pushing any advantage with cunning precision. The two did meet. In a rather short time, Vladimir had convinced Trump that the two were best of friends and that it was in their mutual interest to have the KGB interview Americans, observe and help our election officials and do joint military training. While Congress put the kibosh on these proposals, Trump certainly appeared sincere in his desire to do these things for his "friend."

I have had to give this same social skill lesson time and time again to many of my Autistic students. They had such a longing to belong that it was too difficult for them to realize that others were exploiting them. Saying the right thing, like giving Trump endless compliments that we saw the ex-KGB chief lather on Trump made in their joint conference at the adjournment of the summit, was an expert example of the pitfalls of having a President unable to detect sincerity. Similarly Xi, Kim and others either stumbled onto or already knew that Trump's behavior could be manipulated with simple flattery before laying out a plan which Trump would likely accept with the right amount of encouragement.

Putin and other Russians have expertly kept to the script with Trump, giving him flattery, encouragement and saying all the right things publicly to cultivate trust and comradery. They don't need Trump to know he is working for them, so long as they control as many of the people inside his administration through blackmail or other means. Through these co-conspirators, Russia could persuade Trump easily to agree to do things favorable to the Russian federation.

> *"I never said there was no collusion between the campaign, or people in the campaign … I said the President of the United States. There is not a single bit of evidence the President of the United States committed the only crime you can commit here, conspiring with the Russians to hack the DNC."[156]*

Rudy's CNN interview on January 16, 2019, may have marked the beginning of the throw everybody under the bus phase of Trump's legal defense. As Trump's lawyer, after most of his previous legal counsel had quit, Rudy Giuliani has been quite the interviewer. His job is to protect the President, a man who is at the epicenter of roughly a dozen investigations.

I rather preferred the Trump is too incompetent to organize a conspiracy defense used to argue against a personal interview with Mueller, resulting in a written testimony instead. It still took him and his legal team more than two days to complete the document as the President discussed doing to a press spray on November 18, 2018, and his legal counsel submitted it on November 20.[157][158][159]

Rudy may be right in this defense, as well as Trump's lawyers who successfully lobbied Mueller that Trump was incapable of knowing he was lying or not.

---

[156] Kelly, Caroline. "Rudy Giuliani Says Trump Didn't Collude with Russia but Can't Say If Campaign Aides Did." CNN, Cable News Network, 17 Jan. 2019, www.cnn.com/2019/01/16/politics/rudy-giuliani-cnntv/index.html.

[157] Haberman, Maggie, and Michael S. Schmidt. "Mueller Will Accept Some Written Answers From Trump." The New York Times, The New York Times, 4 Sept. 2018, www.nytimes.com/2018/09/04/us/ politics/mueller-trump-russia-investigation.html.

[158] Hains, Tim. "Full FOX News Interview: President Trump on Divided Congress, Mueller, Foreign Policy, Fake News, More." RealClearPolitics, www.realclearpolitics.com/video/2018/11/18/president_ trump_on_divided_congress_mueller_foreign_policy_fake_news_more.html.

[159] "Trump Submits Written Answers to Special Counsel Robert Mueller's Questions." NBCNews.com, NBCUniversal News Group, www.nbcnews.com/politics/donald-trump/trump-submits-written-answers-robert-mueller-s-questions-n938666.

Trump, while known for insulting people, generally African-American people, as having low IQs really isn't that smart. Rudy, if he is a good lawyer, should have Trump sit down and complete a full cognitive evaluation with two or three of those evaluations measuring his IQ, or Intelligence Quotient, the expected performance of an individual based on a battery of subtests measuring long and short term memory and other metrics. In Special Education I was trained on, but haven't given the Woodcock-Johnson Tests of Cognitive Abilities as part of my certification in Special Education program at Weber State University. I generally was the one in charge of recording and observing behavior as part of any school evaluation for eight years while at a high-performing Charter School in Utah. Give Trump that and either the Stanford-Binet Intelligence Scales or the Wechsler Adult Intelligence Scale.

Based on my own "gut instinct" I would wager Trump would do rather poorly on an IQ test, perhaps low enough to qualify for Special Education under Intellectually Disabled, a category requiring two standard deviations below the normed average at the 50-69 range. Trump is inattentive, doesn't learn things correctly and is mostly a learner through connecting to what he sees and hears on television.

This doesn't mean that Trump isn't "smart," just that he is no "stable genius." I actually put him in the low end of the average range, somewhere in the 87-92 range based on his "angry moments" where he is juiced up and thinking quickly. This is how Trump is at his rallies and when he has felt trapped in a corner. When Trump is more taciturn, like when he is doing a sit-down interview, his crispness is a little delayed. An IQ test is very unlikely to get Trump's cognitive juices running, though he may show that "teacher-pleasing skills" he did in the 2016 deposition mentioned previously, and be fully engaged for some of the measurements.

On actual achievement, a different testing metric used to compare cognitive ability with student academic achievement, Trump lacks the foundation skills of math, reading and writing to do any higher than 80.

One of the more interesting patterns I have seen with these tests is that many of the kids on the Spectrum perform all over the place with some categories at really high and others at really low marks. They almost all did poorly on communication, written, verbal and non-verbal. Trump, if he is listening and engaged, should have several markers above 100, the median score of any bell-curve test and a few that require pragmatic judgment abysmally low, in the 50s and 60s.

Back to Trump and his greatest vulnerability—Social Skills deficits.

Trump is incapable of reading social situations and doesn't know when he is being played. Someone almost always has to explain why things mean what they do, and with how restricted his behavioral patterns are now with Russia, his wanting to be a success and other things included, Trump has been played by a whole lot of people, not just foreign adversaries. Many are his closest "friends," that had agendas of their own.

When allies have played Trump, like when the almost giggling Canadian Prime Minister on June 10, 2018, gave him a photo of Donald's grandfather Freidrich's "hotel," Forty-five was beaming. Well played, Justin. Donald found out later from either media reports or others that his grandfather owned a brothel not a hotel and that was one of the issues pushing the family to immigrate to the United States and not be welcomed back to Germany, Trump was none too pleased.

Trump left the G7 summit early headed to Singapore, failed to sign the summit's communique and blasted Trudeau as dishonest and weak. The relationship was over, and Trump was fuming.[160]

The Queen of England "only" wore a broach given to her by Michelle Obama. That was a much more classy way to troll, far better and less obvious than a diapered baby Trump balloon or the Green Day's song *American Idiot* to the top of the record charts campaign during Donald's July 17, 2018, visit to the kingdom. The Brits do love their politics. Trump was shielded from most of this, and didn't have an epic meltdown.[161] [162] [163]

Even Russia risked trolling Trump with the press coverage "betrayal" of Kislyak and Lavrov meeting him in the Oval Office while the US Press Corps were locked out, more so to fracture US allies trust in Trump than to potentially

[160] Caralle, Katelyn. "Justin Trudeau Trolls Trump with Framed Photo of His Grandfather's Canadian Brothel." Washington Examiner, 16 June 2018, www.washingtonexaminer.com/news/canadian-prime-minister-justin-trudeau-trolls-trump-photo-grandfathers-brothel.

[161] MailOnline, Martha Cliff for. "The Queen Was Reportedly 'Trolling Trump' with Choice of Brooches." Daily Mail Online, Associated Newspapers, 17 July 2018, www.dailymail.co.uk/femail/article-5961705/Did-Queen-troll-Trump-BROOCHES.html.

[162] "Green Day's 'American Idiot' Hits Top of British Charts in Time for Trump's UK Visit." USA Today, Gannett Satellite Information Network, 13 July 2018, www.usatoday.com/story/life/music/2018/07/12/president-trump-may-hear-green-days-american-idiot-during-uk-visit/778414002/.

[163] Lavelle, Daniel. "What Happened Next? The Trump Baby Blimp: 'In Retrospect, We Should Have Ordered a Bigger Balloon'." The Guardian, Guardian News and Media, 17 Dec. 2018, www.theguardian.com/global/2018/dec/17/what-happened-next-the-trump-baby-blimp-in-retrospect-we-should-have-ordered-a-bigger-balloon.

anger him. Had those closest to the President nudged him at this time away from trusting Putin in coordination with the press and intelligence community, perhaps Trump would have made the cognitive break in his thinking, no longer viewing Putin with the respect and admiration he presently does.

If only world leaders *just* trolled Trump instead of exploiting him. And it isn't just world leaders who are doing this. EVERYBODY around him seems to be taking advantage of an essentially vacant Presidency with Trump generally oblivious. Let's get back to the Russians, and the "discredited dossier."

According to some pages of the other less entertaining than the PP tape page dossier, Russia had groomed Trump for the better part of five years, marking the start date around the Moscow pageant. While team Trump likes to say the intelligence gathered has been discredited, any who do, do so omitting that many of the details have since been verified to be true, if spiced up by an over-expressive storyteller trying to make what was discovered through opposition research, seem even flashier than it needed to be.

One recent detail verified came out in the second guilty plea by Michael Cohen, which he had been untruthful to Congress about when the Trump Tower Moscow project plans, including a promised personal fifty-million dollar free penthouse for Vladimir Putin, had been scrapped. Cohen had pursed the agreement well beyond January 2016 as he stated to Congress on three occasions, up to June of that year. [164]

Building Trump Tower Moscow isn't that big of deal from a business perspective. Trump had sought that deal for years, without much success. From a criminal perspective, that deal had enormous potential, like Taj Mahal, the Trump casino potential, for Russia to do a little "laundry" service in another of Donald's businesses. The Taj is as far as documents go back that I can easily access connecting Trump to the criminal enterprise of the Russian mob. Essentially, the mob needed to "legitimize" money gained through generally illegal means such as extortion, prostitution, etc. Trump's casino was used at least since 1998 till its bankruptcy in 2015 to money launder for the mob's activities. Once money has been "cleaned" it is in theory easy to move around

---

[164] Ward, Alex. "Trump Tower Moscow, and Michael Cohen's Lies about It, Explained." Vox, Vox, 27 Feb. 2019, www.vox.com/world/2018/11/29/18117910/cohen-trump-tower-moscow-mueller-buzzfeed.

to other activities. The casino was hit with a ten-million fine on March 5, 2015, and had just been bankrupted a second time.[165]

There are other effective avenues for money laundering activities, including hotels, real estate, and businesses that Trump owns where Russians could in theory be plumping up Trump and friends wallets. With all the holdings that Trump has, it is impossible for him to be aware of where the money comes and goes from, which makes the potential for using his businesses doubly rewarding for the Russians. Not only do they have the opportunity to get cash into the international banking system, they also have the actual crimes linked to Trump! While these "threads" are not fully established they no doubt are part of the investigation into the Trump Organization.

---

[165] "FinCEN Fines Trump Taj Mahal Casino Resort $10 Million for Significant and Long Standing Anti-Money Laundering Violations." FinCEN Fines Trump Taj Mahal Casino Resort $10 Million for Significant and Long Standing Anti-Money Laundering Violations | FinCEN.gov, www.fincen.gov/news/news-releases/fincen-fines-trump-taj-mahal-casino-resort-10-million-significant-and-long.

Chapter Thirteen

"The whole Russia thing is a big nothing-burger."–Van Jones

In the grand scheme of things, the Russian-Trump conspiracy is a nothing-burger compared to the Saudi Arabian conspiracy concocted as part of "Trump's roadmap" for the Middle East, led by Son-in-Law, Mr. 666 Fifth Avenue, Jared Kushner. That's right, Russian interference in coordination with the Trump campaign, the blackmailing US officials, the attacks on democracy and our free elections is rather inconsequential compared to what Trump's Presidency has effected in the Middle East, for one reason only—the staggering body count already achieved.

Eighty-five thousand children died from starvation alone with some ten-million Yeminis expecting the same cruel fate due to the US supported War on Yemen. This isn't including the civilians or militia killed, just those faced with a slow and painful death. While some of the deaths happened before Trump took over (10,000 total), this humanitarian catastrophe was only made possible with his assurances, signature and blessings.[166]

The roadmap to "peace" in the Middle East is a complex conspiracy of interconnected bits and pieces that has elements of genocide, extortion and blackmail, murder and large-scale weapon sales made possible by having an inept and easily persuaded United States President willing to sign off on a deal

---

[166] Bibbo, Barbara. "UN Raises $2.6bn in Donations for Yemen Humanitarian Aid." Yemen News | Al Jazeera, Al Jazeera, 27 Feb. 2019, www.aljazeera.com/news/2019/02/raises-26bn-donations-yemen-humanitarian-aid-190226161139569.html.

without understanding the magnitude or scope of what it meant, with the cover of chaos at home ample enough to obscure the obliteration of potentially millions of Yemenis people.

This tragedy starts with one Jared Kushner, the owner of the underwater New York property sitting on the "mark of the beast" address on Fifth Avenue needing to find a buyer, investor or banker willing to bail him out.

The building was first purchased by Kushner Properties in January 2007, paying a then record price of $1.8 billion. The rents and low occupancy rates made the debt on the property very likely unsustainable. Charles Kushner, Jared's father and ex-felon, met with the Qatari Finance Minister in late April 2017 to secure funding, but was unsuccessful. [167]

Jared Kushner is also the son-in-law of the President of the United States, husband to Ivanka and a high-ranking administration official in the Executive Branch. Something really bad happened to Qatar the next month after Donald Trump made his first foreign visit abroad to Saudi Arabia. Is this a coincidence?

Let's take a look at parts of Trump's prepared remarks, given May 21, 2017. Note how clear and reasonable he sounds compared to everything else detailed in this book:

> *"This landmark agreement includes the announcement of a $110 billion Saudi-funded defense purchase—and we will be sure to help our Saudi friends to get a good deal from our great American defense companies. This agreement will help the Saudi military to take a greater role in security operations."*

This part early on in his speech is where Trump's buy-in to the Saudi scheme is evident. He defines himself and this deal in the same terms, as winning, making big money deals. Trump is completely blind to what he is agreeing to, as the dollar signs he is seeing will soon be bathed in blood.

> *"Young Muslim boys and girls should be able to grow up free from fear, safe from violence, and innocent of hatred."*

---

[167] Brookfield Properties announced Friday afternoon that it has acquired a 100% leasehold interest in the building. "Kushner Companies Offloads Troubled 666 Fifth Avenue Flagship." CNNMoney, Cable News Network, money.cnn.com/2018/08/03/news/companies/kushner-666-fifth-avenue-brookfield/ index.html.

Curious statement considering how Trump's broad strokes against Muslims in his campaign and Presidency has been. Keep in mind that Trump's speech was prepared for him, likely with his input. Trump has no connection to Muslims, and generally overgeneralizes the terror attacks on America by the less than a percent of radical Islam with the entire Muslim world. The "*innocent of hatred*" choice has a dual nature to it. Innocent of hated could mean that Muslims should be protected from terrorists OR that they are inclined TO BE terrorists. Language really needs to be as precise as possible in any diplomatic effort. Later, the author of this speech clarifies its meaning.

> *"But this future can only be achieved through defeating terrorism and the ideology that drives it.*
>
> *"Few nations have been spared its violent reach. America has suffered repeated barbaric attacks—from the atrocities of September 11th to the devastation of the Boston Bombing, to the horrible killings in San Bernardino and Orlando.*
>
> *"The nations of Europe have also endured unspeakable horror. So too have the nations of Africa and even South America. India, Russia, China and Australia have been victims.*
>
> *"But, in sheer numbers, the deadliest toll has been exacted on the innocent people of Arab, Muslim and Middle Eastern nations. They have borne the brunt of the killings and the worst of the destruction in this wave of fanatical violence. Some estimates hold that more than 95 percent of the victims of terrorism are themselves Muslim."*

We see that Trump's speech writer had been referring to protecting Muslim children from becoming victims of a terror attack.

> *"We now face a humanitarian and security disaster in this region that is spreading across the planet. It is a tragedy of epic proportions. No description of the suffering and depravity can begin to capture its full measure. The true toll of ISIS, Al Qaeda, Hezbollah, Hamas, and so many others, must be counted not only in the number of dead. It must also be counted in generations of vanished dreams."*

Extremism isn't only limited to these groups, nor is it only inspired by religion. Radicalization is just as rampant and perverse of a problem in the United States as it is in the Middle East, with Trump at his bully pulpit reciting hate against various racial groups, Muslims and immigrants, inspiring acts of terror within the United States without ever acknowledging or likely comprehending his role in the escalating violence. White terror, once rather limited, has been normalized. That is also a tragedy of epic proportions. We will cover the cult leader effect of Donald Trump in a subsequent chapter.

There were two other lines worthy of note for tragic reasons:

> *"Qatar, which hosts the U.S. Central Command, is a crucial strategic partner."*

Trump was soon to call out Qatar falsely as a state sponsor of terror in agreement with Saudi Arabia and UAE, and to allow a blockade to be formed around our crucial strategic partner sealing them off from Western aid.

> *"And political leaders must speak out to affirm the same idea: heroes don't kill innocents; they save them."* [168]

Trump then in his own words is no hero.

The Qatari Crisis

It still astonishes me that a President of the United States could be so easily persuaded to turn on such a vital Middle East ally. Then again, at the time I had not yet caught on how Trump was severely limited in his abilities as most of his early speeches had masked his Autism disability as they had been prepared by others. Qatar doesn't only hold a vital US military base on Russia and Iran's doorstep; they have similar value systems to America within their Sunni Islam culture. These are great people.

Qatar is very progressive, generous, respectful and caring as any government one would wish to be a US ally. They do a lot of social and charity work influencing the betterment of children, women and society in general. As an

---

[168] "President Trump's Speech to the Arab Islamic American Summit." The White House, The United States Government, www.whitehouse.gov/briefings-statements/president-trumps-speech-arab-is-lamic-american-summit/.

example, Qatar's influence on improving access to a quality education extends well beyond their borders. The emirate was in early talks to learn and implement strategies of the IDEA Charter school system within the Middle East back in 2016 when I worked there. That announcement from our regional director didn't surprise me in the least, as I already knew of their Queen's advocacy for education.

Qatar's Queen Sheikha Moza bint Nasser hired my father as well as others years ago out of Brigham Young University to work on a critically important documentary. She was deeply worried about the perceived breakdown of the familial structure and wanted to know more about how it was caused, to prevent radicalization and to strengthen families, not just Islamic ones. Interviews were conducted worldwide, including several of the families of the 911 hijackers.

What was learned by the team's research is that a father's role in the family is just as vital in a properly functioning family, as none of the hijackers had one they were searching for that sense of belonging that Al-Qaeda provided. The most important discovery-that the family meal tradition, sitting together and sharing a meal, was evident in all the closet knit families. One family did not eat till everyone was at the table, instead electing to search out the missing family member before continuing.

So with this backdrop, Trump dropped the hammer on Qatar, already blockaded since the 5th of June by fellow Gulf States and Egypt at a press conference on June 9, 2017:

> *"The nation of Qatar, unfortunately, has historically been a funder of terrorism at a very high level, and in the wake of that conference, nations came together and spoke to me about confronting Qatar over its behavior. So we had a decision to make: Do we take the easy road, or do we finally take a hard but necessary action? We have to stop the funding of terrorism. I decided, along with Secretary of State Rex Tillerson, our great generals and military people, the time had come to call on Qatar to end its funding—they have to end that funding—and its extremist ideology in terms of funding.*
>
> *"I want to call on all other nations to stop immediately supporting terrorism. Stop teaching people to kill other people. Stop filling their minds with hate and intolerance. I won't name other*

countries, but we are not done solving the problem, but we will solve that problem. Have no choice." [169]

Remember how a group fooled George W. into approving an invasion into Iraq using spiced up reports about children suffering and weapons of mass destruction that turned out to be mostly faked? Trump was given a report similar to that, "proving" Qatar had paid dearly a heavy ransom of 1.15 billion on April 21, 2017, to the Iraqi government to save twenty-six nationals that were taken hostage by "armed militants" while on a hunting party in southern Iraq. The released hostages were all alive, but gaunt. The connection to the Iraqi government in releasing them, and their taking the king's ransom hasn't fully been explained. Trump convinced of Qatari ties to terrorism approves a "second affront" of a trade embargo and blockade to further harm Qatar at Saudi insistence.[170]

Still, the pointed message Trump bellowed to *"stop filling their minds with hate and intolerance,"* a line that easily reflects back on Trump's bombastic and inflammatory rhetoric against Muslims, immigrants and other minority groups, is mind boggling.

Of course there is more to how and why this story evolved, beyond Trump's inability to listen intently to intelligence briefings and make sound decisions. There was a "hack" and false statements attributed to the Emir of Qatar on May 23, 2017, meant to cause a rift between Doha, the capital of Qatar, and the rest of their neighbors, just days after Trump had left the Middle East. Saudi Arabia and UAE blocked Al-Jazeera, who had at times been "critical" in their reporting. The whole Qatari blockade was built on lies in order to remove Al-Jazeera, a press outlet based in Qatar, whose journalists tend to shine the light on what really is going on in the Arab world, something that corrupt leaders tend to hate. One in particular shined up to Trump, Mohammad Bin-Salman, known as MbS, and is a key figure in the shake-up of the whole Middle East.

https://www.reuters.com/article/us-qatar-cyber/gulf-rift-reopens-as-qatar-decries-hacked-comments-by-emir-idUSKBN18K02Z

---

[169] Factbase. "Transcript Quote - Press Conference: Donald Trump Holds a Joint Press Conference with Klaus Iohannis of Romania - June 9, 2017." Factbase, factba.se/transcript/donald-trump-press-conference-romania-iohannis-june-9-2017.

[170] Wood, Paul. "'Billion Dollar Ransom': Did Qatar Pay Record Sum?" BBC News, BBC, 17 July 2018, www.bbc.com/news/world-middle-east-44660369?intlink_from_url=https%3A%2F%2Fwww.bbc.com%2Fnews%2Ftopics%2Fcny6m78kw47t%2Fqatar-crisis&link_location=live-reporting-story.

On June 23, 2017, Saudi Arabia made its list of demands, to be met in ten days. The thirteen are listed here:

1. Curb ties to Iran
2. Sever ties to terror organizations
3. Shut down Al-Jazeera
4. Shut down news outlets that Qatar funds
5. Terminate Turkish military presence
6. Stop funding terrorism
7. Hand over "terrorist figures"
8. End interference in sovereign countries internal affairs
9. Stop contacts with political opposition in other Gulf States
10. Pay reparations caused by Qatar policies
11. Consent to monthly audits for the first year
12. Align with Arab countries economically, militarily, socially and politically
13. Agree to all demands within ten days[171]

MbS really hates the media sources that he cannot control, more so than Donald, as several of these demands are directly connected to ridding him of the "evils" of the free press in the region. His complete takeover as heir of the Kingdom also struck during this critical time.

On June 21, 2017, favored son MbS was named crown prince; replacing a cousin less favorable to Trump, as the heir to the throne should King Salman, his father, pass away. He is currently the most powerful and influential man in the Kingdom and the one able to pull the strings.

The puppet-master ruler-to-be, first began cleaning up "corruption" in the Kingdom during May. Women civil rights activists, clerics and other prominent Saudis were swept up in a crackdown on dissent, which allegedly involved tortures, sexual assault, water boarding and electrocution. When you want to send a message, it needs to be clear and brutal to be effective, such as Union General William T. Sherman's desolation wake in his Civil War March to the Sea. Such a message says you mean business. This preparation was leading up to the MAIN event slated for November 4, 2017.

[171] Wintour, Patrick. "Qatar Given 10 Days to Meet 13 Sweeping Demands by Saudi Arabia." The Guardian, Guardian News and Media, 23 June 2017, www.theguardian.com/world/2017/jun/23/close-al-jazeera-saudi-arabia-issues-qatar-with-13-demands-to-end-blockade.

Ritz Carlton Shakedown

Imprisoning eighty-seven royals and other political targets in the Ritz-Carlton at Riyadh in an "anti-corruption sting" netted a paltry 106.6 billion after all was said and done. The shakedown, though in the nicest of five star prisons, involved psychological torture and abuse needed to consolidate MbS's power, political control and wealth. Only one detainee has died, while many who have been released have been stripped of most of their freedoms as well as their wealth.[172] [173]

The shakedown at the Ritz happened after Jared Kushner traveled to Saudi Arabia in late October 2017, where the Presidential advisor allegedly gave US Intelligence detailing who was disloyal to MbS, an accusation Kushner and the White House deny. The Intel originated from "eavesdrops" by US intelligence officers which included details of what was said in the calls. Kushner could not do this legally without Trump's consent. Kushner's temporary clearance to the highest classified documents was revoked for three months with no explanation, from February 27, 2018, to May 23, 2018, by John Kelly, White House Chief of Staff.[174]

The Crown Prince bragged about how Kushner gave him the Intel, and now had him in his pocket to Abu Dhabi Crown Prince Mohammed bin Zayed, of the United Arab Emirates and others according to sources. [175]

The Killing of *Washington Post* Reporter Jamal Khashoggi

MbS ,with the United States' blessing for the go-ahead, had extended ambitions beyond the Saudi Emirate, crushing regional rivals such as Qatar into submission and cruelly wiping millions of Houthis off the Peninsula into mass

---

[172] "How Saudi Arabia's Crown Prince Crushed His Rivals at the Ritz." NBCNews.com, NBCUniversal News Group, www.nbcnews.com/news/mideast/how-saudi-royal-crushed-his-rivals-shakedown-ritz-carlton-n930396.

[173] agencies, The New Arab &. "Saudi Prince's Ritz-Carlton 'Shakedown' Ends with $106B Netted." Alaraby, The New Arab, 31 Jan. 2019, www.alaraby.co.uk/english/news/2019/1/31/saudi-princes-ritz-carlton-shakedown-ends-with-106b-netted.

[174] Korte, Gregory, and Kevin Johnson. "Jared Kushner, Trump's Son-in-Law, Has White House Security Clearance Restored." USA Today, Gannett Satellite Information Network, 23 May 2018, www.usatoday.com/story/news/politics/2018/05/23/jared-kushner-security-clearance-restored-after-being-downgraded/638127002/.

[175] Ryan Parry West Coast Correspondent For Dailymail.com. "Saudi Crown Prince Brags Jared Kushner Handed Him U.S. Intelligence." Daily Mail Online, Associated Newspapers, 5 Apr. 2018, www.dailymail.co.uk/news/article-5575395/Saudi-crown-prince-brags-Jared-Kushner-handed-U-S-intelligence.html.

extinction. He was conspicuously quiet on a few moves in Israel, like when the US embassy was opened in Palestinian territory, and when Israel's death squad squashed an Arab general in Egypt. These sorts of things always had elicited a strong rebuke before the Kushner-MbS alliance was struck. Then something happened Trump could not ignore, that would reverberate all the way to Washington, D.C., with the planned killing of *Washington Post* reporter Jamal Khashoggi.

Trump spoke of the "deal" on October 23, 2018, from the White House:

> *"They had a very bad original concept. It was carried out poorly. And the cover-up was one of the worst in the history of cover-ups. Very simple. Bad deal. Should have never been thought of. Somebody really messed up. And they had the worst cover-up ever. And where it should have stopped is at the deal standpoint, where they thought about it. Because whoever thought of that idea I think is in big trouble, and they should be in big trouble. Okay?"*[176]

Trump really is a simple man who doesn't think or speak too deeply. Here he is describing the murder of a human being as a bad deal. Murder isn't a deal, well at least to MOST people. Jamal Khashoggi walks into a Saudi Embassy inside Turkey with his fiancé standing outside waiting for him to receive the documents allowing them to marry, is beset by a kill squad that strangle and dismember him. All Trump thinks in is dollars and cents. Trump has no empathy, and is being rather blunt with his response, failing to understand how he comes across due to his disability. Jamal had applied for US citizenship according to his fiancé, and had he been given more time on Earth would be an American citizen.

Trump and Saudi Arabia were strung along in this one by Turkey's Erdogan, likely still bitter over the Saudi demand of Qatar to remove a Turkish base and military from the country, who slow-rolled the painful and deeply disturbing details, timing a release of something newly "discovered" whenever denials were issued or the story seemed to be fading.

Khashoggi seemed to expect something was going to happen when he entered on October 2, 2018, as this was his second attempt to get his consent to

---

[176] Factbase. "Transcript Quote - Remarks: Donald Trump Signs S.3021 on Water Infrastructure and Answers Questions - October 23, 2018." Factbase, factba.se/transcript/donald-trump-remarks-water-infrastructure-october-23-2018.

marry certificate, telling his fiancé to wait outside and call if he didn't return. Turkish intelligence captured audio of the extrajudicial killing inside and video outside of the "body double" sent out of a different entrance from the diplomatic compound. They had every sordid detail worked out, such as who were inside the building, when they arrived and left Turkey and who was the only Saudi with the authority to direct the murder and cover-up.

The Saudi response to the targeted killing evolved over the steady Turkish rollout of the facts from we had nothing to do with it, to eventually, yeah we did it, we have the people responsible and will take care of it ourselves, but it has nothing to do with the Crown Prince, so leave us alone America or we will retaliate against any sanctions by cutting oil! [177] [178]

Trump's responses were more interesting, blaming "rogue killers" early in the month, than arguing that it would be bad to cancel the arms deal the signed because that was a lot of money, again on October 23, 2018:

> *"I will tell you that Russia and China would love to have that military order. I mean, I can say it to my Democrat friends, too. I mean, they would love—this is $110 billion worth of military. And Russia would pick that up very quickly, and China would pick it up very quickly, and France would pick it up very quickly. France makes a lot of military equipment. It's a very competitive market.*
>
> *"I did a great job when I sold them. That's why I went to Saudi Arabia first. I went to Saudi Arabia on the basis that they would by hundreds of billions—many billions of dollars' worth of things. And the ultimate number is around $450 billion; $110 [billion] for military. $450 billion. I think that's over a million jobs. A million to over a million jobs.*
>
> *"So if we do that, we're just hurting ourselves. We're just hurting ourselves. And I know that from a certain standpoint, you could also say, 'Well, it doesn't matter,' because it is a terrible thing. But we would be really hurting ourselves. We'd be hurting*

---

[177] Alkhalisi, Analysis by Zahraa. "Saudi Arabia's Oil Is a Powerful Weapon. But Using It Has Big Risks." CNN, Cable News Network, 15 Oct. 2018, www.cnn.com/2018/10/15/economy/saudi-arabia-oil-prices/index.html.

[178] Hutchinson, Bill. "Timeline of the Disappearance and Killing of Journalist Jamal Khashoggi." ABC News, ABC News Network, 12 Dec. 2018, abcnews.go.com/International/timeline-disappearance-journalist-jamal-khashoggi/story?id=58505659.

our companies; we'd be hurting our jobs. And so we'll see what happens."[179]

Trump is being beyond stupid here, blinded by money. It is part of his restricted personality that defines winning as making a whole lot of money through trade or business deals. Let's pause for a moment and look at the trade issues the US has with China over Trump's insistence that the deficit is harming America. Chinese press released a government-approved response to Mike Pence's speech at the Hudson Institute early October, sagely suggesting a collapse of the difference in goods traded could easily be made:

"The problem is not that China does not buy, but that the United States does not sell. For example, is the US willing to sell its Ford-class aircraft carriers? If one piece is priced at US$15 billion and the US sells four to China, we can immediately narrow the trade gap by US$60 billion."[180]

Would the US agree to sell its best military tech to the Chinese? Honestly, under Trump that is distinctly possible because he did sell high tech weapons to Saudi Arabia, a country that the Obama administration ceased selling to when the foreign nation began indiscriminately blowing questionable targets up with smart bombs, such as hospitals, schools and a funeral procession that killed one-hundred forty mourners. The ban went into effect December 13, 2016, with only 10,000 casualties so far in the then twenty-month offensive against Yemen.[181]

By November 20, 2018, Trump was "convinced" of MbS denials over his own administration, he betrayed the US intelligence community and indeed the nation, by siding with the Crown Prince in this released statement excerpt:

"Representatives of Saudi Arabia say that Jamal Khashoggi was an 'enemy of the state' and a member of the Muslim Brotherhood,

---

[179] Factbase. "Transcript Quote - Remarks: Donald Trump Signs S.3021 on Water Infrastructure and Answers Questions - October 23, 2018." Factbase, factba.se/transcript/donald-trump-remarks-water-infrastructure-october-23-2018.

[180] Post, South China Morning. "China Rips 'Tired' Mike Pence over Trade-Deficit Complaints: 'Is the US Willing to Sell Its Ford-Class Aircraft Carriers?'." Business Insider, Business Insider, 12 Oct. 2018, www.businessinsider.com/china-suggests-us-sell-ford-class-aircraft-carriers-for-trade-deficit-2018-10.

[181] Farmer, David Lawler; Ben. "US Halts Arms Sale to Saudi Arabia over Civilian Casualties in Yemen." The Telegraph, Telegraph Media Group, 13 Dec. 2016, www.telegraph.co.uk/news/2016/12/13/us-halts-arms-transfer-saudi-arabia-civilian-casualties-yemen/.

but my decision is in no way based on that—this is an unacceptable and horrible crime. King Salman and Crown Prince Mohammad bin Salman vigorously deny any knowledge of the planning or execution of the murder of Mr. Khashoggi. Our intelligence agencies continue to assess all information, but it could very well be that the Crown Prince had knowledge of this tragic event—maybe he did and maybe he didn't!

"That being said, we may never know all of the facts surrounding the murder of Mr. Jamal Khashoggi. In any case, our relationship is with the Kingdom of Saudi Arabia. They have been a great ally in our very important fight against Iran. The United States intends to remain a steadfast partner of Saudi Arabia to ensure the interests of our country, Israel and all other partners in the region. It is our paramount goal to fully eliminate the threat of terrorism throughout the world!"[182]

Funny he should mention Israel in a statement about Saudi Arabia, as I said earlier Israel and Saudi Arabia have been notably quiet during most of the Middle East moves regarding each's moves. The CIA had already issued the President their conclusion that the murder of Mr. Khashoggi was carried out with the express consent of the Crown Prince. Other parts of the statement mentioned the money Saudi Arabia had been investing as well as that arms contract. Additionally, Yemen could be left alone if only Iran wasn't involved.

The Houthi Genocide

As mentioned earlier, Yemen's Houthi population is facing eradication from joint Saudi and Yemeni military assaults and starvation, a dual threat enabled further by Trump's desire to make cash, at the massive cost of human lives. The conflict really is a religious genocide, one of the worst in history if the conflict doesn't end soon.

Saudi Arabia and Iran are from two opposing factions of Islam, Sunni and Shiite. The Houthi are Shiite along the same religious lines as Iran is, hence MbS's desire as a Sunni is to remove them by any means necessary, as he views

---

[182] "Statement from President Donald J. Trump on Standing with Saudi Arabia." The White House, The United States Government, www.whitehouse.gov/briefings-statements/statement-president-donald-j-trump-standing-saudi-arabia/.

them as a potential threat, having gained power in Yemen during the Arab Spring of 2011. With a steady supply of weaponry, not just from the US, the coalition to destroy the Houthi has been brutal and deliberate, with one attack leaving the most indelible impression.

On August 9, 2018, a laser-guided US bomb stuck into a school bus full of children in the Yemeni city of Saada. Fifty-one people died including forty children, with seventy-seven others injured in the vicious and deliberate attack. The Saudis had intentionally targeted the school bus with claims that it was a viable military target, calling the strike a legitimate military action.[183] [184]

"The Coalition will take all necessary measures against the terrorist, criminal acts of the terrorist Iranian-Houthi militia, such as recruiting child soldiers, throwing them in battlefields and using them as tools and covers to their terrorist acts."[185]

—*Col. Turki al-Malki*

These were very young kids going on a field trip. They weren't combatants, just young boys that had their whole lives ahead of them till they were butchered to send a message. On September 1, 2018, the coalition's Joint Incident Assessment Team finally admitted the "mistake" causing "collateral damage" had been made, after international condemnation.[186]

The Qatar crisis, the Yemen War, and many of the Ritz captive imprisonments are still ongoing situations as of this writing. These are dramatic impacts directly caused by Trump's need of winning by making money allowing no repercussions to be levied on MbS. Congress invoked the Presidential requirement of making a determination on the responsibility of the murder of

---

[183] Al Jazeera. "Yemen: The Saada Bus Bombing." Yemen | Al Jazeera, Al Jazeera, 22 Dec. 2018, www.aljazeera.com/programmes/specialseries/2018/12/yemen-saada-bus-bombing-181221224132671. html.

[184] Borger, Julian. "US Supplied Bomb That Killed 40 Children on Yemen School Bus." The Guardian, Guardian News and Media, 19 Aug. 2018, www.theguardian.com/world/2018/aug/19/us-supplied-bomb-that-killed-40-children-school-bus-yemen.

[185] Dwyer, Colin. "Saudi-Led Coalition Strikes School Bus In Yemen, Killing At Least 29 Children." NPR, NPR, 9 Aug. 2018, www.npr.org/2018/08/09/637175068/saudi-led-coalition-strikes-school-bus-in-yemen-killing-at-least-29-children.

[186] Al Jazeera. "Saudi-UAE Coalition Admits Yemen School Bus Attack 'Unjustified.'" Yemen News | Al Jazeera, Al Jazeera, 1 Sept. 2018, www.aljazeera.com/news/2018/09/saudi-uae-coalition-admits-yemen-school-bus-bombing-unjustified-180901141048148.html.

Khashoggi under the Magnitsky Act on October 23, 2018, which Trump intentionally failed to submit by the required deadline of February 8, 2019, marking another violation of the law for the President who always appears above the law. The Khashoggi killing, like many flashpoints of the Trump administration would eventually fade as the next crisis would be effectively queued up when the President needed cover from something going on in the many investigations against him or his organizations. [187]

---

[187] Gearan, Anne, et al. "White House Declines to Submit Report to Congress on Khashoggi Killing." The Washington Post, WP Company, 8 Feb. 2019, www.washingtonpost.com/politics/white-house-declines-to-submit-report-to-congress-on-khashoggi-killing/2019/02/08/fdab7f96-2bd4-11e9-984d-9b8fba003e81_story.html.

Chapter Fourteen

The Cult of Donald J. Trump and the "Killing" of the American Media

"The people, my people are so smart. You know what else they say about my people? The polls, they say I have the most loyal people. Did you ever see that? Where I could stand in the middle of Fifth Avenue and shoot somebody and I wouldn't lose any voters, okay? It's like incredible."

-Donald Trump, January 23, 2016[188]

Donald Trump, the man who called the Khashoggi murder the *"worst in the history cover-ups"* planned his own "killing" of an American journalist set for November 7, 2018, the day after the resounding midterm defeat for his party, to show the novice Saudi authoritarian ruler how it really should be done.

Trump stood up at the pulpit sounding off at how well the election the night before had been for his party, then called on a few reporters taking questions, clashing mildly with several for roughly fourteen minutes before he spotted his mark, the unsuspecting journalist of CNN, Jim Acosta. Trump said go ahead, signaling to Acosta. Then Trump "killed" him.

The Don pointed, whipping his short index finger towards the intended target. Jim began asking a question of Trump's campaign ad, sowing fear of an

188 Posted on January 23, 2016. "Trump: 'I Could Stand In the Middle Of Fifth Avenue And Shoot Somebody And I Wouldn't Lose Any Voters.'" RealClearPolitics, www.realclearpolitics.com/video/2016/ 01/23/trump_i_could_stand_in_the_middle_of_fifth_avenue_and_shoot_somebody_and_i_wouldnt_lose_any_voters.html.

immigrant invasion, but was cut off several times mid-sentence by the gangster President. Trump, who had already fielded multiple questions from each of the other journalists so far called upon, made eye contact to his intern, and with a bit of a devilish and delighted grin, said:

"I think you should—honestly, I think you should let me run the country, you run CNN and if you did it well, your ratings would be much better."

Trump tried to move onto a different journalist, while the intern swept in for the kill. She missed. Jim had pulled his hand back as the would-be assassin fumbled between looking at Jim then her boss and ducking, swiping at the mic in his hand, even grabbing Jim's wrist briefly deftly delivering the deathblow her boss had intended. Trump made a "get lost" swirl with his tiny pointer finger, then walked away from the podium briefly, till the mic was removed.

"I'll tell you what: CNN should be ashamed of itself having you working for them. You are a rude, terrible person. You shouldn't be working for CNN. Go ahead."

"I think that's unfair."

"You're a very rude person. The way you treat Sarah Huckabee is horrible. And the way you treat other people are horrible. You shouldn't treat people that way. Go ahead. Go ahead, Peter. Go ahead."

"In Jim's defense, I've traveled with him and watched him. He's a diligent reporter who busts his butt like the rest of us."

"Well, I'm not a big fan of yours either. So, you know."

And just like that, Jim Acosta, fake news CNN reporter, and enemy of people, was dead giving Trump true street cred the next time he met up with Putin, Kim or MbS. Save Jim wasn't dead.

Sarah Saunders, White House designated thug and Press Secretary, was queued next up to take out Jim. She posted an altered video of the exchange, oblivious that perhaps another camera in the venue might have been turned on in the pressroom, declaring this along with the removal of his press credentials:

"President Trump believes in a free press and expects and welcomes tough questions of him and his Administration. We will, however, never tolerate a reporter placing his hands on a young woman just trying to do her job as a White House intern. This conduct is absolutely unacceptable." [189]

---

[189] Stelter, Brian. "White House Pulls CNN Reporter Jim Acosta's Pass after Contentious News Conference." CNN, Cable News Network, 8 Nov. 2018, www.cnn.com/2018/11/07/media/trump-cnn-press-conference/index.html.

Unsurprisingly to no one, everyone else in the room had cameras rolling, and the feed had even been live making the whopper Sanders told so bad even Fox News put out a statement in support of the "dead" Acosta and freedom of the press which the President and his spokeswoman sought to outright kill. CNN sued, and like nearly every suit against this administration, the plaintiff received a favorable ruling, restoring Acosta's "life" on November 16, 2019, forcing the White House to reissue his credentials on the 19th.[190] [191]

This wasn't the first time Trump has drawn blood with the media, as he does this sort of thing deliberately. There was an off-camera briefing a White House official held, that the administration probably planned on using to play into the "fake news" narrative their chief uses for any outlet that had been tricked into covering it. Then there was the press ban of the Guardian, CNN and the *NY Times* from a press briefing in February 24, 2017. These are as close to how Trump can, as President, silence democracy's voice.[192]

The attack on Jim Acosta was rather sophomoric and unsophisticated, indicating that only one foolish as much as Trump could have ever imagined the hapless scheme would work. That others, who seem intelligent, went along with what the President wanted, is the power of Trump, one that has risen him to a cult-like figure able to issue edicts that no matter how crazy, will be picked up on and followed through by one of his "followers."

Trump in the opening lines of this chapter praised his "smart" followers, as willing to allow him even if he brazenly kills someone in public, and they would remain loyal. It is why he attacks the "fake" news, the "so-called judges," the "dirty" FBI and CIA and has been for the most part a boldface liar when given a direct question. Trump, though, is not the one who generally does the dirty work. He issues an edict, and expects that order to be followed, with those entrusted generally to come up with the plan to get things done. If Trump calls the press the enemy of the people, his followers will respond.

[190] Farhi, Paul. "Judge Hands CNN a Victory in Its Bid to Restore Jim Acosta's White House Press Pass." The Washington Post, WP Company, 16 Nov. 2018, www.washingtonpost.com/lifestyle/style/judge-hands-cnn-victory-in-its-bid-to-restore-jim-acostas-white-house-press-pass/2018/11/16/8bedd08a-e920-11e8-a939-9469f1166f9d_story.html.

[191] Michael. "CNN's Jim Acosta Has Press Pass Restored by White House." The New York Times, The New York Times, 20 Nov. 2018, www.nytimes.com/2018/11/19/business/media/jim-acosta-press-pass-cnn.html.

[192] Siddiqui, Sabrina. "Trump Press Ban: BBC, CNN and Guardian Denied Access to Briefing." The Guardian, Guardian News and Media, 25 Feb. 2017, www.theguardian.com/us-news/2017/feb/24/media-blocked-white-house-briefing-sean-spicer.

They hoot and cheer whenever he decries this at any of his bloodthirsty rallies. Some even have launched into action.

In the morning of March 2, 2018, I was preparing to leave for work when I heard a loud boom outside my house in Austin, Texas, off to the South. I figured a garbage truck had dropped a heavy dumpster on the other side of the wall separating our street from the back of several warehouses even though I could not hear the truck. Thinking nothing of it, I hopped into my car and headed to work. My wife later complained of not being able to easily get out of the neighborhood, as the police had shut down the main entrance most of the morning.

That was the beginning of a terrifying month for everyone in the Austin area, as a domestic terrorist later revealed to live about two miles from my home, was setting bombs on doorsteps that killed two and injured three others.

When I looked up the location of the bombing a week later, I found that it had been adjacent to our favorite park where I often take my three beautiful mixed-race daughters, and that was the source of the loud boom. I cried that night thinking of those "what-ifs." My wife gets many packages that I take inside and leave for her to open. My two older girls tend to open these every so often that I began dreaming nightly that one of them opened a package shrieking in terror as the package explodes, and I was always too late to save them. Terrorism, a term almost never used with these white men mass killers by the Trump administration as it conflicts with their stereotyped agenda of dehumanizing minorities, had hit home in a big way for me personally. My wife and I set up a system till the "danger" had passed. While the Austin bomber's motive wasn't ever given, we see more and more cases of domestic terrorism and hate crimes now under Trump, where the associations to what he and his radicalized right wing media supporters are saying, that his cult influence is killing America.

The next US bomber, known simply as the MAGA bomber for his fervent following and belief in Trump and his "teachings," was indeed influenced by his doctrine of MAGA, America first and anti-immigrant propaganda. His targets were all named on Fox News or by Mr. Trump, designated as threats to America.

George Soros, billionaire philanthropist and Holocaust survivor, received the first package on October 22, 2018. Soros is a boogeyman of sorts by the radicalized right because his charity pushes liberal and progressive movements around the world, including education, poverty reduction, and to increase transparency through journalism. His influence helped undermine Communism replacing it with Democracy in many Eastern European countries.

The conspiracy theorists at the time had been pushing a false narrative that Soros funded the caravans that were fleeing violence and economic stagnation in Central America. This and Trump's attacks that month on Soros as the funder of campaign actors, made it quite clear how Trump's cult has radicalized violent and dangerous domestic terrorists ready to act. Trump had attacked Soros four times (one at a rally, twice in different interviews, and once on Twitter) that month about placing paid protestors at rallies and the Kavanagh hearing, another minor-conspiracy pushed at the time against Soros.

October 5, 2018, 6:03 A.M. EDT on Twitter:

"The very rude elevator screamers are paid professionals only looking to make Senators look bad. Don't fall for it! Also, look at all of the professionally made identical signs. Paid for by Soros and others. These are not signs made in the basement from love! #Troublemakers"

October 6, 2018, on Air Force One:

"When you see their signs, you notice yesterday—I talked about the signs all week, today they're all different because they said oh, we can't do the same sign made by a manufacturer, paid for by Soros or whoever. So I think Republicans are going to do incredibly well, although history always says that whoever's president it goes a little bit the other way. I think we're going to do really well. We have the greatest economy in the history of our country. We have an economy like no other."[193]

October 11, 2018, on Fox and Friends:

"The Democrats and Soros and they came from all over. And we'd have protesters. And I would say this, that it wasn't so successful

---

[193] Canty, Jennifer. "Transcript Quote - Press Gaggle: Donald Trump Speaks to Reporters on Air Force One - October 6, 2018." Factbase, CantyMedia, factba.se/transcript/donald-trump-press-conference-af1-in-flight-gaggle-october-6-2018.

for those protesters. But they have to be careful with the rhetoric, because it's very dangerous what Holder says. And Holder was held in contempt by Congress, Holder went after Christians, he went after our great evangelicals, he went after the Tea Party people."[194]

October 18, 2018:

"You ever see their signs? Resist. They say what are you going to resist? I don't know. Do you ever see when the fake news interviews them? And then they try and cut it, but they—they'll go to a person holding a sign who gets paid by Soros or somebody, right? That's what happens. Well, did you see with—with now Justice Kavanagh, did you see—and, by the way, also, with Justice Neil Gorsuch."[195]

What each of these quotes reminds of is that Trump, other than he is being extremely anti-Semitic associating money and a prominent Jew with all these "problems," has a fascination with conspiracy theories, an element of his personality and disability. He is convinced that these things are true and presents them as facts, which in turn is reported on and that reporting reinforces his belief. It is a nasty "alternative fact cycle" that spreads to his people, like the MAGA bomber.

Hillary Clinton, former President Barak Obama, Maxine Waters, former CIA Director John O. Brennan, former US Attorney General Eric Holder, US Rep. Debbie Wasserman Schultz, Robert De Niro, former VP Joe Biden, former National Intelligence Director James Clapper, US Senator Cory Booker, US Senator Kamala Harris, Tom Steyer and CNN all had bombs addressed to them. When the MAGA bomber was caught, his van had been covered in pro-Trump and anti-Clinton stickers, making it obvious to everyone where his allegiance lies. Then video of him proudly holding a sign at a Trump rally in Florida was pulled up.

---

[194] Factbase. "Transcript Quote - Interview: Donald Trump Calls In to Fox and Friends for An Interview - October 11, 2018." Factbase, factba.se/transcript/donald-trump-interview-fox-and-friends-october-11-2018.

[195] Factbase. "Transcript Quote - Speech: Donald Trump Holds a Political Rally in Missoula, Montana - October 18, 2018." Factbase, factba.se/transcript/donald-trump-speech-maga-rally-missoula-mt-october-18-2018.

Trump's extensively controlled media network, fueled by the likes of Rush Limbaugh, Candace Owens, Ann Coulter and other hacks, pushed out a "false flag" narrative that the MAGA bomber was a DNC operative trying to harm the GOP before the election, as none of the bombs detonated.[196]

The MAGA bomber wasn't the only terrorist inspired by Trump. A forty-seven-year-old, former Marine, white nationalist Coast Guard lieutenant charged on February 19, 2019, had amassed an arsenal since 2017 with the intent to clear out reporters and Congress people on the side of the aisle opposing Individual 1:

> *"Liberalist/globalist ideology is destroying traditional peoples esp white. No way to counteract without violence. It should push for more crack down bringing more people to our side. Much blood will have to be spilled to get whitey off the couch. For some no amount of blood will be enough. They will die as traitors who actively work toward our demise. Looking to Russia with hopeful eyes or any land that despises the west's liberalism. Excluding of course the muslim sum. Who rightfully despise the west's liberal degeneracy…"*

An extensive hit list left on his computer of Democrats and CNN/MSNBC media folk some listed with derogatory or racist names were his targets. His internet searches on January 17, 2019, interested me:

8:54 A.M."what if trump illegally impeached"

8:57 A.M."best place in dc to see congress people"

8:58 A.M."where in dc to congress live"

10:39 A.M."civil war if trump impeached"

11:26 A.M."social democrats usa"[197]

As crazy as it sounds, the Cult of Donald Trump, as I have called them, has been planning an insurrection in the event Trump is overthrown from power. I have heard this from a Trump supporter multiple times (brother of a friend on Social Media) without sufficient evidence that he was ready to "join"

---

196 Nguyen, Tina. "'Too Coincidental': MAGA-Land Calls Bombing Threats a False Flag." The Hive, Vanity Fair, 24 Oct. 2018, www.vanityfair.com/news/2018/10/cnn-obama-clinton-bomb-threats-false-flag-theories.

197 Myre, Greg, and Vanessa Romo. "Arrested Coast Guard Officer Allegedly Planned Attack 'On A Scale Rarely Seen.'" NPR, NPR, 21 Feb. 2019, www.npr.org/2019/02/20/696470366/arrested-coast-guard-officer-planned-mass-terrorist-attack-on-a-scale-rarely-see.

such an uprising. There is plenty of material on the radicalized media sources on the right to suggest that this is happening, and it is a dangerous movement I am sure the FBI is already on thanks to the Coast Guard militant's arrest. This explains two of the five searches, while the other three are intelligence gathering for his planned strike that appeared to be imminent before his arrest. The Cult believes Trump and Russia in a sense will establish a white homeland, which makes these quotes on October 23, 2018, from Donald "inspiring" to his people:

> *"So I'm proud—I'm proud of our country. And I am a nationalist. It's a word that hasn't been used too much. Some people use it, but I'm very proud. I think it should be brought back. I'm somebody that wants to help other countries of the world, but I also have to take—we have to take care of our country. We cannot continue to allow ourselves to be duped on military and also duped on trade, with the European Union, as an example.*
>
> *"For many years, other countries that are allies of ours—so-called allies—they have not treated our country fairly. So in that sense, I am absolutely a nationalist, and I'm proud of it."*

The question asked was all important adding this context:

> *"Mr. President, just to follow up on your comments about being a nationalist, there is a concern that you are sending coded language or a dog whistle to some Americans out there that what you really mean is that you're a white nationalist."*[198]

The question was asked BECAUSE of Trump's rally in Houston, Texas, the night before on October 22, 2018, leaving "doubt" of how Trump understands the word's meaning.

> *"But radical Democrats want to turn back the clock for the rule of corrupt power-hungry globalists. You know what a globalist is,*

---

[198] Factbase. "Transcript Quote - Remarks: Donald Trump Signs S.3021 on Water Infrastructure and Answers Questions - October 23, 2018." Factbase, factba.se/transcript/donald-trump-remarks-water-infrastructure-october-23-2018.

right? You know what a globalist is? A globalist is a person that wants the globe to do well, frankly, not caring about our country so much. And you know what? We can't have that. You know, they have a word. It sort of became old-fashioned. It's called a nationalist. And I say, really, we're not supposed to use that word. You know what I am? I'm a nationalist, OK? I'm a nationalist. Nationalist. Nothing—use that word. Use that word."[199]

Does Trump know of other Nationalists and the horrors they have wrought on humanity when they seized power? Like Hitler, Mao? Trump has, but in his fixed-mindedness, Trump wants to use that word as an antonym to globalist. That is not how language works.

Language has many layers, intentional and unintentional with hidden meaning, something Trump with his weak cognition does not effectively grasp. People are telling him, likely those in the White House, that he shouldn't use the word nationalist. It's bad. Trump REALLY wants to. He is stubborn AND he is going to get others to use the word the way he wants it to be used.

Sorry, Donald. Nationalist IS a bad word, and you should never use it to describe yourself if you do not want to be compared to Hitler and other self-proclaimed Nationalists.

The problem is he did a couple of times over the course of two days, and his Cult picked up on his use of the word, but ignored the context as the media went crazy with his pragmatic error. And that is a bigger problem, fueled by a President who does not have the ability to regulate his pragmatic speech, much less his thoughts, and in so doing endangers Americans. Trump may have learned his lesson as he hasn't tried to use the "antonym" of globalist since those cringeworthy quotes.

This Trump behavior though has been seen before, in the days and weeks surrounding the removal of Confederate monuments in Charlottesville, North Carolina. He had called the rallygoers "very fine people."

In the aftermath of the August 12, 2017, Charlottesville attack by a white nationalist, instead of rallying Americans together for shared grief and mourning, President Trump instead focused on blame with the statement of "both

---

[199] Factbase. "Transcript Quote - Speech: Donald Trump Holds a Political Rally in Houston, Texas - October 22, 2018." Factbase, factba.se/transcript/donald-trump-speech-maga-rally-houston-tx-october-22-2018.

sides." The both sides statement, the refusal for days to acknowledge the mistake, the apology written by a staffer then delivered by Trump and the next day retracted by a fiery and defiant man has so many elements of intentional and unintentional behavior.

First, Trump does not recognize suffering that isn't directly related to him. He has no emotional connection to the people injured, or the white nationalists, only understanding that he is compelled as the President to say something about the event. His lack of filter discussed in detail further in the article was on display. Why say both sides were to blame? To Donald, they probably were as he had seen and heard reports on the news and likely drew up this conclusion himself after seeing the anger and hostility. It is also possible that at the direction of Steve Bannon that statement was intentionally added. We don't know whether it was intentional or unintentional, but to actually say something was caused by the victims using the "both sides" jargon is socially unacceptable, unnecessary and dangerous as it further emboldened a fringe group of supporters. Second, Trump dug in. That behavior is very characteristic of individuals with Autism, as they often present with extreme rigidity. Third, Trump never hit the emotional tone for Americans that makes suffering easier by making grief a shared connection and experience. Instead of sorrow, anger and hostility followed. This clearly demonstrates Trump's lack of empathy, poor judgement and ability to connect with the American people.

Here is what Trump said at the press conference given three days after the crisis on August 15, 2017:

> *"I am not putting anybody on a moral plane, what I'm saying is this: you had a group on one side and a group on the other, and they came at each other with clubs and it was vicious and horrible and it was a horrible thing to watch, but there is another side.*
>
> *"There was a group on this side you can call them the left. You've just called them the left that came violently attacking the other group. So you can say what you want, but that's the way it is."*

Trump identifies the "left" as attacking the first group. Using that term, associating the group of Antifa, short for anti-fascist, the counter-protestor groups responding to the Nationalist groups marching with Democrats, was likely very intentional. It is a Trump Us versus Them moment.

"You said there was hatred and violence on both sides?"

"I do think there is blame—yes, I think there is blame on both sides. You look at, you look at both sides. I think there's blame on both sides, and I have no doubt about it, and you don't have any doubt about it either. And, and, and, and if you reported it accurately, you would say."

Trump actually is correct here given his context of the events and what he likely has seen on Fox or other channels. He had seen people attacking each other, some from the "left," others from the "right." He isn't even thinking about the guy who smashed through all those protestors in a car when he says it. Whether it was a correct observation is NOT the point. Someone died. That murderer, a "Unite the Right" rally-goer, was a man on the "right" of his thinking, along with all the other rallygoers who were KKK, Neo-Nazi or run-of-the-mill White Nationalists. Trump lacking filter, says things bluntly as he sees it.

"The neo-Nazis started this thing. They showed up in Charlottesville.

"Excuse me, they didn't put themselves down as neo-Nazis, and you had some very bad people in that group. But you also had people that were very fine people on both sides. You had people in that group—excuse me, excuse me.

"I saw the same pictures as you did. You had people in that group that were there to protest the taking down, of to them, a very, very important statue and the renaming of a park from Robert E. Lee to another name."

Trump's statements show his disconnect of the rally events to the carnage, injuring thirty-eight and killing Heather Heyer. When he says they didn't put themselves down as neo-Nazis, he is making a pragmatic error leaving out the likely detail that he was referring to the permit on file with the city to hold the event.

"George Washington and Robert E. Lee are not the same.
"Oh no, George Washington was a slave owner. Was George

Washington a slave owner? So will George Washington now lose his status? Are we going to take down—excuse me. Are we going to take down, are we going to take down statues to George Washington?

"How about Thomas Jefferson? What do you think of Thomas Jefferson? You like him? Okay, good. Are we going to take down his statue? He was a major slave owner. Are we going to take down his statue?

"You know what? It's fine, you're changing history, you're changing culture, and you had people—and I'm not talking about the neo-Nazis and the white nationalists, because they should be condemned totally—but you had many people in that group other than neo-Nazis and white nationalists, okay?"

Trump is simply stating what he knows (and it isn't a lot by typical standards) about History. Lee, Jefferson and Washington all owned slaves. They were all people in US history. What he is also doing, very possibly unintentionally, is signaling support to his "base" at the Unite the Right. Trump is VERY stubborn and has been getting very agitated at this point making his Autism traits more apparent.

"And the press has treated them absolutely unfairly. Now, in the other group also, you had some fine people, but you also had troublemakers and you see them come with the black outfits and with the helmets and with the baseball bats—you had a lot of bad people in the other group too."

Is Trump incorrect here? There clearly were many on both sides engaged in peaceful protests, and because some were violent they were all grouped together as "bad" by the media. These are the people he is identifying as "fine people," and Trump is upset that others do not understand his point of "fairness." This belief is of course without Trump considering that the Unite the Right is entirely made up of various hate groups coming together. He missed that context as well as the deadly attack in his arguments of being fair.

"I just didn't understand what you were saying. You were saying the press has treated white nationalists unfairly?"

"No, no. There were people in that rally, and I looked the night before. If you look, they were people protesting very quietly, the taking down the statue of Robert E. Lee. I'm sure in that group there were some bad ones."

"The following day, it looked like they had some rough, bad people, neo-Nazis, white nationalists, whatever you want to call 'em. But you had a lot of people in that group that were there to innocently protest and very legally protest, because you know, I don't know if you know, but they had a permit."

"The other group didn't have a permit. So I only tell you this: there are two sides to a story. I thought what took place was a horrible moment for our country, a horrible moment. But there are two sides to the country." [200]

Trump REALLY came off bad in this one due to his disability, to just about everyone save the racist groups that clearly feel emboldened and supported by him. He had tried to argue a factual point that SHOULD NOT be argued, that not all the white nationalists were breaking the law. All that accomplished was giving a "dog-whistle" of support to the most dangerous factions in the United States, the "marginalized" and "militant" white nationalists.

---

[200] Factbase. "Transcript Quote - Press Conference: Donald Trump on Infrastructure + Charlottesville - August 15, 2017." Factbase, factba.se/transcript/donald-trump-press-conference-infrastructure-charlottesville-august-15-2017.

Chapter Fifteen

*"I am self funding and will hire the best people,
not the biggest donors!"*

Trump bragged about his bringing along the "best people" into the administration and draining the swamp with their help, yet somehow Washington seems swampier than ever. Each character in his inner circle seems out to "get" each other, and many are willing to do whatever it takes to move up in the organization. It is like a reality show gone bad in the White House, which considering Trump starred in one for a long time isn't the least bit surprising.

When the White House and Campaign rolls are filled with cartoonish villains as impressive as any rogue's gallery, greater villains outside will seek to corrupt and influence to further their grander agendas. It is even easier when the Kingpin is sending his small fry to hook up with the bigger fish. With Individual One, his singlemindedness and extreme fascination over Hillary's emails driving his illicit behavior, he would definitely be reaching out for Putin's help with more than a business deal to build Trump Tower Moscow.

Trump, as everyone working around him describes, is a "hard worker" and a micromanager. He gets the "big idea" of what he wants to do, his lieutenants come up with the plan then he signs off on the job. Trump lavishes praise on those he feels are loyal, and cuts loose those that are not or are too much of a liability, but rarely works as the grunt getting his hands dirty in the process.

As I have described previously, the times where Trump has been at the center of any of his dirty tricks, they are plainly obvious, simplistic and bungling. He sends Pence into a football game as a stunt then flubs the delivery in a Tweet. Trump sets up Acosta, makes Jim a hero that even Fox News supported, while Mr. Trump looked churlish and brooding. Donald brags about lying to the PM of Canada at a campaign fundraising event, is recorded and winds up with egg on his face. Trump's sheer incompetence combined with his penchant as a loud-mouth boldface cheat and liar, makes for an interesting crime lord. Yet here we are.

Most of schemes, both legal and illegal, that have been successful over the years appear to be more because of the thugs Trump has recruited or inherited from his father's "business" dealings. Trump also I assume has hired some *"very fine people"* too. But even very fine people can be corrupted and influenced by a manipulator that has been surprisingly effective as Trump has been over the years.

Before we go to the people encircled around Forty-Five, Trump lied to get himself on the first Forbes Fortune 400 list. Calling in on May 17, 1984, in a recorded lie posing as John Barron, Vice President of Finance, speaking to journalist John Greenberg, Trump pulled one of his earliest known cons.

> *"Most of the assets have been consolidated to Mr. Trump, because you have down Fred Trump and I'd like to talk to you off the record if I can just make your thing easier."*
>
> *"Okay sure," replies Greenburg.*
>
> *"But, but I think you can really use Donald Trump now and you can just consolidate it. I think last year someone showed me the article and I think he had two hundred and two hundred and the other's been pretty well consolidated now for the most part as I also think somebody had mentioned that you had asked about that or somebody had and it's been pretty well consolidated, okay?"*

The voice is deeper than Trump typically speaks, showing that Don was at least smart enough to "disguise" his voice somewhat. His language fingerprints in the recording were impossible to hide. His "okay" added in at the end is vintage Trump-speak, like a characteristic verbal tick used frequently in his speech. According to Factba.se where I have viewed and listened to for most of the audio I am reporting, a search for "okay" turned up more than 4,250 times. His twice *"I think," "asked about the other day"* as well his unspecific use of *"somebody"* are hallmarks of Trump-speak.

Trump also recruited his personal lawyer Roy Cohn to make an additional call to Greenburg, convincing him of inclusion. Trump was only worth less than five million dollars at the time, and was placed in the Fortune 400 List fraudulently based on this con with a net value about 400 million, allowing him access to bank loans he could not otherwise afford. The more wealth Trump's syndicate could acquire the bigger the schemes he could pull off duping banks, investors and other suckers along of the way.[201]

This is why Trump Tower Moscow was a critical "investment" to broadening the Trump Empire connecting his Organization to the Russian Government instead of the Russian mob as he had with the Trump Taj Mahal. That tower deal was vital to keep the money running smoothly, but also very "inconvenient" in the scheme of building brand Trump as a Presidential Candidate, so he sought to hide ties to the project and Russia until after he lost the election. There was one big problem with his Trump branding plan. He didn't lose.

Russia was why. They were critically invested in Trump, likely well before the "five years out" claim of the Steele dossier, as having "their guy" in charge of America while subverting the United States and European Democracies with infiltration, voter suppression and Social Media campaigns.

Trump has had plenty of statements "flirting" with running for President over the years, and the Russians knew this. They also knew exactly the kind of women Trump sleeps with from the Howard Stern recordings. Trump likes big-breasted, skinny, fair-skinned women who take off their clothes for a living that he can direct and treat like trash. He is a known cheat, having slept around on all three wives, so throwing a couple lanky model-quality women at him flashing a smile then listening to him for a minute is all that was needed to arouse his faculties and gain his interest. This Trump "Intel" is just based on publicly available recordings out there.

We know Trump was offered five Russian prostitutes in 2013 based on testimony given by one of his security detail Keith Schiller to Congress on November 9, 2017, who stated he turned them away. The problem is that Schiller told Trump of the offer, and wasn't present the rest of the night.

Trump, based on what we know of his personality, fixates on stuff like this, and by just mentioning to him that he was offered FIVE PROSTITUTES all

---

[201] "Reporter: Trump Lied to Get on Forbes 400 List - CNN Video." CNN, Cable News Network, 20 Apr. 2018, www.cnn.com/videos/politics/2018/04/20/jonathan-greenberg-intv-forbes-400-trump-john-barron-recording-sot-newday.cnn.

at the same time for his own personal depravity and use is going to gnaw at him for a long time for his "missing" that deal. Who is to say Trump didn't get on the phone and made that deal after choir boy Schiller left for the night?[202]

The Russians likely have more than PP sex tapes on the Donald. He is an open book when among "friends" so I would assume compromising conversations aplenty exist also. But none of that matters in the context of controlling Trump. Russia only needed Trump to know of the reports of compromising material while controlling the people around him to get the best effect for their coercive measures. That was accomplished when Trump was told by FBI Director James Comey about Moscow 2013 in their first meeting. During the campaign they lined up several "recruits," Trump's "best," which we will now discuss.

George Papadopoulos, who first met Trump on March 31, 2016, at a meeting with all of Trump's National Security advisors, was the first minor villain to plead guilty and serve twelve days in prison for lying to federal investigators about campaign contact attempts with Russians. His task was to open a backdoor channel to Vladimir Putin as a foreign policy adviser to the campaign. In his efforts he "hears" about damaging information relating to Clinton emails stolen by Russians on around April 26, 2016, from the *"professor"* based in the UK and shares that information with multiple members of the campaign. These were an earlier batch of DNC emails the Russians already had before Trump requested a specific attack to get Hillary's.

While a minor rogue, it was his later approaching of a US Diplomat about needing to contact Putin that triggered the FISA request to surveil several members of the Trump Campaign. His mentioning of Clinton emails piqued Trump's interest as that "thread" already has him entirely fixated on enlisting help in getting all her emails. Quite frankly, Papadopoulos wasn't a high-level target within the campaign for the Russians to "acquire," so his contacts were limited to two individuals, the "professor" and the "Russian Woman."[203]

The next in Trump's gallery of rogues is the conniving duo of twin convicted felons Campaign chairman Paul Manafort and Rick Gates, Deputy

---

[202] "Bodyguard Rejected Russian Offer of 5 Women for Trump." NBCNews.com, NBCUniversal News Group, www.nbcnews.com/news/us-news/trump-bodyguard-testifies-russian-offered-trump-women-was-turned-down-n819386.

[203] Owen, Paul. "George Papadopoulos Timeline: Trump Campaign Adviser Details Russia Links." The Guardian, Guardian News and Media, 30 Oct. 2017, www.theguardian.com/us-news/2017/oct/30/george-papadopoulos-timeline-trump-campaign-adviser-russia-links.

Campaign chairman. Both failed to register as lobbying on behalf of foreign governments in a timely manner. This cadre of cronies cut different paths when details emerged of what they did and when, for the Trump campaign and how they were already Russian comprised for their work in Ukraine and Russian oligarchs (billionaires). Gates plead guilty while Manafort fought and lost in court on most of the counts. While these crimes are mostly financial and other charges stemming from before their involvement in the campaign, having the tie-ins established with Russia through Manafort and Gates has been revealed in court filings of why they are important to the Mueller investigation.

Manafort was the prime target in the Russian Trump campaign influence operation, and boy did that pay off in a BIG way, that you might not have even noticed or suspected. That payoff required another villain to get the goods—Steve Bannon, Campaign Advisor and Republican Nationalist.

Republican Nationalist Steve Bannon, shown as the Angel of Death on SNL, and known as *"Sloppy Steve"* now by Trump after the two cut ties over comments in the book *Fire and Fury*, is by far the most dangerous and intelligent of Donald's gallery of longtime rogues. Most know the guy for Breitbart, an obscure nationalist radical right website that shot up the charts during the Trump campaign and abruptly died after the falling out with Trump. Breitbart is nothing. His other venture he was involved in, Cambridge Analytica is.

During the fall of 2015, Bannon set up shop near D.C. with a Cambridge Analytica office in Alexandria, Virginia. What this business was doing has been the subject of Congressional investigation, mostly focusing on Facebook and social media companies that the company "harnessed" information from. The company worked for *"Lying Ted Cruz"* for a spell, till Trump took him behind the woodshed insulting his manhood and his father for having something to do with the assassination of JFK, then Cambridge Analytica worked heavily with his campaign. Bannon was made Trump's Campaign Chief Executive and all that Facebook data came along with him at the insistence of the Mercer family, the billionaire family backing the Trump campaign, Brexit, Breithart and other such "populist ventures." [204]

That Russian payoff with Manafort "indebted" first reported accidentally in a January 8, 2019, document from the lawyers representing him, stated that

---

[204] Mayer, Jane. "New Evidence Emerges of Steve Bannon and Cambridge Analytica's Role in Brexit." The New Yorker, The New Yorker, 18 Nov. 2018, www.newyorker.com/news/news-desk/new-evidence-emerges-of-steve-bannon-and-cambridge-analyticas-role-in-brexit.

Manafort shared internal campaign "polling data" with Konstantin Kilimnik, a Russian Intelligence officer. The law firm hadn't redacted then scanned the document, instead posting it in a manner that redactions could be lifted revealing the blocked out words. That polling data likely included Cambridge Analytica Facebook data including passwords, which was then shared further to lower level hackers within the Federation for smaller cyber-crime.[205]

I mention Facebook passwords and petty Russian cyber-crime with annoyance, simply because this connection from Cambridge Analytica to Trump Campaign to Manafort to the GRU (Russian intelligence) via Kilimnik to their organization of hackers may explain how my own accounts were successfully infiltrated by at least one Russian hacker early 2017 based on shared password vulnerability that could not be easily done otherwise.

In my case, the Russian hacker took digital gaming valuables from my account and shuffled them to mule accounts. I estimated the worth of these to be roughly $2,000, which is rather small for online gaming communities. The hack happened in the middle of the night, and a gaming friend of mine recalled the oddity of "me" asking about values of certain things, as I was one who routinely "set" values for the higher priced stuff.

I had European and Asia based friends then watch out for my best items as I knew the stats of several by heart, and contacted at least one game developer who helped restore my lost items to my account, at least the ones not "dropped" and destroyed during the theft. My items showed up very quickly on a sketchy Russian site, known to process card skimming and other scams to steal actual cash. While the theft of $2000 was small, the potential growth from that was in the tens of thousands, still petty cyber-crime, but likely a reliable source of illicit money for an unscrupulous government or mafia.

Manafort gave the Russians other benefits. He lobbied heavily likely on behalf of Russian interests, getting the Republican Party to weaken support to pro-Western forces working to protect Ukraine in its platform, consistent with what best suits the needs of the Kremlin that had "annexed" Crimea, a portion of the country of Ukraine, and not the US's. [206]

---

[205] AP Staff, and Associated Press. "Unredacted Manafort Filing Detailing Lying Allegations in Russia Probe." DocumentCloud, www.documentcloud.org/documents/5677676-Unredacted-Manafort-filing-detailing-lying.html.

[206] Johnson, Carrie. "2016 RNC Delegate: Trump Directed Change To Party Platform On Ukraine Support." NPR, NPR, 4 Dec. 2017, www.npr.org/2017/12/04/568310790/2016-rnc-delegate-trump-directed-change-to-party-platform-on-ukraine-support.

Former Trump National Security Adviser Michael Flynn, Retired General, was never deeply compromised by Russian intelligence officials, though he had met and sat adjacent to Russian President Vladimir Putin at a RT gala, a news organization in Russia, on December 10, 2015, for a $33,750 paid speaking engagement. He isn't the same level of rogue as others previously mentioned in regards to Russia.

Flynn made some incredibly poor choices along the way regarding Turkey, whom he lobbied on behalf of, and with speaking four times in December during the Trump transition to Russian ambassador Kislyak while the current President was implementing sanctions, the last on the 29th of December, 2016. On the 30th Putin opts to not retaliate in a public statement electing for the next administration to restore relations, which Trump giddily goes on Twitter to heap praise:

> *"Great move on delay (by V. Putin) - I always knew he was very smart!"*
>
> -Donald J. Trump
> December 30, 2016

The Trump administration's attempts to circumvent the US Government are extremely problematic as Flynn and other Trump officials had no legal authority to conduct US policy at the time with Russia or Saudi Arabia which will be discussed in a later chapter. Flynn knew this, yet discussions took place and Flynn lied about those discussions to the FBI, Vice President Mike Pence, and *The Washington Post* saying sanctions were not discussed. Trump's reaction may indicate that he directed Flynn in this manner or that at least he was aware of the discussions as he seems to be aware of everything that is going on that should not be going on.

Sanctions WERE discussed, and that is a big deal. Flynn resigned after twenty-four days in service as National Security Adviser as reports began surfacing that intelligence eavesdrops on Kislyak had intercepted the Flynn conversations.[207]

You see, as odd as it sounds, I too have been eavesdropped on by the US government just like Flynn was here. I guess I am indeed a lucky guy. My

---

[207] Trump, Donald. "Michael Flynn Timeline: Trump Aide to Mueller Witness." PolitiFact, 12 May 2017, www.politifact.com/truth-o-meter/article/2018/dec/05/detailing-michael-flynns-turn-trump-mueller/.

friend, originally from Idaho calls to talk about an upcoming event we were going to together. I was on a cordless, he on a cell.

"Click-click. Click-click."

My friend also hears that odd sound, which I had only heard one time before—in the Boy Scouts when visiting the Scout Leader's business at the telephone company where we were allowed to tap into a couple phones to check the wires. My friend says, *"Okay."*

I respond, *"So tell me again about those felonies that Battelle and the DOJ committed?"*

I am never one to miss an opportunity that presents itself, and the chance that I was being recorded and have that evidence be useful was not going to be wasted. It was recorded, as evidenced by a Freedom of Information Act request that showed our conversation heavily redacted. The point of reference of that conversation was the first of multiple large doses of nuclear radiation leaked (at least six so far) in the Idaho Falls area that my pal's family had been harmed by. The government downplayed the amount released, the "heaviness" and half-life of the material discharged into and around the community meaning the contamination would last a couple of generations and not days as they would have the community believe. If you are interested in what happened there I suggest you check out the article on the Idaho Statesman, dated August 11, 2017, 7:38 A.M. (see citation). [208]

Flynn, having done what Trump wanted and was seemingly loyal to him said the following as documented on page ten of the James Comey memos on February 14th:

> *"He began by saying he wanted to 'talk about Mike Flynn.' He then said that although Flynn 'hadn't done anything wrong' in his call with the Russians (a point he made at least two more times in the conversation), he had to let him go because he misled the Vice President, whom he described as a 'good guy.' He explained that he just couldn't have Flynn misleading the Vice President and, in any event, he had other concerns about Flynn, and had a great guy coming in, so he had to let Flynn go."[209]*

---

[208] Malone, Patrick, and Peter Cary. The Center for Public Integrity. "Unheeded Warnings, Repeated Mistakes Put Workers' Health at Risk at Idaho Nuclear Lab." Idahostatesman, Idaho Statesman, 11 Aug. 2017, www.idahostatesman.com/news/northwest/idaho/article166418912.html.

[209] Day, Chad, and Associated Press. "Ex-FBI Director James Comey's Memos." DocumentCloud, www.documentcloud.org/documents/4442900-Ex-FBI-Director-James-Comey-s-memos.html.

Those other concerns likely had to do with Turkey, which I will explain shortly. This comment, made in private between the two men, is highly unusual given the independence and integrity of the FBI. The fact Trump was asking essentially for a favor of the FBI director in dropping anything regarding Flynn was an immediate red flag.

The first Turkish connection that was bothersome to Trump had to do with Flynn's objection to arming Kurdish groups designated as a terrorist organizations by Turkey and the US State Department. Trump wanted these groups to fight for the US in Syria knowing full well the implications of doing so. Trump would go on to training and arming these Kurdish forces in May souring US-Turkey relations.[210] [211]

The second problem with Flynn's work on behalf of Turkey which he later files as a foreign agent for was the efforts to extradite highly influential religious cleric Fethullah Gulen from the US to Turkey. While I do not know Gulen personally, I know of the Charter School network which is connected to his Gulen movement, which ranges across the United States. Beehive Academy in Utah with an emphasis on Math and the Sciences, had chronic under-enrollment due to suspicion the school was an "indoctrination center" instead of just a school. Beehive was in imminent jeopardy of abruptly closing, something that rarely has happened in Utah Charter schools, due to large funding gap and a state school board decision based on religious intolerance and fear that was later removed. Through donations, mostly likely from Turkey and the surrounding community, the $300,000 gap was closed and kept the school in operation, which has continued to this day. Sure there are some problems, like most of the staff being Turkish at these schools across the US, but they really are just schools, and generally good ones at that. As my daughter hit kindergarten age, we applied to have her enrolled at a Harmony Math and Science Academy here in Texas as well as a number of other schools. [212]

---

[210] "State Department Maintains Foreign Terrorist Organization (FTO) Designation of the Kurdistan Workers' Party (PKK)." U.S. Department of State, U.S. Department of State, 1 Mar. 2019, www.state.gov/r/pa/prs/ps/2019/03/289833.htm.

[211] Snow, Shawn. "US Still Arming Kurdish Allies in Syria." Military Times, Military Times, 27 Nov. 2017, www.militarytimes.com/flashpoints/2017/11/27/us-still-arming-kurdish-allies-in-syria/.

[212] Stuart, Elizabeth. "Islamic Links to Utah's Beehive Academy Probed." DeseretNews.com, Deseret News, 1 June 2010, www.deseretnews.com/article/700036619/Islamic-links-to-Utahs-Beehive-Academy-probed.html.

Gulen is accused of plotting a failed coup against the Turkish President Erdogan that happened in 2016. As Enis Kanter, NBA star, was also accused of being part of the same "terror group," the Gulen movement, by that same Turkish government on January 16, 2019, I have my reservations. Unless I see the *"smoking saw"* that Turkey provided when the criminal evidence roll-out was meant to embarrass both the Trump administration and Saudi Arabia over the Khashoggi murder, I will continue to be suspicious.[213]

The FBI did NOT let Flynn go, as Trump requested, and his guilty plea for lying under oath was filed on December 1, 2017. Many questions about the substantial assistance Flynn has provided the Mueller investigation warranting their recommendation of no prison time likely won't be known until Trump is out of office and indictments presumed to be sealed will finally be opened. A lot of that may have to do with the Saudi Conspiracy where the transition team, then administration worked on the Marshall Plan likely circumventing multiple laws. As I said, Russia is a nothing-burger compared to what these goons were doing on the Arabian Peninsula.[214] [215]

---

[213] Sommeryesterday, Allison Kaplan, et al. "Turkey Seeks Arrest Warrant for NBA Star They Allege Is Part of Terror Organization, Report Says." Haaretz.com, 16 Jan. 2019, www.haaretz.com/us-news/turkey-seeks-arrest-warrant-for-nba-star-report-says-1.6848453.

[214] Cox Media Group National Content Desk. "Mueller Investigation: Michael Flynn Requests No Jail Time in Court Filing before Sentencing." Ajc, Cmgsharedcontent.com, 12 Dec. 2018, www.ajc.com/news/national/mueller-investigation-michael-flynn-attorneys-make-sentencing-recommendation/BVC1YsccCCDyh8mSuarjJN/.

[215] United States, Congress, District Court for the District Court of Columbia. "US Vs. Michael T. Flynn." US Vs. Michael T. Flynn, District Court for the District Court of Columbia, 2017, pp. 1–6.

Chapter Sixteen

"By the way, that's a treasonous act."

"*The three senior guys in the campaign thought it was a good idea to meet with a foreign government inside Trump Tower in the conference room on the 25th floor—with no lawyers. They didn't have any lawyers.*

"*Even if you thought that this was not treasonous, or unpatriotic, or bad shit, and I happen to think it's all of that, you should have called the FBI immediately.*"[216]

-Steve Bannon

The above quote about the Trump Tower meeting given to Michael Wolff in the book *Fire and Fury* sums up just how compromised the Trump campaign was at the time. It also shows how badly Trump wanted to get the Hillary emails he will publicly ask Russia to obtain for him against US law the following month. For his son Trump Junior, son-in-law Jared Kushner and Campaign Manager Paul Manafort to go to such a meeting without Trump's knowledge is absurdly laughable considering the man talked so much about it on the campaign trail.

Donald Trump Junior is much like his father, flat affect, poor judgment and all. Autism is known to run in families and all three of the Trump boys as well as dad show the outward presentations of the disorder in their facial expressions.

I am glad though Junior was "transparent" without consulting his lawyer first laying out the evidence against him as to why the meeting was arranged Tweeting out his email exchange with Rob Goldstone arranging the Trump Tower meeting for June 9, 2016, before journalists would be able to, that were presumed to have obtained them from someone inside the administration. (Leakiest White House in history.)

June 3, 2016

> *"Emin just called and asked me to contact you with something very interesting. The Crown Prosecutor of Russia met with his father Aras this morning and in their meeting offered to provide the Trump campaign with some official documents and information that would incriminate Hillary and her dealings with Russia and would be very useful to your father.*
>
> *"This is obviously very high level and sensitive information but is part of Russia and its government's support for Mr. Trump-helped along by Aras and Emin. What do you think is the best way to handle this information and would you be able to speak to Emin about it directly? I can also send this info to your father via Rhona, but it is ultra-sensitive so wanted to send to you first."*

June 3, 2016, Junior replies:

> *"Thanks Rob. I appreciate that. I am on the road at the moment but perhaps I just speak to Emin first. Seems we some time and if it's what you say I love it especially later in the summer. Could we do a call first thing next week when I am back?"*[217]

Other messages back and forth from that point forward on different days set up the logistics of the eventual meeting. The important details were why the meeting was being set up—to get dirt on Hillary to the Trump campaign and that Jr. took the meeting. It is also important that Goldstone stated, *"Russia*

---

[217] Owen, Paul. "Full Text of the Emails between Donald Trump Jr and Rob Goldstone." The Guardian, Guardian News and Media, 11 July 2017, www.theguardian.com/us-news/2017/jul/11/donald-trump-jr-emails-full-text-russia-rob-goldstone.

and its government's support for Mr. Trump," which implies preference as to whom they want in control after the election.

According to Federal guidelines listed on the Federal Election Commission website, fec.gov, it is illegal to receive or solicit campaign contributions from foreign nationals.

> *The Act and Commission regulations include a broad prohibition on foreign national activity in connection with elections in the United States. 52 U.S.C. § 30121 and generally, 11 CFR 110.20. In general, foreign nationals are prohibited from the following activities:*
>
> *Making any contribution or donation of money or other thing of value, or making any expenditure, independent expenditure, or disbursement in connection with any federal, state or local election in the United States;*
>
> *Making any contribution or donation to any committee or organization of any national, state, district, or local political party (including donations to a party nonfederal account or office building account);*
>
> *Making any disbursement for an electioneering communication;*
>
> *Making any donation to a presidential inaugural committee.*
>
> *Persons who knowingly and willfully engage in these activities may be subject to an FEC enforcement action, criminal prosecution, or both.*

So does *"high level and sensitive information"* offered by a foreign national considered a campaign contribution?

Contribution: A gift, subscription, loan, advance or deposit of money or anything of value given to influence a federal election; or the payment by any person of compensation for the personal services of another person if those services are rendered without charge to a political committee for any purpose. 11 CFR 100.52 (a) and 100.54. [218]

As the Federal Government already charged Michael Cohen under this statute for the conspiracy involving the *National Enquirer* catch-and-kill scheme to hide Trump affairs, this "gift" of information would indeed be illegal had it been "officially" offered to the campaign.

---

[218] "Foreign Nationals." FEC.gov, www.fec.gov/updates/foreign-nationals/.

Trump, anticipating the scheduled meeting and the batch of emails he expects to get, runs the following ill-advised Tweet about three hours before the "delivery" is to take place:

> *How long did it take your staff of 823 people to think that up—*
> *and where are your 33,000 emails that you deleted?*[219]
>
> *-Donald J. Trump*
> *1:40 P.M., June 9, 2016*

At the meeting the "dirt" on Hillary Clinton that had been offered by the Russians according to Goldstone wasn't given directly, at least according to testimony given by those interviewed. According to Junior's testimony to Congress, the Russian lawyer described documents that would connect an alleged tax fraud scheme with Ziff Brothers Investments and British investor directing money to a Clinton campaign in an illegal donation then spoke about Russian adoptions then the Magnitski Act and the desire to have that repealed. Junior called the whole meeting a "bait and switch." [220]

I guess Junior has never watched the show *To Catch a Predator.*

Donnie Junior might have felt duped as he got nothing out of the crime that he clearly expected. That is exactly how all those men feel when the "girl" walks out one a door to change and in comes several law enforcement rushing in for the arrest. The other two officials from the campaign clearly understood the meaning-remove those sanctions in order to get our help. That information would likely be relayed to the boss by all three who attended the meeting.

Let's be very clear about the material that was being offered. Russia has indeed been funneling money into US politicians' and other people's pockets for years for real-estate, speaking engagements and other things. It is how the Russians "got" Manafort and Flynn using loans and lucrative speaking engagements. In a sense it is also how Russia "got" Trump with investment, real-estate purchases and laundered money and his businesses. Until the US blocks candidates or officials who accept foreign money from hold-

---

[219] Trump, Donald J. "How Long Did It Take Your Staff of 823 People to Think That up—and Where Are Your 33,000 Emails That You Deleted? Https://T.co/GECLNtQizQ." Twitter, Twitter, 9 June 2016, twitter.com/realDonaldTrump/status/741007091947556864.

[220] Herb, Jeremy, and Marshall Cohen. "The Trump Tower Meeting: A Timeline." CNN, Cable News Network, 31 July 2018, www.cnn.com/2018/07/31/politics/trump-tower-meeting-timeline/index.html.

ing public office or lobbying entirely, our Government will continue to fall prey to foreign influence.

With every discrete crime, there is always a cover-up. The Trump Tower meeting was not known about publicly for more than a year until the *"failing" New York Times* broke the story originally on July 8, 2017. By this time, Trump was President and had been lying about contacts and business deals with Russians continually directly or through surrogates like Kelly Anne Con away.

Times reporters are consummate professionals. When they knew of the meeting, they reached out to Junior for comment. He did. And that was a HUGE legal problem as his father then gave this for him to deliver:

"I was asked to have a meeting by an acquaintance I knew from the 2013 Miss Universe pageant with an individual who I was told might have information helpful to the campaign. I was not told her name prior to the meeting. I asked Jared and Paul to attend, but told them nothing of substance. We had a meeting in June 2016. After pleasantries were exchanged, the woman stated that she had information that individuals connected to Russia were funding the Democratic National Committee and supporting Ms. Clinton. Her statements were vague, ambiguous and made no sense. No details or supporting information was provided or even offered. It quickly became clear that she had no meaningful information. She then changed subjects and began discussing the adoption of Russian children and mentioned the Magnitski Act. It became clear to me that this was the true agenda all along and that the claims of potentially helpful information were a pretext for the meeting. I interrupted and advised her that my father was not an elected official, but rather a private citizen, and that her comments and concerns were better addressed if and when he held public office. The meeting lasted approximately 20 to 30 minutes. As it ended, my acquaintance apologized for taking up our time. That was the end of it and there was no further contact or follow-up of any kind. My father knew nothing of the meeting or these events."[221]

---

[221] Pramuk, Jacob. "Here's Donald Trump Jr.'s Full Statement on His Meeting with a Russian Lawyer." CNBC, CNBC, 10 July 2017, www.cnbc.com/2017/07/09/donald-trump-jr-full-statement-on-meeting-with-a-russian-lawyer.html.

This statement is a key piece of evidence, as it is the first public accounting of what went on at the meeting. It was also intentionally misleading. While adoptions were discussed, that was brief. The majority of the time was spent discussing repealing the Magnitski Act. In Junior's statement, the Act was *"mentioned."*

The next day's follow-up Times piece claimed correctly that the intent of the meeting was to gain "dirt" on Hillary, not Russian adoptions, likely spooking Junior. Junior dumps out his messages with Goldstone to be "transparent" two days later realizing someone was "squealing" to the press. That full-disclosure showed "intent" to receive Russian assistance on behalf of the campaign.

Then came the denials from Trump officials of the President's involvement in crafting the tower statement:

> *"I do want to be clear that the president was not involved in the drafting of the statement and did not issue the statement. It came from Donald Trump Jr. So that's what I can tell you because that's what we know."*
>
> —*Attorney Jay Sekulow*
> *July 16, 2017, on* Meet the Press

> *"The president weighed in, as any father would, based on the limited information that he had. He certainly didn't dictate, but like I said, he weighed in, offered suggestions like any father would do."*[222]
> —*Press Secretary Sarah Sanders*
> *August 1, 2017*

On January 29, 2018, Trump's legal counsel John M. Dowd sent a letter to the Office of the Special Counsel answering specific questions pertaining to the President, and a possible interview, which they argued against. The leak of the intended secretive document likely originated with those so-called resistance staff within the administration.

His lawyers argue many intriguing points such as Trump could not obstruct himself, because hey, he is the President. He could also terminate the investigation or pardon himself. Essentially Trump is all-powerful and cannot be held accountable as President.

---

[222] Kiely, Eugene. "A Timeline of Trump Tower Meeting Responses." FactCheck.org, 4 June 2018, www.factcheck.org/2018/06/a-timeline-of-trump-tower-meeting-responses/.

None of these arguments make any sense to any law-abiding person. Can a criminal President have absolute immunity? The chief concern here was whether Trump had obstructed justice, which his actions of covering up the secret meeting and what it was about certainly reeks of.

Then they attack the credibility of the FBI and the DOJ. Anyone wonder at that point why the White House may have been inclined to leak this? His lawyers at the end of the first letter concede Trump dictated the letter—BUT doing so wasn't obstruction:

STATEMENT OF JULY 8, 2017,
TO **THE NEW YORK TIMES**

You have received all of the notes, communications and testimony indicating that the President dictated a short but accurate response to The New York Times *article on behalf of his son, Donald Trump, Jr. His son then followed up by making a full public disclosure regarding the meeting, including his public testimony that there was nothing to the meeting and certainly no evidence of collusion.*

This subject is a private matter with The New York Times. *The President is not required to answer to the Office of the Special Counsel, or anyone else, for his private affairs with his children. In any event, the President's son, son-in-law, and White House advisors and staff have made a full disclosure on these events to both your office and the congressional committees.[223]*

So why did Trump "jump in" and dictate a statement for his son potentially obstructing justice in the process? Trump has an overwhelming compulsion to control all things connected to him, part of his autism spectrum disorder's restricted behaviors, especially when it comes to the media. Like most of Trump's control schemes, they eventually unravel like all the Trump Tower meeting lies did. Trump went from the definitive no one in the campaign made contacts with Russians statements to this meeting did happen but this is the first time I am hearing about it, to discussing the meeting being set up with his son in the presence of Michael Cohen.

---

[223] The New York Times. "The Trump Lawyers' Confidential Memo to Mueller, Explained." The New York Times, The New York Times, 2 June 2018, www.nytimes.com/interactive/2018/06/02/us/politics/trump-legal-documents.html.

There is a BIGGER problem for Trump. There are at least one hundred tapes of "stuff" seized from the raid of Cohen's office.

> *"Inconceivable that the government would break into a lawyer's office (early in the morning)—almost unheard of. Even more inconceivable that a lawyer would tape a client—totally unheard of & perhaps illegal. The good news is that your favorite President did nothing wrong!"[224]*
>
> 5:10 A.M., July 21, 2018

Did nothing wrong? Trump can't help but dig in-restricted patterns of behavior—even when he knows there is a high probability things will eventually crash down on him. Then a couple days later Trump claims again he did not know about the Trump Tower meeting:

> *Fake News reporting, a complete fabrication, that I am concerned about the meeting my wonderful son, Donald, had in Trump Tower. This was a meeting to get information on an opponent, totally legal and done all the time in politics—and it went nowhere. I did not know about it![225]*
>
> 5:35 A.M., August 5, 2018

If only Trump could control the "fake media."

---

224 Trump, Donald J. "Inconceivable That the Government Would Break into a Lawyer's Office (Early in the Morning) - Almost Unheard of. Even More Inconceivable That a Lawyer Would Tape a Client - Totally Unheard of & Perhaps Illegal. The Good News Is That Your Favorite President Did Nothing Wrong!" Twitter, Twitter, 21 July 2018, twitter.com/realDonaldTrump/status/1020642287725043712.

225 Trump, Donald J. "Fake News Reporting, a Complete Fabrication, That I Am Concerned about the Meeting My Wonderful Son, Donald, Had in Trump Tower. This Was a Meeting to Get Information on an Opponent, Totally Legal and Done All the Time in Politics - and It Went Nowhere. I Did Not Know about It!" Twitter, Twitter, 5 Aug. 2018, twitter.com/realdonaldtrump/status/1026084333315153924? lang=en.

Chapter Seventeen

"The media is very dishonest with–of course,
"Fox & Friends" is exclued, OK?"

Donald Trump's rise from a virtual nobody rich conman elevating all the way to "stealing" the job President of the United States could not have been done without his ability to manipulate others through the media, coercion, threats and the occasional meltdown.

> *"While CNN doesn't do great in the United States based on ratings, outside of the U.S. they have very little competition. Throughout the world, CNN has a powerful voice portraying the United States in an unfair....*
>
> *"....and false way. Something has to be done, including the possibility of the United States starting our own Worldwide Network to show the World the way we really are, GREAT!"* [226]
>
> 11:47 A.M., November 26, 2018

Trump does NOT like CNN, as well as a few other news outlets because they refuse to join his rather dystopian view of the world, instead reporting things he has for decades used tactics to bludgeon and kill. CNN has angered him so much that

---

[226] Trump, Donald J. "....And False Way. Something Has to Be Done, Including the Possibility of the United States Starting Our Own Worldwide Network to Show the World the Way We Really Are, GREAT!" Twitter, Twitter, 26 Nov. 2018, twitter.com/realdonaldtrump/status/1067142820388052993? lang=en.

"

his wife turned the channel on just to spite him after the "FOURTH" time the Stormy Daniels story surfaced and finally broke.[227] The first two times Trump killed that story, he had conspired with the *National Enquirer* to "catch-and-kill" and then the report also was "squelched" twice internally at Trump's state run TV, Fox News just prior to the election. Turning on CNN was a much more effective "message" than say slapping away Donnie's hand or that time she wore the "I really don't care, do u?" jacket on the way to visit imprisoned children separated by Trump's inhumane zero-tolerance policy from their families.[228]

Trump is ALL about the control. It is why he was caught peeking to see WHO his wife was voting for in his "photo-op voting booth" shot.[229]

> *"The American Media has changed forever. News organizations that seemed like a big deal are now extinct. Those that remain have now degraded themselves beyond recognition, like the New Yorker—or they've been purchased by Jeff Bezos to conduct unregistered lobbying for.........*
>
> *"....Amazon, like The Washington Post. It's hard to remember that not so long ago America had prestige media outlets, but not anymore." @TuckerCarlson The Fake News Media is the true Enemy of the People!*[230]
>
> *6:04 P.M., March 4, 2019*

The most definitive piece I have read on Trump's infiltration and takeover of the American media is Jane Mayer's exceptional *The Making of the Fox News White*

[227] Ralph, Pat. "Melania Trump's Spokeswoman Says She Watches 'Any Channel She Wants' after Report Said Trump Was Irate Her TV Aboard Air Force One Was Set to CNN." Business Insider, Business Insider, 25 July 2018, www.businessinsider.com/melania-report-trump-was-irate-she-watched-cnn-2018-7.

[228] Jennings, Rebecca. "Melania Trump Wears 'I Really Don't Care, Do u?' Jacket on Trip to Migrant Children." Vox, Vox, 21 June 2018, www.vox.com/2018/6/21/17489632/melania-trump-jacket-zara-i-really-dont-care-do-u.

[229] Bowerman, Mary. "Internet Goes Crazy over Photo of Trump Appearing to Look at Melania's Ballot." USA Today, Gannett Satellite Information Network, 9 Nov. 2016, www.usatoday.com/story/news/politics/onpolitics/2016/11/08/donald-trump-melania-ballot-voting/93491398/.

[230] Trump, Donald J. "'The American Media Has Changed Forever. News Organizations That Seemed like a Big Deal Are Now Extinct. Those That Remain Have Now Degraded Themselves beyond Recognition, like the New Yorker - or They've Been Purchased by Jeff Bezos to Conduct Unregistered Lobbying for........." Twitter, Twitter, 5 Mar. 2019, twitter.com/realDonaldTrump/status/1102751706444636160.

House published online March 4, 2019, then in print on March 11, 2019, *The New Yorker* magazine. I had seen the "pivot" too, where Fox had been mostly ambivalent and dismissive of Trump to becoming enthusiastic cheerleader, and taking on all his "traits" and "core messaging." Meyer connected all the threads expertly, and Trump is none too happy, as evidenced by his shout out advertising something big came out in *The New Yorker* magazine in his Tweet. This inability of Trump's to self-regulate his own behavior and speech when something bad is newly revealed about him must make his lawyers and advisors cringe ALL the time.

Trump and Fox News are intertwined, married and inseparable where he calls and speaks with hosts, frequently Tweets live and completes a feedback reinforcement loop with himself. According to the article, Sean Hannity is Trump's daily call-in routine each night before going to bed. Considering that the man shared Michael Cohen as a lawyer and has appeared on stage at a rally with Trump, pointing at the real media and calling them fake, this is no surprise. Hannity is a Trump thug through and through. [231]

Remember that guy Hitler I mentioned a few chapters back? His line of thought was mostly out of whack with the socialist organization he was sent to infiltrate by the German Army, yet the common ground of hate, fear-mongering and racism were the same. As an obvious outsider, with a strong-will and power to influence others, Adolf went in then carved out the parts he didn't like and rebranded the party nationalist.

Like Hitler, Trump found his political audience with his voice spreading far-right-wing nut job conspiracy theories, such as the ridiculous "birther theory" that Obama was born in Kenya, as a weekly guest on Fox News, starting in 2011. He also showed up on other networks, such as CNN, where he said this on April 7, 2011:

> *"There's no birth certificate. There's only a certificate of live birth, which is a totally different thing and a much, much lower standard. There are no hospital records. His own family doesn't know what hospital he was born in in Hawaii. But have you no hospital records in any of the hospitals that he was born there."[232]*

[231] Darcy, Oliver. "Sean Hannity Said He Wouldn't Campaign on Stage at Trump's Rally. Hours Later, He Did Exactly That." CNN, Cable News Network, 6 Nov. 2018, www.cnn.com/2018/11/06/media/trump-rally-missouri-hannity/index.html.

[232] agencies, The New Arab &. "Saudi Prince's Ritz-Carlton 'Shakedown' Ends with $106B Netted." Alaraby, The New Arab, 31 Jan. 2019, www.alaraby.co.uk/english/news/2019/1/31/saudi-princes-

Suzanne Malveuax who had done her research corrects Trump showing the transcript of the interview where the conspiracy originated. She points out that the grandmother stated Obama was born in the United States. Trump, who is as fixed-minded in his beliefs can't make that cognitive break despite having proof given to him, and continues to argue.

Trump eventually wore down the being corrected at Fox. It was like they, for the most part, just stopped being journalists, gave up and gave the child what he demanded. Ratings climbed. Trump would say more stupid outlandish things. Ratings would go up further. As Fox was built to support more of a right-wing leaning audience anyhow, a lot of Trump's Nationalism, particularly the fear of immigrants and Muslims, was connecting with viewers who were naturally more fearful and intolerant of others. This made for a strange brew. No matter how farcical the claim Trump blurts out unfiltered, Fox runs it, does not retract falsehoods often enough, and this causes those claims to be accepted as alternative facts.

Other claims made in *The New Yorker* piece were that Trump hated CNN so much he intentionally pushed parts of his administration to block the Time Warner and AT&T merger. This was already pretty obvious since Trump on November 21, 2017, the day after the suit had been filed, said this:

> *"Personally, I've always felt that that was a deal that's not good for the country. I think your pricing is going to go up. But I'm not going to get involved. It's litigation."*[233]

The piece went on to claim that Trump told John Kelly he asked Gary Cohn to get the lawsuit filed. If true, that would counter the *"I'm not going to get involved"* shtick he had fed to the media. When it came time for Fox to face regulator's scrutiny in a sale to Disney that was approved the following month, Trump reached out first to make sure the news division wasn't part of the sale, likely pushed approval internally then congratulated Murdoch, December 14, 2017.[234]

---

ritz-carlton-shakedown-ends-with-106b-netted.

[233] "Personally. "President Trump Speaks on AT&T-Time Warner Deal: 'Not Good for the Country.'" CNNMoney, Cable News Network, money.cnn.com/2017/11/21/media/trump-comments-att-time-warner/index.html.

[234] Higgins, Tucker. "Trump Congratulated Rupert Murdoch on the Fox-Disney Deal." CNBC, CNBC, 14 Dec. 2017, www.cnbc.com/2017/12/14/trump-congratulated-rupert-murdoch-fox-disney-

The most scintillating reveal of *The New Yorker* piece was that Fox had the Stormy Daniels story in October just before the election. Considering the timing of the piece being completed and the Access Hollywood *"Grab them by the pussy"* tape the iron was burning hot for such a release. Diana Falzone took the completed story, independent of the *National Enquirer* one that Pecker, Cohen and Trump caught and killed, and submitted it to the editors of Fox. It was dead, killed at the highest levels. Falzone then found out about the *National Enquirer* angle, and pitched that to Fox too. Fox was too invested in seeing Trump winning to run either story. Seems Trump gutted any journalistic integrity at Fox before he was elected, and had at least partial control over what was happening at the network. The Stormy Daniels story broke for real, a year into Trump's reign.[235]

The umbilical cord that connects between Fox and Trump apparently runs both ways. Sometimes it is the hosts that work over the President to get what they want. This is how it went when Fox tormented the beleaguered President for agreeing to sign off on the continuing resolution funding the government announced on December 19th and fear-mongered him into closing the government while in control of House, Senate and Presidency for thirty-five days.

The real *"nasty woman"* made him do it. And Rush Limbaugh helped.

That woman is the crazed Ann Coulter, a tall, sharp-tongued blonde woman so thin if you sneezed in her direction she might break.

> *"He is dead in the water if he doesn't build that wall. Dead, dead, dead."*
>
> *"Trump will just have been a joke presidency who scammed the American people, amused the populists for a while, but he'll have no legacy whatsoever."*

Trump likely was consumed by the criticism, especially since these people were inside his "safe space" he had created for himself on the far right media outlets. On top of that, Coulter had written flattering stuff in her book, *In Trump We Trust*. So hearing he was going to DIE probably caught Donald's attention.[236]

deal.html.

[235] Mayer, Jane. "The Making of the Fox News White House." The New Yorker, The New Yorker, 8 Mar. 2019, www.newyorker.com/magazine/2019/03/11/the-making-of-the-fox-news-white-house.

[236] Gray, Sarah. "Ann Coulter Doubles down: Trump Will Be 'Dead in the Water' If He Doesn't Build the Wall." New Haven Register, Business Insider, 17 Jan. 2019,

Rush wasn't as terrifying.

> *"It's what the drive-by media calls compromise: Trump gets nothing and the Democrats get everything! Including control of the House in a few short weeks."*
>
> *"In fact... Trump is going to get less than nothing because this compromise strips out the $1.6 billion for the wall that the Senate Appropriations Committee had already approved weeks ago, that's gone too."*
>
> *"Not a penny!" Limbaugh shouted. "Forget wall, think border security!"*[237]

Trump caved under the pressure, mostly because of these two personalities Trump has long been "friends" with. He doesn't get it. I used to listen to Rush and Glen Beck for years during my drives to and from work until a day I spotted something obviously fishy in the back to back radio casts. That rotten fish was both media influencers peddling a falsehood that gold was the best current investment in the economic climate at the time. I knew a bubble when I see one having been fixated on business reports and tracking prices for gold as well as the stock market well before I had any skin in the game. I realized these guys would likely benefit from a surge of late investors, and that likely explained their behavior. I tuned them out from that day forward as I hate scammers preying on others, and found myself instead listening to sports radio. The bubble popped, along with housing, stocks and just about everything months later as the economy entered the Great Recession.

In the end, Trump got even less than what was on the original continuing resolution while Nancy Pelosi came out *wearing "two blue balls on a chain"* to the eventual State of the Union address, perhaps the best "burn" of the feeble President yet, clapping with sarcasm at all the women elected in Congress thanks to him. Most of how the longest shut down in US history saw Pelosi in control, firmly scolding Trump on cameras, then in private and lastly cutting off the original State of the Union address while Donnie sulked and tweeted

www.nhregister.com/technology/businessinsider/article/Ann-Coulter-doubles-down-Trump-will-be-dead-in-13540320.php.

[237] Zhao, Christina. "Rush Limbaugh Furious about Border Wall: Trump Got 'Less than Nothing' and 'Democrats Get Everything!'" Newsweek, 20 Dec. 2018, www.newsweek.com/rush-limbaugh-angrily-rants-about-border-wall-trump-got-less-nothing-and-1265987.

about being alone in the White House (with his wife also there, probably just as alone as he was). That is the difference between a grandmother who is so kind you wouldn't even know she had cut off your head, and a President with the cognitive maturity of a twelve-year-old.

Trump pulled his own "power" move the day after Nancy suggested Trump give his Speech from the White House with security not being adequate with furloughs and the shutdown. He did so via Sarah Sanders on Twitter:

> *"Due to the Shutdown, I am sorry to inform you that your trip to Brussels, Egypt, and Afghanistan has been postponed. In light of the 800,000 great American workers not receiving pay, I am sure you would agree that postponing this public relations event is totally appropriate. Obviously, if you would like to make your journey by flying commercial, that would certainly be your prerogative."[238]*

Pelosi's tough-guy image of vacationing in war zones makes Chuck Norris look soft. I halfway expected Nancy to go coach, save Trump's choice to reveal a classified trip to the public put the delegation at serious risk should they even try.

After intense pressure with the potential airports would have to shutter, many of his base realizing that having a government shutdown hurt them too, Trump signed the papers giving Pelosi a victory. But that isn't how the lore-crafters spun it to the in-tuned TV President. Like the Netflix All Hail King Julian's own state TV gossiping Toucan Xixi who speaks from a box in front of the diminutive lemur dictator, members of the Faux News Network lined up to applaud Trump's triumph on live TV for saving the government and making the Democrats look so bad. At least Ann Coulter had burned her "bridge" of influence to the President.

> *"Good news for George Herbert Walker Bush: As of today, he is no longer the biggest wimp ever to serve as President of the United States."*
>
> *1:55 P.M., January 25, 2019*
> *-Ann Coulter, FORMER Trump influencer*

---

238 Sanders, Sarah. "President @RealDonaldTrump's Letter to @SpeakerPelosi Concerning Her Upcoming Travel Pic.twitter.com/TtBCvwp080." Twitter, Twitter, 17 Jan. 2019, twitter.com/PressSec/status/1085978219872964608.

"I wish people would read or listen to my words on the Border Wall. This was in no way a concession. It was taking care of millions of people who were getting badly hurt by the Shutdown with the understanding that in 21 days, if no deal is done, it's off to the races!"[239]

6:33 P.M., January 25, 2019
-Donald J. Trump

https://www.foxnews.com/politics/trump-slams-claims-he-gave-in-on-partial-shutdown-this-was-in-no-way-a-concession

---

[239] Zwirz, Elizabeth. "Trump Signs Bill to End Partial Government Shutdown." Fox News, FOX News Network, www.foxnews.com/politics/trump-slams-claims-he-gave-in-on-partial-shutdown-this-was-in-no-way-a-concession.

Chapter Eighteen

"They are nothing but thugs and criminals and predators."

"I've *known Jeff for fifteen years. Terrific guy. He's a lot of fun to be with. It is even said that he likes beautiful women as much as I do, and many of them are on the younger side. No doubt about it—Jeffrey enjoys his social life."*[240]

-Donald J. Trump
New York *Mag, 2002*

It is very telling going back and reading quotes from Trump then looking at what is currently known and being able to "read" the deeper meaning with the newer added context. Trump gives "tells" about what he is thinking constantly as he is unable to filter correctly to keep up a ruse when he feels comfortable, as part of his overall disorder. In this quote about convicted child serial rapist and Trump's social life buddy Jeffery Epstein, Trump connects EVERYTHING that he really shouldn't have if any of his past escapades emerge from the shadows. These things Donald said are simply young girls, fun and Trump BEING there.

Facts matter. While there were actual recordings of Trump and his reflective admiration for then twelve-year-old Paris Hilton's body after having seen her adult sex tape, and his disturbing comment about his going to be dating

---

[240] Jr., Landon Thomas. "Jeffrey Epstein: International Moneyman of Mystery." NYMag.com, nymag.com/nymetro/news/people/n_7912/.

that child in ten years by the escalator, there isn't known audio or video to confirm what Trump did or didn't do when having "fun" with his teen-sex-crazed buddy. All we have are some threads and accusations, which give a strong impression, particularly with known suppression tactics of threats and intimidation or payoffs by the Trump mob, that these sultry things surely must warrant further investigation.

First fact, in 2005 someone finally went to the police about Epstein molesting her stepdaughter.

Second fact, in 2008 Epstein pleads guilty to solicitation of prostitution and procurement of minors for prostitution. The prepared indictment was extensive carrying a possibility of life in prison. Epstein would use girls to get more girls, using alcohol and cocaine to get them to do things for him, which pretty much was whatever he wanted to do with them at the time. I'll let your imagination paint its own picture. He'd have a cadre of these mostly young "ladies" that would impress the likes of friends Bill Clinton, Kevin Spacey and Donald J. Trump.

Third fact, Alexander Acosta, then US attorney in Miami, and now Labor Secretary in the Trump administration, arranged a plea deal with Epstein that boggles the mind. Epstein "served" a scant thirteen months for some eighty sexual assaults, with around thirty being underage girls, in a private wing of a Palm Beach County jail with six-days-a-week, twelve-hour work release. As part of the deal Epstein and any co-conspirators were granted immunity, "killing" a potentially broadening FBI investigation which considering some of the names connected to Epstein and his sex parties is wrong on many levels for his many victims in his child prostitution ring.[241]

Fourth fact, Trump was accused of being one of those co-conspirators in the abuse of a thirteen-year-old girl. Trump was required to give a deposition in December after the election then suddenly the now adult woman dropped the case on November 4, 2016, citing threats and intimidation.[242]

At this point, forget Pizza-Gate, the wildly circulated and debunked Clinton child-sex ring conspiracy theory that many of Trump's followers fell for,

---

[241] Coaston, Jane, and Anna North. "Jeffrey Epstein, the Convicted Sex Offender Who Is Friends with Donald Trump and Bill Clinton, Explained." Vox, Vox, 22 Feb. 2019, www.vox.com/2018/12/3/ 18116351/jeffrey-epstein-trump-clinton-labor-secretary-acosta.

[242] Crockett, Emily. "The Lawsuit Accusing Trump of Raping a 13-Year-Old Girl, Explained." Vox, Vox, 5 Nov. 2016, www.vox.com/policy-and-politics/2016/11/3/13501364/trump-rape-13-year-old-lawsuit-katie-johnson-allegation.

as the Epstein story was the real deal. Actually, DON'T forget Pizza-Gate, as like many of these conspiracy theories that are believed by Donald's cult, they seem to be BUILT to deflect from the actual stories that have come up against the right (false flag with the MAGA bomber and claiming the Vegas Shooter was a Democrat are other noteworthy examples). The Pizza-Gate conspiracy was formed near the end of October 2016, when a woman who claimed to have been thirteen at the time of one of those parties had come forward to accuse Donald Trump and Epstein of some pretty serious stuff.

What she said if true was very shocking, violent and frankly uncharacteristic of what is known about Trump's behavior as he has never been violent, just grabby with every other assault claim. For this reason, I believe that this unknown accuser, who had forced a December deposition in the case where Trump would answer questions, was likely not telling "truth." She dropped the suit on November 4, 2016, and the President-elect never testified. That doesn't mean Trump is in the clear, only that that one woman was probably a false accuser, in a sea of many likely real ones.

Trump himself held quite a few of the same sort of wild parties in the suites at the Plaza Hotel that seem eerily similar to the ones buddy Epstein held during the 80s and 90s. I mean what could people possibly accuse you of when you are mixing drugs and young girls looking for model industry contacts at a party? Here is how an industry male model who lined up willing girls for the shebang described it, reported by Michael Gross who has covered Trump since 1985, on October 24, 2016, reported in the *Daily Beast*:

> *"There was cocaine around. I never saw him do that. Donald Trump does not do cocaine. He's in control of himself.*
>
> *"A lot of girls, 14, look 24. That's as juicy as I can get. I never asked how old they were; I just partook. I did partake in activities that would be controversial, too."*
>
> *-Andy Lucchessi*

Trump also doesn't smoke or drink, not allowing others to smoke at his parties. Additionally an unnamed "photographer" who also partied with Trump had these things to say:

"I was there to party myself. It was guys with younger girls, sex, a lot of sex, a lot of cocaine, top-shelf liquor.

"They exchanged information, facilitated each other. Trump was in and out. He'd wander off with a couple girls. I saw him. He was getting laid like crazy. Trump was at the heart of it. He loved the attention and in private, he was a total fucking beast."

And more importantly what did Trump say years after the event:

"If I hadn't got married, who knows what would have happened? You had drugs, women and booze all over the fuckin' place."[243]

-Donald J. Trump

These party details of his single days give Trump a mythical sex beast type of status alongside his banging Porn Star Stormy Daniels and Playmate Karen McDougal. That plays well on Fox, which at any given time has two or more sex-oriented "news" stories covered on its website. It is more of the *"locker room talk," "boys will be boys,"* and the objectification of women sort of mindset that likely endears his character more to his adoring base. But to those who are "religiously conservative," this level of debauchery should have been disqualifying. That may be why he resorted to mob-type tactics to silence accusations and stories including his conspiracy with the *National Enquirer*. Trump needed to look Presidential, and his past was anything but. His lawyer of ten years and personal "fixer" would clear all that up after lying for him on all sorts of things.

Recall also that Trump was recorded commenting on a pre-teen girl that he would be dating her in ten years at this point. It was the only audio recording found so far, however there was at least one mention of him saying it directly to two fourteen-year-old girls in a newspaper clipping from the *Chicago Tribune*, December 1992. If this sort of "joke" as the clipping and audio suggested were a pattern, Trump's behavior is clearly disturbing. These sorts of "fishing" statements are grooming behaviors designed to probe a child's level of vulnerability or potential interest in the predator. Depending on the reac-

---

[243] Gross, Michael. "Inside Donald Trump's One-Stop Parties: Attendees Recall Cocaine and Very Young Models." The Daily Beast, The Daily Beast Company, 25 Oct. 2016, www.thedailybeast.com/inside-donald-trumps-one-stop-parties-attendees-recall-cocaine-and-very-young-models?fbclid= IwAR0gy1tzHIn3KFAn_od8juwLx8i2D0WhNY5mI06RhUIjYo5QqdcHyEwo5e8.

tion, the predator will change the subject, leave or give directional comments or compliments to build trust and work to further their objectives.[244]

This is how a predator attempted to bag one of my friend's twelve-year-old daughters before I half-asleep figured out what was going on and took action. It was at US Nationals for a game I play called Magic. I had been a bit disconnected that year from the Magic scene locally, only playing online so when she and I were watching another player in the group competing, this blonde young man comes over, leans in very close and says something to her I can't hear. I briefly look over towards the two just as he approached and abruptly left. Her shoulders had raised a little and she appeared tense.

Weird, so I asked her what he said. As a teacher I do that pretty much automatically when something seems off as perhaps I need to explain expectations or re-teach something.

He said, *"Does everyone know you are only twelve years old?"*

I hadn't slept in almost forty hours at this point. I had never seen this guy before so didn't think of asking a follow-up question to something so out of place as that one-liner. I got some floor space to sleep for a couple hours and came down the next morning and was in a circle standing next to her father when the same dude wanders by and again leans towards her and says much more audibly, *"Twelve years old!"* My head whipped in his direction as he shot off and I connected what just happened and the previous odd statement. I reacted pointing at the kid leaving saying something likely a little incoherent, if any of the group sees that kid to keep an eye on him. I asked anyone if they knew him in the circle, none did save the only child in the group whom he made the comment to. My reaction was laughed at (I was VERY dizzy and sleep deprived, making my own Autism traits more apparent), but fortunately recognized by my friend's daughter. This guy was "friends" with another twelve-year-old girl also on site playing that weekend.

Later, my friend's daughter sought me out with this other girl. Short backstory—I knew of her too since she was ten, but do not interact with children who are neither related to me or I have limited responsibility for unless there is a need. She and my friend's daughter met and played Magic together two years previous. My friend's daughter didn't go the next year. Her friend did.

---

[244] Mehta, Seema. "Donald Trump Once Told 14-Year-Old Girls, 'In a Couple of Years, I'll Be Dating You.'" Los Angeles Times, Los Angeles Times, 13 Oct. 2016, www.latimes.com/nation/politics/trailguide/la-na-trailguide-updates-trump-spoke-of-dating-underage-girls-1476377294-htmlstory.html.

When she sat down across from me this was our first introduction, so I wasn't expecting her to open up to me as she did.

This adorable little blonde girl explained that he was her "stalker." With that one word my vacation changed, as I had "teacher" work to do instead. I asked questions and listened. I asked a few more. I pulled in my friend then had him pull in the other girl's parents (whom I also didn't know) after the "bomb" of his pitch was dropped from this innocent twelve-year-old girl's mouth:

"You can come up to my room if you want, as there are two of you and since you are together you will be safe."

I was sure he had interest in her from the year previous, made a plan then had a change of plans when he found there were two targets to choose from. The year she was eleven and alone, I wasn't even sure if it was the same girl due to her make-up and dress made her look around like a trendy fourteen. While he was still interested in this other girl, my friend's daughter was physically more mature and he mostly targeted getting her attention. I thought he was fifteen, so took appropriate actions considering his age.

The stalker was banned from the tournament floor. I was right behind him the next morning, fully rested for once, when he was being explained to by the tournament official of where he could and could not go in the building. I then mentioned "JSS stalker" to the official, and he asked me how I knew about all that. I told him that I was the one who informed their parents and gave him the details verbally then written (there was more than what I have mentioned here). That was when I found out he was eighteen. Dang! It was just a little too late to file police charges as my friend "sugar-coated" what was said.

He didn't leave the hotel, just the convention floor. While getting ready to play a team event, my friend's daughter came in visibly shaken. She had encountered him briefly at the door. Conversations were had with him, his two friends, me and my friend. With what I said about thanking the two boys with him for understanding the seriousness of what he had done without specifying it directly, and bringing him to the head tournament official so he could explain himself, showed they were true friends. Their expressions indicated a bigger discussion would take place shortly after my friend and I left.

While the JSS stalker didn't get either of his targets up to the "safety" of his room, his actions had caused short-term damage. My friend's daughter's childhood was shattered as she put the pieces together that weekend of what he might have done to her had he gotten her alone. She seemed sad and scared the rest of the weekend and after we got back to Utah she stopped coming to events with her dad. I wouldn't see her next till she was fifteen.

This world is full of sexually exploitive perverts like the JSS stalker. He wasn't rich or knowledgeable of how to do what he wanted more effectively. That isn't the case for the likes of Trump, Epstein and Harvey Weinstein, another of Trump's buddies who operated freely and openly for decades using mostly aspiring actresses as his pool of targets instead of models. Each of these rich and powerful men set themselves in positions where they would have access to young attractive girls and women that they could exploit a networked system of grooming, influence and power over. All they needed was silence as they worked a system to recruit and exploit girls and women in succession, occasionally shunting used girls to others in the network with promises of industry contracts and potential work. The system worked well until the powerful *Me Too* movement started rolling finally exposing all this stuff. Get the girl to consent using offers of connections, or using drugs and alcohol to lower their resistance to sexual advancement then *"grab them by the pussy,"* as Trump said to Billy Bush.

When they are rich and powerful like Epstein, Weinstein or Trump they can groom girls openly and the general public will generally ignore it. That is why a grooming statement like *"In a couple years I'll be dating you"* could be so easily dismissed as a joke, allowing Trump to move freely to gauge a different girl's susceptibility instead. Just call it what it is—sexual networking and grooming. While no one has so far credibly accused Trump of sexually assaulting them as children his reported behavior of attending and hosting sex parties where drugs and alcohol is used to increase older men's likeliness to score with the women and girls did have all the pining's of a sex-ring, procuring the girls and women he doesn't want potentially for others who do. The parties were MOSTLY a few older men and a lot of young women, with many underaged girls. Even if Trump didn't get with any of the children invited or snorted a line of drugs at his or Epstein's sex parties, serving alcohol to minors and possession and distribution of cocaine alone was and still would be breaking several laws.

Trump Models, opened in 1999 while Trump was dating then model Melania Knauss, and like many of Trump's ventures has been accused of violating US laws, specifically in undermining US immigration statutes employing undocumented labor. Several models have come forward saying that they were instructed to lie to immigration officials when arriving saying they were officially visiting a friend and give an address of a Trump model booker. They were also told by Trump Models to not take "evidence" they performed work while stateside such as carrying their portfolios when they left the country. One of the models third gig left her in debt to the company due to "industry practices of exploitation" of paying less than what they charge for flights and housing expenses.

Former Trump Model Rachel Blais called the sham company this in a Mother Jones article dated August 2016:

> *"Honestly, they are the most crooked agency I've ever worked for, and I've worked for quite a few."*

She described the Trump accommodations in stark terms. Girls packed like sardines on bunks with two basement rooms shared by eleven or more, a bathroom smelling of burnt hair and charges of up to $1600 per month back to the agency. Nearby accommodations could be had in the surrounding area without roommates for less than that. As she had a tourist VISA, which allowed entry but not the ability to work legally, she didn't want to risk getting in trouble if she spoke up. Most of the girls are foreign and cannot work legally, so Trump Models, which Donald made roughly two-million off from his 85% stake according to financial disclosures exploited them. Blais eventually got an H-1B VISA through the company allowing her to legally work and not fear deportation. At the end of her Trump Models work, Blais received a check for $8,427.35, after all the fees had been extracted for the rent, VISA and other expenses. Not bad for three years of work! The system Trump employed to get these young foreign beauties indebted to him is similar to the Indentured Servant programs of the early United States before the first ship of Africans arrived on our shores. Blais at least wasn't "owned" by debt to the company at the end of her "employment" as many other girls were.

Model Maggie Rizer stated this on Instagram quitting the agency election eve:

> *"As a woman, a mother, an American and a human being, I cannot wake up Wednesday morning being the least bit related to the*

*Trump brand; win or lose. I owe it to myself and to my children to
proudly stand up for what I believe in and that is a world where
Donald Trump has no voice for the future of our country."*

For these alleged and clearly easily proven crimes looking at the timing of photoshoots and immigration records, Trump as the employer of each foreign national working illegally in the country in this particular scheme could face $16000 fines per employee and up to six months in prison. [245] [246]

The Trump Organization, which is under investigation for criminal activity including the allegations involving Trump Models, announced the closure of the company April 10, 2017.[247]

Trump also acquired other noteworthy sexually oriented "assets" from his ownership of the Miss Universe Organization as part of his overall portfolio in 1996. This included Miss Universe, Miss USA and Miss Teen USA.

It was in 1997 where Trump surveyed the contestants of the Teen pageant backstage in the dressing rooms, according to six contestants. While Trump didn't mention that he walked in on the teens to Howard Stern, he did admit to doing it on the adult contestants.

*"I remember putting on my dress really quick because I was like,
'Oh my god, there's a man in here.'"*
-Miss Vermont Teen USA, 1997, Mariah Billado[248]

*"The time that he walked through the dressing rooms was really
shocking. We were all naked."*
-Miss New Hampshire, 2000, Bridget Sullivan[249]

---

[245] Jacobs, Sarah. "2 Models Who Worked for Trump's Controversial Agency Tell What It Was like for Them." Business Insider, Business Insider, 14 Feb. 2017, www.businessinsider.com/former-trump-models-tell-their-story-2017-2.

[246] West, James, and Max J. Rosenthal. "Former Models for Donald Trump's Agency Say They Violated Immigration Rules and Worked Illegally." Mother Jones, 23 June 2017, www.motherjones.com/politics/2016/08/donald-trump-model-management-illegal-immigration/.

[247] Jacobs, Sarah. "Trump's Controversial Modeling Agency Is Shutting Down." Business Insider, Business Insider, 10 Apr. 2017, www.businessinsider.com/trump-models-is-closing-2017-4.

[248] Taggart, Kendall. "Teen Beauty Queens Say Trump Walked In On Them Changing." BuzzFeed News, BuzzFeed News, 13 Oct. 2016, www.buzzfeednews.com/article/kendalltaggart/teen-beauty-queens-say-trump-walked-in-on-them-changing#.gs4JxObZm.

[249] "'We Were All Naked' When Donald Trump Walked Through Beauty Queen Dressing Room." BuzzFeed News, www.buzzfeednews.com/article/jessicagarrison/we-were-all-naked-when-donald-

His behavior wasn't limited to just gawking at the contestants naked in the dressing rooms. "Miss Housekeeping" and "Miss Piggy" Miss Venezuela and 1996 Miss Universe winner Alicia Machado was showcased exercising in front of Trump and reporters. He kissed Miss Utah Temple Taggart on the lips without consent in 1997, then again at Trump Tower when suggesting Taggart lie about her age to be younger to succeed in the entertainment industry.

2009 Miss California, Carrie Prejean Boller, wrote a memoir, *Still Standing*, which shared another view of the owner of the pageants:

> *"Donald Trump walked out with his entourage and inspected us closer than any general ever inspected a platoon. He would stop in front of a girl, look her up and down, and say, 'Hmmm.' Then he would go on and do the same thing to the next girl. He took notes on a little pad as he went along. After he did this, Trump said: 'O.K. I want all the girls to come forward.'...*

> *"Donald Trump looked at Miss Alabama. 'Come here,' he said. She took one more step forward. 'Tell me, who's the most beautiful woman here?' Miss Alabama's eyes swam around.*

> *"'Besides me?' she said. 'Uh, I like Arkansas. She's sweet.'*

> *"'I don't care if she's sweet,' Donald Trump said. 'Is she hot?' ...*

> *"It became clear that the point of the whole exercise was for him to divide the room between girls he personally found attractive and those he did not. Many of the girls found the exercise humiliating. Some of the girls were sobbing backstage after he left, devastated to have failed even before the competition really began to impress "The Donald."[250]*

---

trump-walked-in#.alvYNNpJ8.

[250] Stuart, Tessa. "A Timeline of Donald Trump's Creepiness While He Owned Miss Universe." Rolling Stone, 25 June 2018, www.rollingstone.com/politics/politics-features/a-timeline-of-donald-trumps-creepiness-while-he-owned-miss-universe-191860/.

She recanted a bit on Fox News with Sean Hannity on May 17, 2016, saying that her comments in her book were twisted by the *New York Times* as Trump helped her tremendously, as well as thousands of women. So did Harvey Weinstein. Let's be clear, the comments she made and intentionally were included in her book were either factual or not. She did NOT dispute those comments only downplayed them as inconsequential, a behavior that "justifies" and "normalizes" what she witnessed Trump doing. Was she one who was sobbing? Was she one who found the exercise humiliating? Which group did she wind up on? With her comments to Hannity and the likelihood she received high marks on her "hotness" I believe people will come to their own conclusions on all three questions. What I don't understand is why she, Melania and other women loyal to Trump keep on doing it, allowing the predatory behavior to increase and continue.[251]

TMZ had audio of Trump posted on November 12, 2009, 12:50 P.M. PST, that backed up Carrie's remarks. Like a great deal of Trump-related material once on the internet, *"Deep State"* operatives have managed to remove or corrupt the file. The article still remains, and describes "The Trump Rule" separating the girls into two groups based on who the ladies felt were the most beautiful. The whole demeaning separation exercise reminds me of the Dr. Seuss classic *The Sneetches*. Those that had their stars upon thars, looked down upon those without. From a psychological standpoint, Trump strengthened his connection to one group at the expense of the other; similar to how that guy Adolf did in his power building network stage. Here is what was said on the now deleted audio:

> *"We get to choose a certain number. You know why we do that? Because years ago when I first bought it, we chose ten people, I chose none and I get here and the most beautiful people were not chosen. And I went nuts. So we call it the Trump Rule."[252]*

2013 Miss Washington Cassandra Searles recalled women who did not look Trump in the eye had to redo introductions posted this on Facebook on June 17, 2016:

---

[251] "Carrie Prejean Says NY Times Twisted Her Story: 'I Have Nothing Bad to Say About Trump.'" Fox News, FOX News Network, 18 May 2016, insider.foxnews.com/2016/05/17/carrie-prejean-says-ny-times-twisted-her-story-i-have-nothing-admiration-and-respect.

[252] Staff, TMZ. "Trump Rule — Hot Chicks Required in Miss USA." TMZ, TMZ.com, 9 Apr. 2010, www.tmz.com/2009/11/12/trump-rule-hot-chicks-required-in-miss-usa/.

> *"Miss USA Class of 2013: Do ya'll remember that one time we had to do our on stage introductions, but this one guy treated us like cattle and made us do it again because we didn't look him in the eyes? Do you also remember he proceeded to have us lined up so he could get a closer look at his property? Oh I forgot to mention that guy will be in the running to become the next President of the United States. I love the idea of having a misogynist as the President…#HeWillProbablySueMe #iHaveWorseStoriesSoComeAt-MeBro #Drumpf"*

And in the comments Searle wrote:

> *"He probably doesn't want me telling the story about that time he continually grabbed my ass and invited me to his hotel room."*[253][254]

Trump after his 2016 campaign rhetoric against Mexicans went full-tilt Nazi, caused most sponsors for his pageants to flee harming his bottom line. The pageant was off-loaded in 2015, and that is a great thing. My wife and I LOVE the Miss Universe pageant as it showcases mostly positive examples of intelligent, usually kind (looking at you, 2018 Miss USA, to change) and talented women. We always cheer for the most intelligent English-speaking woman in the pageant, and have been pleased that twice, Miss Philippines was crowned since watching together in 2015. My favorite parts are the Q&A and the native dress portions, my wife evening gowns. Neither of us really cares for the swimsuit portion, perhaps because we both come from conservative upbringings. Swap that out for the talent portion and it smartens up instead of focuses on the attributes of womanhood that matter the least—her appearance.

With some of Trump's predatory behavior, sexual assaults and voyeurism associated with walking in on naked girls during his ownership of the pageant, it is only he who seems to be above the Me Too movement that caught up most of his friends. These were crimes, serious ones too, that can't easily be

---

[253] Tuck, Lauren. "Donald Trump Reportedly Treated Miss USA Contestants Like 'Property.'" Yahoo!, Yahoo!, 17 June 2016, www.yahoo.com/lifestyle/donald-trump-reportedly-treated-miss-000000927.html.

[254] Stuart, Tessa. "A Timeline of Donald Trump's Creepiness While He Owned Miss Universe." Rolling Stone, 25 June 2018, www.rollingstone.com/politics/politics-features/a-timeline-of-donald-trumps-creepiness-while-he-owned-miss-universe-191860/.

dismissed by compliant or complicit women and men invested in Trump's position who continues to block or provide cover for his behavior.

What I find remarkable in all this is the concept of "sex as currency" the use of criminal organizations like the Russian mob, MS-13, the Zetas and others appears to be consistent within how the Trump realm also operates. Get the girls young, often holding power over them through "contracts," drugs, VISAs or threats in order to build more wealth using them. Trump signed many of the models personally, some directly from his pageant portfolio of assets, others from overseas that would be easier to exploit as he could hold more power over those. He used some models personally to promote other schemes like Trump Vodka which he pitched to "sucker investors" with essentially an indentured and ogle-worthy slave on each arm.

Trump Vodka was launched October 2006 with the likes of porn stars Stormy Daniels, Tera Patrick and Kim Kardashian in attendance at several cities according to Max Abelson's April 20, 2016, article on Bloomberg. The advertising on this thing was solid, especially Overit Studio's Russian commercial for Drinks America, the company partnered with Trump on the Vodka. Is it strange mentioning BOTH Stormy Daniels and Russia connected to one of Trump's enterprises way back in 2016? At a 2008 Super Bowl party a topless seventeen-year-old with the Vodka logo on her billboard chest, serving the liquor, was also part of the marketing—though Trump wasn't present. He instead appeared via pre-recorded message. When TMZ ID'd the girl a Trump rep said this:

> *"We are appalled. Given the circumstances, we can only guess that she crashed the event to seek publicity."*

Generally when someone is in the act of an alcohol =-serving hostess for a company, they generally know the age of that person, and are legally required to do so. Both Trump Vodka and the modeling company contracted for the op (not Trump Models) denied they "knew" Chanell Elaine Hallett was a child. Even I who doesn't drink know the law with alcohol and minors, and that Vodka is a type of alcohol. She was seventeen and half-naked serving alcohol—hence sex as currency, just another discard-able girl in how Trump seeks building his fortunes. [255]

---

[255] Staff, TMZ. "Trump Flaunts Teen for Vodka Party?" TMZ, TMZ.com, 7 Apr. 2016, www.tmz.com/

A series of other failures followed after the financing dried up near the end of 2008. With most upfront debt ventures, businesses burn through cash to advertise and build distribution or recognition. Without the cash the liquor dried up as Drinks America owed many people and companies on the manufacturing side. While the company Drinks America crawled around till 2012, it was dead as a business back in the first quarter of 2009. [256]

No chapter on Trump subtitled "Sex as Currency" could be complete without Stormy Daniels, one of Trump's trysts about four months after Melania's birthing son Barron in 2006, who wrote *Full Disclosure*. Trump banged Stormy the first "meet" after showing pictures of the baby before showing his other "baby" and getting in on. The next day Trump, Big Ben Roethlisberger and Stormy were together in a VIP section at Lake Tahoe, and instead of Trump being a gentleman and escorting his new lover back to her room, he enlisted Big Ben. Ben walks her back and asked for a kiss. Nope. He didn't get in her room either, despite waiting at the door after it had closed for several minutes. While Stormy never got paid for sex with Trump (they hooked up occasionally the next few months), his sending a friend to potentially score with her has that sex as currency vibe to it that was suggested by his association with Epstein. [257]

2008/03/18/trump-flaunts-teen-for-vodka-party/.

[256] Bloomberg.com, Bloomberg, www.bloomberg.com/features/2016-trump-vodka/.

[257] Sidner, Sara. "Stormy Daniels Shares XXX-Rated Details of Her Alleged Affair with Trump in New Book." CNN, Cable News Network, 19 Sept. 2018, www.cnn.com/2018/09/18/politics/stormy-daniels-book/index.html.

Chapter Nineteen

Don the Two-Bit Con

In the Michael Cohen testimony before Congress on February 27, 2019, his former lawyer presented evidence supporting why Trump's Foundation was nothing more than a "piggy bank" for Trump, raking charitable contributions and buying personal stuff, like a painting of himself up for auction, then putting it in his country club.

> *"Mr. Trump directed me to find a straw bidder to purchase a portrait of him that was being auctioned at an Art Hamptons Event. The objective was to ensure that his portrait, which was going to be auctioned last, would go for the highest price of any portrait that afternoon. The portrait was purchased by the fake bidder for $60,000. Mr. Trump directed the Trump Foundation, which is supposed to be a charitable organization, to repay the fake bidder, despite keeping the art for himself."[258]*

The Trump Foundation was dissolved December 19, 2018, for "shocking pattern of illegality," which this illegal painting purchase from charitable funds confirms. These were State crimes, something a President cannot pardon for

---

[258] "Testimony of Michael D. Cohen." Scribd, Scribd, www.scribd.com/document/400649065/Testimony-of-Michael-D-Cohen#from_embed.

making those crimes very perilous to those running the Foundation scheme, his children, should New York continue to pursue.[259]

Cohen also confirmed the known payments to the *National Enquirer* as hush money in-kind campaign donations, and described the process of reimbursement over twelve months with signed checks and total making such a payment look "good" on the books. At least when Trump turned on Fox and Friends and live-tweeted their coverage of the story, he was no longer lying about the payment happening, only lying about what it was.

> *"It was not a campaign contribution, and there were no violations of the campaign finance laws by me. Fake News!"*
> *6:24 A.M., March 7, 2019[260]*

Cohen also made this statement, about his false testimony to Congress after stating, Trump did NOT direct him to lie to Congress, as that isn't how he operates.

> *"You need to know that Mr. Trump's personal lawyers reviewed and edited my statement to Congress about the timing of the Moscow Tower negotiations before I gave it."*

That is how Individual 1, also confirmed by Cohen as Mr. Trump, operates. Causing someone to knowingly lie before Congress is a big deal, as is threatening them the day before they testify (witness tampering) through thugs like Republican Representative Matt Gaetz's now deleted Tweet:

> *"Hey @MichaelCohen212, Do your wife & father-in-law know about your girlfriends? Maybe tonight would be a good time for that chat. I wonder if she'll remain faithful when you're in prison. She's about to learn a lot..."[261]*

---

[259] Underwood, Barbara D. "So-Ordered Stipulation Concerning the Dissolution of the Donald J. Trump Foundation." Ag,Ny.gov, Attorney General of the State of New York, Barbara D. Underwood, 19 Dec. 2018, ag.ny.gov/sites/default/files/stipulation_re_dissolution_execution_version.pdf.

[260] Trump, Donald J. "It Was Not a Campaign Contribution, and There Were No Violations of the Campaign Finance Laws by Me. Fake News!" Twitter, Twitter, 7 Mar. 2019, twitter.com/realDonaldTrump /status/1103662776424132608.

[261] Cillizza, Chris. "Florida Rep. Matt Gaetz Just Straight-up Threatened Michael Cohen." CNN, Cable

Cohen who stated he had gone with directed threats and intimidation on behalf of Individual 1 that numbered more than five-hundred such instances, shrugged off the obvious mob-like tactics he once employed. The biggest reveal was that Cohen was in the room when Stone called.

> *"As I earlier stated, Mr. Trump knew from Roger Stone in advance about the WikiLeaks drop of emails.*
>
> *"In July 2016, days before the Democratic convention, I was in Mr. Trump's office when his secretary announced Roger Stone was on the phone. Mr. Trump put Mr. Stone on the speakerphone. Mr. Stone told Mr. Trump that he had just gotten off the phone with Julian Assange and that Mr. Assange told Mr. Stone, that within a couple of days, there would be a massive dump of emails that would damage Hillary Clinton's campaign.*
>
> *"Mr. Trump responded to the effect of 'wouldn't that be great.'"*[262]

This admission Trump had worked through Stone to time the release of stolen government documents procured through Russian espionage at his request is probably not a surprise to anyone reading this book. Trump can't leave things alone. It isn't his nature. Trump had been fixated on Hillary's emails well before he knew Russia was working to support him using hacks and influence campaigns. Trump had sent messengers to get those documents. Donald had approved the Trump Tower meeting to get those documents, and when he found that the Russians didn't have them decided to ask directly for their assistance in his campaign he was currently losing, *"Russia, if you are listening..."*

Trump has a compulsion to control, without the ability to predict possible outcomes of his actions, lacking any inhibition that would normally prevent most people from setting on such a dangerous course. He is all about the "deals" and the putting on the "show" that gets him the deals, much less so the "details" of how he is going to accomplish what he sets out to do. And people keep falling for it.

News Network, 27 Feb. 2019, www.cnn.com/2019/02/26/politics/matt-gaetz-tweet-michael-cohen/index.html.

[262] "Testimony of Michael D. Cohen." Scribd, Scribd, www.scribd.com/document/400649065/Testimony-of-Michael-D-Cohen#from_embed.

One of Trump's worse scams was getting into "education" offering up Trump University in 2005. Trump U bilked around 6,000 "students" looking for an education in real estate investment. It wasn't even a University, only a highly controlled "sales" environment where there was no actual product.

"In just 90 minutes, my hand-picked instructors will share my techniques, which took my entire career to develop. Then, just copy exactly what I've done and get rich."

The above was the free pitch to lure in the suckers to spend on seminars and coaching if they bit. A three-day seminar cost $1495 with prices for the courses climbing up to $34,995. The lure of riches and meeting the celebrity Mr. Trump were quite a bit for many of those in attendance that they signed up for the paid pitches. These events were all behavior driven; looking for body language cues to scan the field for potential marks ready to empty out their wallets, setting the temperature, music and room arrangements to maximize the illusion. They even had fake diplomas, and a name change to The Trump Entrepreneur Initiative.

Trump University was never accredited nor had a charter. Trump never showed up, nor the promised real estate experts that worked with him. What did were the credit card bills from those his fraud suckered. Trump in a rare move settled, giving back $25 million of his pilfered "earnings" just before being sworn in on January 18, 2017.[263] [264]

Trump had a number of other defunct businesses, a lot of them started in 2006-2007 with his name on it. Trump Steaks, Trump Ice, Trump Magazine, GoTrump.com, Trump Mortgage were all destined for failure along with Trump Vodka previously discussed due to bad timing with the economy as well as Trump having zero business sense.[265]

From the archived Trump Mortgage website comes this:

"At Trump Mortgage, we have passion for what we do—helping other people's dreams come true. As the strongest and safest resi-

---

[263] McNichol, Tom. "The Art of the Upsell: How Donald Trump Profits From 'Free' Seminars." The Atlantic, Atlantic Media Company, 17 Mar. 2014, www.theatlantic.com/business/archive/2014/03/the-art-of-the-upsell-how-donald-trump-profits-from-free-seminars/284450/.

[264] Gerstein, Josh, et al. "Trump Pays out $25 Million to Settle Trump University Litigation." POLITICO, 18 Jan. 2017, www.politico.com/story/2017/01/trump-university-lawsuit-settlement-233772.

[265] "12 Donald Trump Businesses That No Longer Exist." Yahoo! Finance, Yahoo!, 10 Oct. 2014, finance.yahoo.com/news/12-donald-trump-businesses-that-no-longer-exist-204923129.html.

> *dential and commercial mortgage company in the industry, we know that trust is the most important element in the process. Our business is about developing and securing relationships, not just loans. Trusted relationships—forged by a unique consultative, educational approach that enables our clients to make confident, truly informed decisions."*

I am not sure how anyone would think that a brand-new company claiming itself as *"strongest"* and *"safest"* in the industry would "trust" that company for something as big as making a home purchase. The whole *"educational approach"* isn't how I see myself spending time when I just want to know the cost of origination and the timing of the loan either. Just his starting up such a company at the end of the housing bubble, with that bubble cresting and showing weakness ready to pop, shows how little Trump understood the basics of the economy. In an April 2006 CNBC interview Trump spoke to his "power" of seeing a bubble before others.

"I've been hearing about this bubble for so many years from you and everybody else in your world, but I haven't seen it. I will let you know when I see it."[266]

None of his business failures can compare to Trump Entertainment Resorts, with Trump Taj Mahal at the center of the portfolio. The Taj connects Trump to Russia and likely explains one of the avenues Trump got filthy rich taking in Russian mob money, along with his real estate gobbled up by Russian "investors." The casino opened April 1990. In the first year and a half, the Taj racked up one hundred six anti-money-laundering rule violations according to a 1998 IRS settlement where Individual 1's company "gave back" the government $477,000 without admitting liability. That fine at the time was a record under the Bank Secrecy Act. Compared to the filthy lucre that likely lined Trump's pocket, that almost half-million was peanuts. Trump bankrupted it, sold a 50% stake to sucker bank bondholders in late 1991 and kept on going. The Russian mob money was still flowing in using better "accounting" methods I'd assume.

At a second of Trump's casinos Don's father Fred sent a loan via a certified check deposited by Howard Snyder for 3.35 million on December 18, 1990,

---

[266] But that didn't deter Donald Trump from getting into the mortgage business. "Trump Mortgage...in 2 Minutes." CNNMoney, Cable News Network, money.cnn.com/2016/03/14/pf/trump-mortgage/ index.html.

walking out with 670 casino chips shortly before an interest payment was due. This broke the state's Casino Control Act, and that amounted only to a $30,000 fine. Keep in mind that Trump was already looking to transfer his father's assets to his in a manner to avoid estate taxes, and this scheme in that light makes more sense as a test run of one avenue to steal taxes from Uncle Sam. Getting away with these financial crimes only emboldened Trump for his run at the US Presidency where he could tap campaign funds as a new piggy bank and claim others were doing it too and only got fined.

The next fine for the Taj was settled for ten million in 2015 for the period of 2010-2012. The money was instead laundered through smaller transactions from slot machine tickets, essentially putting the mob money on a plastic card at the window and cashing out at the next. Trump only held a stake in the parent company at that time having cashed out in 2009 of the casino that bore his name and Russian mob connections.

The casino went bankrupted in 1991, 2004 (1.8 billion in debt) and 2008-2009 when Trump cashed out, and finally September 2014. That first bankruptcy should have been the end of Trump's empire, as he was in debt about 3.4 billion (1 billion on the Taj) and the banks that had been suckered into giving him the financing based on his fraud getting on the early Forbes list were also in big trouble. Deals were made. Trump survived losing half ownership to the banks and kept going. The King of Debt the next year hit a $550 million snag with his Trump Plaza Hotel and Casino. The banks took forty-nine-percent stake in that failed Trump purchase. Then in 2004 the 1.8 billion failures knocked down the Don's ownership level to 25%. That deal gave Trump an additional $500 million loan and was the same year the Trump brand was revived on TV through the staged *The Apprentice*. 2008 hit, and again failure, with Trump reduced to 10% ownership. [267] [268]

So who lost the most on Donald's Trump Entertainment brand scheme? Banks and bond holders who trusted in the name Donald Trump who financed then lost most if not all of their investment in a series of poorly managed, often

---

[267] Pagliery, Jose. "Trump's Casino Was a Money Laundering Concern Shortly after It Opened." CNN, Cable News Network, 22 May 2017, www.cnn.com/2017/05/22/politics/trump-taj-mahal/index.html.

[268] Bingham, Amy. "Donald Trump's Companies Filed for Bankruptcy 4 Times." ABC News, ABC News Network, 21 Apr. 2011, abcnews.go.com/Politics/donald-trump-filed-bankruptcy-times/story?id=13419250.

criminally invested Trump enterprises, made possible by Trump's name and false reputation.

The Don was conning other investors as well as being so smart he wasn't paying Federal taxes (considering the staggering financial loses, he could do so legally). Three Trump Tower properties, in Baja, Tampa and Philadelphia, had investors depositing money on the Trump brand, getting them wiped out in the process, as the banks that trusted the Don also were. Trump marketed and personally showed up, which added cred to the grift. Trump made off well on that scheme, to the likely tune of $4 million and wished those the best who lost life-savings with this quote:

"They were better off losing their deposit."[269]

Trump's other con Michael Cohen described on Capitol Hill was supported with detailed bank disclosures over several years that Trump used to attempt to take out loans to keep his pyramid scheme rolling longer. These disclosures as Cohen stated, inflate Trump's net worth compared to how Trump would file for tax purposes where he would deflate values. In 2013, the name Trump was affixed with a four-billion value.[270] [271]

Sure, let him HAVE that one. Trump needs to pay taxes on that 2013 gain of four billion.

Making false reports to a bank is a felony as is failure to report a four-billion gain on his taxes. Take your pick. The disclosures were sent to Deutsche Bank, the German bank that according to *"Low IQ"* Rep. Maxine Waters as the only bank willing to still loan to Trump:

> *"We know that Deutsche Bank is one of the biggest money laundering banks in the country, or in the world perhaps. And we know that this is the only bank that will lend money to the president of the United States because of his past practices. He won't show his tax returns and we have a certain information that leads*

[269] Barbaro, Michael. "Buying a Trump Property, or So They Thought." The New York Times, The New York Times, 13 May 2011, www.nytimes.com/2011/05/13/nyregion/feeling-deceived-over-homes-that-were-trump-in-name-only.html.

[270] Bush, Daniel. "Cohen Releases Trump Financial Documents, Claims President Inflated Net Worth." PBS, Public Broadcasting Service, 27 Feb. 2019, www.pbs.org/newshour/politics/cohen-releases-trump-financial-documents-claims-president-inflated-net-worth.

[271] Bush, Daniel. "Cohen Releases Trump Financial Documents, Claims President Inflated Net Worth." PBS, Public Broadcasting Service, 27 Feb. 2019, www.pbs.org/newshour/politics/cohen-releases-trump-financial-documents-claims-president-inflated-net-worth.

*us to believe that there may have been some money laundering ac-
tivity that might have been connected with Mr. Manafort, with
some people in his family."*

Maxine is obviously smart, at least two, if not three standard deviations on a bell curve smarter than Trump is. Trump usually associates dark skin with low intelligence, just another of his obvious racist beliefs. Further along in the CNBC interview given on January 31, 2019, Waters is asked if Trump is corrupt:

"I believe that this is a problematic president who has proven that he has taken advantage of others in the past. I know that he was fined and I do know that the attorney general of New York made him reimburse at least $25 million. We know that he has had bankruptcies. We know that there are a lot of stories he hasn't paid contractors, he hasn't paid subcontractors. We know a lot about the history of this president and it doesn't look good.... So, we think that in addition to what Mr. Mueller is doing and now what we are able to do with our subpoena power, we'll find out more and we'll be able to answer that question directly."[272]

---

[272] Harwood, John. "Maxine Waters Talks about the Potential for Trump's Impeachment." CNBC, CNBC, 1 Feb. 2019, www.cnbc.com/2019/01/31/maxinwhat-maxine-waters-hopes-to-uncover-about-deutsche-bank-money-laundering-and-trump.html.

Chapter Twenty

"What a lousy deal; that's a terrible deal."

The only thing that changed in regards to Don the Con once he assumed control of first the GOP, next the right-wing media and last the country, is that his cons changed his address. Trump touted himself as deal-maker, trashing and destroying America's many critical trade and security deals prior US Presidents had secured over the years, with the claim that only he could fix everything broken that he had inherited. Trump is a two-bit con. It is part of his nature, and not his Autism disability that has made him such. While he has no ability to plan or work within the confining system of laws and regulations he has shown some ability to organize long term schemes by convincing others to go out and connect with Putin to secure Hillary's emails. Most of that conspiracy wasn't well organized and seems to be built in stages with coordinated help and support from others. But surely Trump's acumen as a successful businessman would result in a plethora of deals favoring the US on trade.

> *"When a country (USA) is losing many billions of dollars on trade with virtually every country it does business with, trade wars are good, and easy to win. Example, when we are down $100 billion with a certain country and they get cute, don't trade anymore— we win big. It's easy!"*
>
> *-Donald J. Trump*
> *5:50 A.M., March 2, 2018[273]*

---

[273] Trump, Donald J. "When a Country (USA) Is Losing Many Billions of Dollars on Trade with Virtu-

I really feel that the Warburton School of Finance SHOULD be asking Donald to turn back in his diploma each time Trump explains his understanding of economics. Trade wars from a historical perspective have never been good for the United States. The Great Depression saw some short term gains from the Hawley-Smoot act followed by economic collapse as trade works both ways. But to Don the con, he could win a trade war with just about every country the US currently traded with including allies such as Canada and foes like China.

The administration would set off a series of trade actions over the course of his first two years, withdrawing from the TPP (Congress had yet to approve) and NAFTA while institutionalizing US Government subsidizing every export on a grand scale under the Tax, Cuts and Jobs Act violating international laws on trade, and eventually instituting large-scale taxes on US consumers and manufacturers in the form of tariffs.

Is the US winning under Trump?

With his authoritarian fixed mindset telling his "gut" he is right over all his economic advisors, the rest of the US would be collateral damage to each and every Trump move. Lawsuits were filed in international courts, and the US should they lose, will see historic financial losses for damages sustained under Trump's trade violations of the law. Growth in Stocks, the hallmark of praise and adoration of Trump during the first year, had a net yearly loss on the Dow Jones Industrial Average for 2018. Companies while showing great bottom lines with a trillion-dollar Trump stimulus paid down debt or bought back stocks, and that still had no positive effect on the economy or really the stock market. Jobs gained in 2017 and 2018 were on par with previous years, meaning the stimulus only added to debt and did in fact not create jobs as it was purported to do from the GOP. Record store closures were topped in 2017[274] and almost again in 2018, hitting the record of square footage of retail space closed instead[275] with 2019 looking to easily

---

ally Every Country It Does Business with, Trade Wars Are Good, and Easy to Win. Example, When We Are down $100 Billion with a Certain Country and They Get Cute, Don't Trade Anymore-We Win Big. It's Easy!" Twitter, Twitter, 2 Mar. 2018, twitter.com/realdonaldtrump/status/969525362580484098? lang=en.

[274] Thomas, Lauren. "Store Closures Rocked Retail in 2017. Now 2018 Is Set to Bring Another Round of Them." CNBC, CNBC, 26 Dec. 2017, www.cnbc.com/2017/12/26/store-closures-rocked-retail-in-2017-and-more-should-come-next-year.html.

[275] George-Parkin, Hilary. "2018 Set a New Record for Retail Closures by Square Footage." Footwear News, Footwear News, 4 Jan. 2019, footwearnews.com/2018/business/retail/retail-store-closures-

top 2017s and 2018s losses. US debt piled on two-trillion-plus in his first two years.[276]

No, the US is not winning on the economy under Trump.

Tariffs came into effect in Trump's second year starting with solar panels and washing machines on January 23, 2018.[277] The second tariff Trump slapped on America's consumers and businesses announced March 1, 2018, focused on steel and aluminum with some initial exceptions that have mostly been phased out.[278] In May 31, Trump removed exemptions to our allies such as Canada. Canada, China and others lawfully retaliated to Trump's likely illegal tariffs citing National Security as the rationale for implementation and that added to the mess Trump has created.[279]

The funny thing about tariffs is how they tend to adversely harm more than the intended industry they are targeting. While Trump aimed at steel and aluminum, manufacturers in the US who were dependent on those imports had to eat the tax or pass the tax onto consumers. This affects US manufacturing disproportionately leading to greater need to outsource production to maintain profit margins. Sure, internal consumption if quality metal products were both available and affordably made stateside in theory would boost economic output, but exports would be better made elsewhere considering the cost.[280]

As companies adjusted, made announcements to their investors, Trump attacked. Harley-Davidson, a motorcycle company whose sales outside the US are greater than within, made the responsible choice incurring Trump's childlike wrath such as his broadsides to Maria Bartiromo, Fox News, on July 1, 2018. Here are a few snippets:

2018-1202725407/.

[276] Watson, Kathryn. "National Debt Tops $22 Trillion for First Time in U.S. History." CBS News, CBS Interactive, 13 Feb. 2019, www.cbsnews.com/news/us-national-debt-tops-22-trillion-for-first-time-in-history/.

[277] Roberts, Ken. "Washing Machine Imports Plummet, Prices Soar With Tariffs." Forbes, Forbes Magazine, 21 Aug. 2018, www.forbes.com/sites/kenroberts/2018/08/20/__trashed/.

[278] Bloomberg.com, Bloomberg, www.bloomberg.com/news/articles/2019-01-30/why-trump-s-tariffs-didn-t-help-create-more-steel-jobs.

[279] Klingel, Leia. "Dow Lower as US Removes Steel, Aluminum Tariff Exemptions on Some Allies." Fox Business, Fox Business, 31 May 2018, www.foxbusiness.com/markets/stock-rebound-may-continue-ahead-of-eu-tariff-decision.

[280] Aeppel, Timothy. "Trump's Steel Tariffs Create Big Profits but Few New Jobs." Reuters, Thomson Reuters, 13 Nov. 2018, www.reuters.com/article/us-usa-trade-nucor-insight/trumps-steel-tariffs-create-big-profits-but-few-new-jobs-idUSKCN1NI1FC.

"And one of the things I'm doing that you have been reporting on—although I'm not sure that you're a believer, but I think you are getting there—look what's happening with the steel companies. They are doing—they are expanding. They are going wild...

"I think they trust me. And the farmers trust me..."

Trump's penchant for over exaggeration and simplistic thinking believes what he says as he is often reinforced by Fox News in his daily cycle. Trump says something. They repeat it, so it must be true. Steel manufacturing did increase roughly 3,400 jobs according to Reuters. That is far less than the jobs likely lost due to the tariffs which are in the hundreds of thousands across multiple Trump tariff additions.

"Well, actually, it's 20 percent. Tell them to get their numbers right. Look, Maria, what's going to really happen is, there's going to be no tax. You know why? They're going to build their cars in America. They're going to make them here."

Manufacturing cars or really any manufacturing industry was not going to be made better increasing the cost of commodities needed. All adding the Trump tariff taxes does is increase costs, which in turn means companies look to offshore production where wages and other factors are more competitive. No manner of taxes Trump could create would bring back large scale manufacturing.

"First of all, I love free trade. Do you know, when I was at the G7, I said, I have an idea, everybody. I'll guarantee you we'll do it immediately. Nobody pay anymore tax, everybody take down your barriers. No barriers, no tax. Everybody, are you all set? No more tax. Canada, you're not going to get 275 percent for your dairy, and you're going to take down all your barriers. We're going to take all our barriers. We're going to down all our taxes, right?

"You know what happened? Everybody said, 'Uh, can we get onto another subject?' Because America, our country, lost last year $817 billion in terms of deficit. We had a trade deficit, Maria, of 817 billion—with a B—dollars last year. Before that, it was $800 billion."

Have I mentioned Trump has severe cognitive and communication deficits connected to his disability? I could only imagine Trump giving this oration to those assembled at the G7, standing up and blurting out those exact words, and their choice to ignore and tune him out. Little of what Trump says here makes sense because of pragmatic errors and language skills similar to that of a young child. Can a twelve-year-old, a low-functioning one at that, represent the United States appropriately in these sorts of affairs? Trump's track record of international embarrassment indicates that answer is no. Incidentally, the TPP removed most of those barriers Trump was decrying, yet he threw out the trade pact for no other reason than because Obama had signed it. Had he kept it instead of ceding trade control to China as he did, those dairy farmers would be in a lot better shape.

"One of the hard things is, our presidents and our business leaders, they were missing in action—not so much the business leaders. You know, some business leaders benefit by allowing this stuff to go on. That's the problem. They benefit. They're more for their business than they are for the United States. I had a great company, the head of a great company come up to me. He's very seriously affected by the tariffs. He said: 'Mr. President, it's not for me right now. Ultimately, it is, but you're doing the right thing on tariffs.'"

A real journalist upon hearing such bull would normally follow-up by asking what the name of the company was. Not Maria Bartiromo. She is a "journalist" missing-in-action playing tee-ball with the President. Just put the question on the stand and hope the President hits it when he swings. All she did was praise: *"Well, you're doing the right thing on pushing back on China as well."* Trump is making this business leader up, like he makes up a lot of conversations that cannot be verified. Maria knows this, but is complicit in the larger scheme with Fox and Trump so isn't going to move outside of her designated mission. Later she asks why tariffs were so broad: *"That's why you had to do it on everybody, even our friends."*

"I want—I want everybody to do it. Same thing with the tariffs on the steel. If we don't have it on everybody, then what happens is, they—you know, they put it through these other countries that don't have it, and you're wasting a lot of time."

Trump DOES have some sense in this regard. He never makes the full association, though, failing to generalize the rule to Chinese export tariffs that he did with steel. China is more expensive for labor than Vietnam, so many clothing and low-end manufacturing has been leaving China to Vietnam and other countries. Trump's China tariffs weren't broad based as the steel ones were allowing ample work around to keep goods flowing, though that would take weeks if not months to get business fronts up in neighboring countries to ship to the US indirectly. This has happened for both imposed sanctions and tariffs making what the administration has done only really hurting America's interests to be harmed in the long term. After a break Maria set the tee-ball back on the stand and dropped the ball as Trump swung before it was set missing her: *"Would it be better to actually have our allies together to go against China instead of…*

"Because—because the allies—excuse me. The European Union is possibly as bad as China, just smaller, OK? It's terrible, what they do to us. European Union, take a look at the car situation. They send a Mercedes in. We can't send our cars in. Look what they do to our farmers. They don't want our farm products. Now, in all fairness, they have their farmers. So, they want to protect their farmers. But we don't protect ours, and they protect theirs.

"The European Union last year made, if you look at a trade surplus, which I think is a very important thing, $151 billion. Now, we all sort of love the European Union. You know, I was there many, many years ago, meaning, my parents were born in the European Union—"

Trump when it comes to trade views everybody in the same bad light. Maria placates Trump with praise saying the EU loves him and reduces his agitation. Trump says he loves those countries, then this:

"Germany, and all of the countries, Scotland—you know, you have Scotland. They're still in there. They're still hanging in there, right? We will see what happens with Brexit."[281]

Is Scotland a country? I asked my five-year-old and she said no. Trump, my kindergartener, knows that Scotland is part of the United Kingdom and is not an independent country. It is no wonder Don threatened all his schools to stay silent on how well of a student he was before the election. Scotland is part of the United Kingdom, and is the region his mother hails from. Trump's parents emigrated from the United Kingdom and Germany which is likely why Trump mentions both, and he somehow learned an incorrect "fact" in his childhood that makes him staunchly believe Scotland is a country. With these incorrect facts and his Autism, Trump will likely always believe this falsehood as true.

Brexit, another Russian, supported political asset alongside Trump in this statement, connects to Scotland and Trump's Turnberry golf course he visited praising the original Brexit vote on June 24, 2016. The Scots for the most part rejected Brexit, and Trump's lack of social connection led to some disastrous

---

[281] Factbase. "Transcript Quote - Interview: Maria Bartiromo Interviews Donald Trump on Fox News - July 1, 2018." Factbase, factba.se/transcript/donald-trump-interview-maria-bartiromo-fox-july-1-2018.

remarks that day praising Brexit in front of a region that was disgusted with it and his being there to "rub salt" in their eyes.

> *"Just arrived in Scotland. Place is going wild over the vote. They took their country back, just like we will take America back. No games!"*
>
> *10:21 A.M., June 24, 2016*[282]

Maria saunters on bringing up Harley-Davidson's decision to increase production overseas. She asks him if he should be calling out specific US companies:

> *"Yes. Yes, I should. Look, I devoted a lot of time to Harley-Davidson. I treated them good. I guarantee you, everybody that ever bought a Harley-Davidson voted for Trump. I don't know if you know that. I would have to—they call them bikers for Trump. There's—there's hundreds.*
>
> *"I think that Harley is an American bike. It's an American motorcycle. And they should build them in this country. They shouldn't play cute. And I had them for lunch six months ago."*

The thing about Trump's behavior in regards to making comments specific to attacking US business is that he crosses ethical boundaries and exposes himself personally to class action lawsuits. If he says something that then causes Apple to lose 10% value in the stock market, the American mom-and-pops who own shares in that company take a hit to their 401(k). Trump might be held liable for causing such losses as the market hits are easily tracked as happening in coordination with his actions. Trump continues:

> *"I think I taught them more about tariffs than I could ever learn. I was saying, let me ask you a question. How much do you pay in India? One hundred percent. Oh, really? Do you do much business? No. Why? Because the tariff's too high. I'm the one telling them. I said, that's a shame. I got them to reduce the tariffs in*

---

[282] "Donald Trump in Scotland: 'Brexit a Great Thing.'" BBC News, BBC, 24 June 2016, www.bbc.com/news/uk-scotland-glasgow-west-36606184.

India, because I used that as an example. All of the sudden, Harley leaves. Everyone else is coming in."

Trump thinks he is smart. He thinks he knows how tariffs work and is too rigid in his thinking that anyone is going to be able to correct him. Harley who sells more product overseas needs to do what is best to reduce harm from Trump's trade actions. In this case it is to produce more American bikes overseas where they will be sold. Trump has no right to complain, as he himself produces most of his own products offshore and has employed low-wage and often illegal workers within the United States such as the case with Trump Models and recent allegations at Mar Largo.

> *"You know, they are one of the few that's—everyone else is coming in. I have feeling that maybe Harley, I think they're going to take a big hit. I just think it's a great American product. And our people have more pride then they used to have. I really believe that Harley's going to take a—the people that are buying Harley-Davidson, you know, they don't want—they don't want it built in another country."[283]*

Harley is going to be fine. It is the stock shareholders who Trump harmed that won't.

Trump's next wave of trade actions were against China, something anticipated as he had heavily decried the trade deficit with the Middle Kingdom for at least a decade. These were announced March 22, 2018, as targeting Chinese theft of intellectual property. Let's be honest, Trump was conflating his own difficulties with Chinese business restrictions over the issues US companies are having with China, and his behavior consistently has shown that. China buttered him up awarding trademarks he had sought for decades beginning with the first batch on June 14, 2017, gave him praise, flattery and distinction with his being invited to the Forbidden Palace, the first US President to do so on November 8, 2017, as more trademarks had been given to his family. Eventually, though, Trump was

---

[283] Factbase. "Transcript Quote - Interview: Maria Bartiromo Interviews Donald Trump on Fox News - July 1, 2018." Factbase, factba.se/transcript/donald-trump-interview-maria-bartiromo-fox-july-1-2018.

going to show just how smart he is on trade besting Xi, no matter the cost. [284] [285]

The tariffs started at fifty billion and were met with tariffs against Trump's base, farmers who as Trump puts it, were willing to sacrifice for America's business sector. There have been escalations, all initiated by Trump, with some 200 billion currently targeted. The Chinese tariffs closed Chinese markets completely from American agricultural products that included soybeans and other cash crops. In a socialist welfare move Trump offered to bailout farmers with a $4.7-billion package, perhaps enough to allow the farms to survive another year. This was coming from the same man who decried the auto bailout under Obama should not have happened. [286]

The trade deficit in goods continued to increase each month, while US farmers and others interest and livelihoods are sacrificed. Meanwhile Trump's administration had slapped sanctions mid-April 2018 on Chinese tech giant, ZTE and inadvertently brought that company grinding to a halt in the first, and short-lived, triumph for American business interests under Trump. The seven-year ban of parts sales to the company, for being a US security threat, working around US sanctions to Iran and North Korea and acquiring US technology should have been the end of it. Trump had other ideas.

Trump decided to save it.

> *President Xi of China, and I, are working together to give massive Chinese phone company, ZTE, a way to get back into business, fast. Too many jobs in China lost. Commerce Department has been instructed to get it done!*
>
> *10:01 A.M., May 13, 2018*[287]

---

[284] Shanghai, Associated Press in. "China Approves Nine Trump Trademarks It Had Previously Rejected." The Guardian, Guardian News and Media, 14 June 2017, www.theguardian.com/world/2017/jun/14/china-trump-trademarks-beijing.

[285] Griffiths, James. "Trump to Become First Foreign Leader to Dine in Forbidden City since Founding of Modern China." CNN, Cable News Network, 9 Nov. 2017, www.cnn.com/2017/11/07/politics/trump-forbidden-city-beijing-china/index.html.

[286] "'Trade, Not Aid:' Farmers Are Pushing Back Against Trump's $4.7 Billion Trade War Bailout." Fortune, fortune.com/2018/08/28/trump-trade-war-farmer-aid/.

[287] Trump, Donald J. "President Xi of China, and I, Are Working Together to Give Massive Chinese Phone Company, ZTE, a Way to Get Back into Business, Fast. Too Many Jobs in China Lost. Commerce Department Has Been Instructed to Get It Done!" Twitter, Twitter, 13 May 2018, twitter.com/realdonaldtrump/status/995680316458262533?lang=en.

Considering the most costly trade grievance with China is forced intellectual property transfer, Trump's cash grab of a $1.2-billion fine probably didn't sit too well with Silicon Valley. For years tech was developed then "copied" in China and sold globally reducing American profits. ZTE and Huawei have been the most accused companies, as they are the largest and direct competitors to some of our biggest tech enterprises. On February 22, 2019, Trump said this:

> *"Well, ZTE paid a big fine of $1.2 billion, which nobody has ever even heard of before. And we want everybody to compete. And I guess it will be somewhat of a subject that we're talking about here, Bob. We'll be talking about it. We may or may not include that in this deal.*
>
> *"Well, I'd like to have all companies be able to compete. I don't want to artificially block people out based on excuses or based on security. I don't want to have a security problem.*
>
> *"Wait. I'm talking about everybody, really—including. But I'm talking about everybody. I don't want to use artificial blocking. We want to have great 5G. Ultimately, that's going to morph into 6G. And probably 6G will be obsolete in about two months, the way it's going—you know, the way that whole world moves.*
>
> *"But 6G, at some point in the future, will be obsolete. But I want to have competition with China. Fair competition. I don't want to block out anybody if we can help it. Now if there's going to be a security reason or something, then we have no choice, but that is one of the things we'll be discussing today. We want to have open competition. We've always done very well in open competition."* [288]

It is one thing to let ZTE off the hook, and another to announce he is willing to allow 6G development here in the US by Chinese companies, as well as 5G, despite security issues. US complaints allege these tech companies allow China the ability to spy on the US, and have even banned sales of their smart phones in some cases. Either Trump doesn't "get" security risks or there isn't a security risk with ZTE and Huawei.

---

[288] Factbase. "Transcript Quote - Remarks: Donald Trump Meets with Liu He (　) of China at The White House - February 22, 2019." Factbase, factba.se/transcript/donald-trump-remarks-bilat-china-liu-he-february-22-2019.

I believe both are true.

Trump after all has poor awareness as part of his ASD disability, such as when he had classified reports in full view of guests at Mar Lago on February 13, 2017, during a North Korean missile launch. He also can't help break habits, using his personal phone that Russia and China are alleged to already have compromised. Trump likely has limited ability to see the credible threat if one exists despite being told by his intelligence advisors. [289] [290]

ZTE and Huawei setting up shop in the US is likely just as much as a security risk as Apple, Sprint, Google or others are because the interconnectivity of the communication system already has vulnerabilities that can and are exploited. Even the encryption on Apple devices have been broken into by the US government to access a phone used by the San Bernardino suspect,[291] and recent problems have surfaced where "accidental" eavesdropping occurred in the Facetime app. [292] If you have smart technology or are connected to the internet, its best to assume you are tracked and listened in to anyhow and behave accordingly. This essentially means that ZTE and Huawei are likely no more a security threat than other tech companies which makes the arrest and detainment of Huawei CFO executive Meng Wanzhou a very poor "bargaining chip" for trade negotiations. Let's call her detainment what it is, a hostage taking.

Many behaviors of Trump as US President parallel the way he acted as mob boss of the Trump Organization, and frankly Wanzhou being held as an economic hostage is simply the most mob-like thing Trump has done since taking office. She was seized December 1, 2018, in Vancouver, Canada, on Trumped-up charges of undermining sanctions on Iran. Last I checked only the US voided their obligations under the treaty when Donald despite evidence contrary to his "determination" had said Iran had violated its part, while

[289] Borger, Julian. "Missile Crisis by Candlelight: Donald Trump's Use of Mar-a-Lago Raises Security Questions." The Guardian, Guardian News and Media, 14 Feb. 2017, www.theguardian.com/us-news/2017/feb/13/mar-a-lago-north-korea-missile-crisis-trump-national-security.

[290] "U.S. Officials Concerned Trump Discussing Sensitive Information on Unsecured Cellphone." NBCNews.com, NBCUniversal News Group, www.nbcnews.com/politics/donald-trump/u-s-officials-concerned-trump-discussing-sensitive-information-unsecured-cellphone-n924376.

[291] Fox-Brewster, Thomas. "The Feds Can Now (Probably) Unlock Every IPhone Model In Existence — UPDATED." *Forbes,* Forbes Magazine, 28 Feb. 2018, www.forbes.com/sites/thomasbrewster/2018/ 02/26/government-can-access-any-apple-iphone-cellebrite/.

[292] Franceschi-Bicchierai, Lorenzo. "Anyone Can Spy on You With FaceTime, Here's How to Turn It Off [Updated]." *Motherboard,* VICE, 29 Jan. 2019, motherboard.vice.com/en_us/article/3kgqvn/facetime-apple-bug-how-to-turn-off.

everyone else has honored their commitments. Trump has bullied and threatened allies over staying in the Iran treaty while slapping the Middle Eastern country with sanctions. [293]

If Trump's administration did indeed feel the actions of Wanzhou warranted her arrest, why have they not also sought to arrest Russians that undermined US sanctions of North Korea? North Korea attacked Sony, leaking movies online, as well as committed other cyber-crimes such as robbing easy to still digital currency like bitcoin. Yet the Trump administration said nothing as the Russians completed a second connection to the hermit kingdom around October 1, 2017, during heavy US sanctions. Trump, to his credit, is the only US President to get Russia and China to approve and briefly support US sanctions on North Korea. Initially ghost ships of dead North Koreans washed up on shore in Japan, indicating the sanctions were effective as ship captains had to meet quotas on the high seas. That type of story has faded as enforcement of sanctions became an illusion. Both China and Russia likely no longer follow the sanctions and Trump remains silent.[294]

Wanzhou's arrest has been answered with arrests within China of thirteen "corrupt" Canadian business men, as well as sentenced a previously detained drug dealing Canadian to death during the month and a half following Huawei's CFO being detained. The US is moving forward with extradition, formally filing on January 28, 2019, and should that extradition happen expect collateral US damage for business and our citizens traveling or living in China.[295]

---

[293] Horowitz, Julia. "Huawei CFO Meng Wanzhou Arrested in Canada." *CNN*, Cable News Network, 6 Dec. 2018, www.cnn.com/2018/12/05/tech/huawei-cfo-arrested-canada/index.html.

[294] "Russian Firm Provides New Internet Connection to North Korea." *Reuters*, Thomson Reuters, 2 Oct. 2017, www.reuters.com/article/us-nkorea-internet/russian-firm-provides-new-internet-connection-to-north-korea-idUSKCN1C70D2.

[295] Reuters. "Canada Says 13 Citizens Detained in China since Huawei CFO's Arrest." *The Guardian*, Guardian News and Media, 4 Jan. 2019, www.theguardian.com/world/2019/jan/04/canada-says-13-citizens-detained-in-china-since-huawei-cfos-arrest.

Chapter Twenty-One

The Constitution Hangs by a Thread

The United States Constitution created three co-equal branches of government. These are the Judicial, Legislative and Executive branches. Each has a distinct purpose; the judicial to interpret, the executive to enforce and the legislative to create. With Trump's "surprise" win, he was in charge of filling many positions within the executive branch as well as the judicial branch. In this June 26, 2018, excerpt Trump from a round table discussion, Mick Mulvaney says, *"We need the border security money."* Trump in his most simplistic and idiosyncratic way rambles:

> *"That's all we need. Border security. We need to get going. A lot of*
> *bad things are happening and I think we're doing it incredibly well.*
> *We have no tools. We have bad laws. We have the worst immigra-*
> *tion laws in the history of the world, okay? It's a joke. People can't*
> *believe it. Other countries look at us and they say, 'How is that pos-*
> *sible?' Somebody touches our land, we now take them to a court, to*
> *a judge.*
>
> *"They want us to choose 5,000 judges. How do you choose*
> *5,000 judges? Can you imagine the corruption just from a normal*
> *standpoint? Just common sense. Can you imagine the corruption?*
> *Go to the barbershop. Grab somebody. Make them a judge. Every-*
> *body is being made a judge. They want 5,000 judges more. It's*

crazy. Other countries it's called, 'I'm sorry. You can't come in. You have to leave.' This one, we have judges. If they step on our land, we have judges. It's insane. So we're going to have to change our whole immigration policy."[296]

As a factual-based matter, the US Constitution, the foundation of our laws, is not "bad" or the "worst in the history of the world," as Trump lacking a filter attacks. Trump likely doesn't realize he is verbally assaulting the Constitution each time he takes umbrage to our laws like this because it is very unlikely he has read it, or knows the civic basics expected of a fifth grader.

Trump as President has a "check" on the judicial branch in the form of being able to appoint judges, who then are vetted in Congress and either accepted or rejected. For the most part this process works out relatively smooth. Trump has appointed a load of judges, I assume from others recommendations and not from his time at the barbershop. The hilarity of Trump's statement is that he implies that what he is doing is corrupt connecting his record judge placements with his intent to change immigration policy.

What Trump is actually trying to say, which is lost in his pragmatic skills deficit, is that judges are corrupt because they are blocking his moves on immigration. Trump has lost most of his immigration court battles because he has ignored Constitutional requirements and eliminated a need for Congress using executive orders.

Donald Trump hated executive orders on the campaign trail, frequently using the phrase *"illegal Obama executive order"* which he used twenty-six times over the last two weeks of the campaign according to search at factba.se. The most blistering attack on executive order usage came via this Tweet following DACA:

"Repubs must not allow Pres Obama to subvert the Constitution of the US for his own benefit & because he is unable to negotiate w/ Congress."

-Donald J. Trump
8:36A.M., November 20, 2014[297]

---

[296] Factbase. "Transcript Quote - Remarks: Donald Trump Attends Lunch With Members of Congress - June 26, 2018." Factbase, factba.se/transcript/donald-trump-remarks-lunch-members-congress-june-26-2018.

[297] Trump, Donald J. "Repubs Must Not Allow Pres Obama to Subvert the Constitution of the US for His Own Benefit & Because He Is Unable to Negotiate w/ Congress." *Twitter*, Twitter, 20 Nov. 2014,

Donnie kept his pen busy signing in thick black up and down strokes executive orders, signing fifty-five in his first year in office and thirty-seven his second. He also issued a pile of Presidential memoranda, which do not carry the same weight or requirements of an executive order.[298]

Considering Trump's willingness to sign things placed on his desk without reading them, one should wonder why the Trump resistance within the White House never put the Re-Sign Nation Act in front of him and *"see what happens."* Just a suggestion. ;)

Trump has done many of these signings on camera, acting like they are a big deal. Most are rather mundane, not worthy of any fanfare. In contrast, the Emancipation Proclamation Abraham Lincoln signed, one of the most significant executive orders to date was signed to no fanfare, alone one evening apart from the group at the White House, shows how humble a past Republican great has been before the party went the route it has with Trump.

Donald's ire with POTUS's use of executive orders subverting the Constitution vanished when he took office. The Republicans with control of both the House and Senate failed to get almost anything permanent other than removing past laws and protections through Congress that he campaigned on, with just one partisan bill of significance reaching 45th's desk over the course of two years. After 150 days in office Trump went to Twitter to pat himself on the back:

> *"I've helped pass and signed 38 Legislative Bills, mostly with no Democratic support, and gotten rid of massive amounts of regulations. Nice!"*
>
> *4:39 A.M., 23 June, 2017*

Of the thirty-eight, fifteen were repeals of Obama era legislation. Among the pillars of Republican ideals of good governance was re-allowing miners to dump waste into streams, reducing requirements for effective teacher training, removing business requirements to make and report accidents and injuries, and elimination of some federal requirements regarding background checks

---

twitter.com/realDonaldTrump/status/535441553079431168?ref_src=twsrc%5Etfw%7Ctwcamp%5Et weetembed%7Ctwterm%5E535441553079431168&ref_url=https%3A%2F%2Fwww.businessin-sider.com%2Ftrump-2014-Tweet-obama-executive-action-hypocrisy-2019-2.

[298] "Executive Orders." *Federal Register*, www.federalregister.gov/presidential-documents/executive-orders.

for gun purchases. Most laws signed were designation bills, such as three naming board of regent members to the Smithsonian or funding resolutions to fund parts of the government.[299]

Considering the list of early legislative achievements lacked a signature win, his sheer number of executive orders was expected. One of Trump's earliest, nicknamed as the so-called Muslim ban, was blocked quickly. Trump derided the judicial branch's constitutional role in interpreting our law with the following Tweet:

> *"The opinion of this so-called judge, which essentially takes law-enforcement away from our country, is ridiculous and will be over-turned!"*
>
> 7:12 A.M., February 4, 2017[300]

Trump had campaigned on racist xenophobia and delivered early for his base enacting the ban via executive order on January 27, 2017. The title, *"Protecting the Nation From Foreign Terrorist Entry Into the United States,"* sought to immediately block entry of Syrian refugees indefinitely and block foreign nationals from Iran, Iraq, Libya, Somalia, Sudan, Syria and Yemen for 120 days. Chaos ensued at the airports as the administration dropped the order out without a delayed implementation. People were in transit and with their VISA now nullified by the President they could not enter "legally" into the country. [301]

The courts blocked Trump's first attempt ruling it unconstitutional so the administration filed a second almost identical executive order to the first on March 6, with the same name. This one was also blocked. Trump signed a third one on September 24, 2017, that eventually made its way to the Supreme Court where after two failures Donald finally was successful in a 5-4 ruling June 26, 2018.[302]

---

[299] "What Are the Bills Donald Trump Has Signed?" CBS News, CBS Interactive, www.cbsnews.com/news/what-are-the-bills-donald-trump-has-signed/.

[300] Trump, Donald J. "The Opinion of This So-Called Judge, Which Essentially Takes Law-Enforcement Away from Our Country, Is Ridiculous and Will Be Overturned!" *Twitter*, Twitter, 4 Feb. 2017, twitter.com/realdonaldtrump/status/827867311054974976?lang=en.

[301] Trump, Donald J. "Protecting the Nation From Foreign Terrorist Entry Into the United States ." Federal Register, Federal Register, 27 Jan. 2017, www.govinfo.gov/content/pkg/FR-2017-02-01/pdf/2017-02281.pdf.

[302] "Timeline of the Muslim Ban." *ACLU of Washington*, 26 Nov. 2018, www.aclu-wa.org/pages/timeline-muslim-ban.

This decision could not have been possible without Neil Gorsuch, the first appointment under Donald J. Trump. Gorsuch, while a stable and honorable right-leaning jurist, leapfrogged the Presidential nomination of centrist Merrick Garland who has yet to appear for confirmation hearings since his nomination in March of 2016 by then President Barack Obama. McConnell brazenly blocked the nomination of Merrick, and then changed Senate rules going nuclear, eliminating the filibuster in 2017 in order to pass Gorsuch through. Trump seeing unprecedented power in the so-called nuclear option for getting everything through Congress he desired while the GOP had full control wanted that change to be widespread. Mitch understood, while he stole a SCOTUS seat, each move will have an inverse effect when the other party gains control, and that giving such power for a short term effect could be disastrous to the long term future of the conservative movement.

> *"Border Patrol Agents are not allowed to properly do their job at the Border because of ridiculous liberal (Democrat) laws like Catch & Release. Getting more dangerous. 'Caravans' coming. Republicans must go to Nuclear Option to pass tough laws NOW. NO MORE DACA DEAL!"*
>
> *7:56 A.M., April 1, 2018*[303]

Donnie really has a fixation for Wall Trump, something he promised Mexico was going to pay for. He wants his wall so bad he was briefly willing to give back one of those things he damaged, DACA. Trump has wiped out most of the protected status allowing refugees to stay legally in the United States since taking office. As most of these immigrants anticipated his Nationalist agenda, an unprecedented number of people filed for Citizenship. As an example, my wife and her friend both filed for naturalization about a week apart, with my wife filing around December 1, 2015, and her friend the following week. There was a year difference between the two being sworn in as United States citizens. The main difference in processing times between my wife and her friend likely was attributed to the San Bernardino shooting on December 2, 2015, and sudden fear of a Trump presidency and retaliation on immigrants.

---

[303] Trump, Donald J. "Border Patrol Agents Are Not Allowed to Properly Do Their Job at the Border Because of Ridiculous Liberal (Democrat) Laws like Catch & Release. Getting More Dangerous. 'Caravans' Coming. Republicans Must Go to Nuclear Option to Pass Tough Laws NOW. NO MORE DACA DEAL!" *Twitter*, Twitter, 1 Apr. 2018, twitter.com/realDonaldTrump/status/980443810529533952.

Trump's war on immigrants isn't just the building of an arcane wall. He has spent most of his campaign and presidency attacking both the legal and non-legal avenues while his businesses exploited the very people Trump sought to keep out. In a series of connected reports describing Trump's business practices at his Bedminster golf club, accusations of the Trump company providing false documentation on behalf of two "illegal aliens" so they could work have come out starting December 6, 2018.

A lawyer representing two workers in the case against the Trump property stated:

> *"My clients and others were repeatedly subjected to abuse, called racial epithets and threatened with deportation. Ironically, the threats often came from the same supervisor who had employed them despite knowing their undocumented status and even provided them with forged documents."[304]*

After the suit and negative publicity from the alleged crimes, the Trump Organization began firing those it had illegally hired, starting January 26, 2019, some who had worked for up to twenty years.[305]

Donald continued his assault on the Constitution with more of his executive actions. Courts blocked his transgender military ban initially, but SCOTUS bypassed lower appeal courts without hearing arguments allowing the ban to finally take effect around January 22, 2019, by a 5-4 vote. At this point Trump had placed the swamp creature Brett Kavanagh to the court after the most contentious and political spectacle. [306]

Let's be clear. I thought Kavanagh initially was a good pick but wanted Amy Barrett as she would be historic as the first female conservative justice on the court and was younger. Hearings were going well then the credible Me Too accusations of Professor Christine Blasey Ford changed the whole tone. Trump really should have picked Barrett.

---

[304] Stewart, Ian. "Trump Golf Club Allegedly Employed Undocumented Immigrants." *NPR*, NPR, 7 Dec. 2018, www.npr.org/2018/12/07/674576373/trump-golf-club-allegedly-employed-undocumented-immigrants.

[305] Llorente, Elizabeth. "Undocumented Workers Reportedly Fired from Trump Golf Club." *Fox News*, FOX News Network, www.foxnews.com/us/dozen-undocumented-workers-were-fired-from-trump-golf-club-in-new-york-report.

[306] *Bloomberg.com*, Bloomberg, www.bloomberg.com/news/articles/2019-01-22/supreme-court-lets-trump-s-transgender-military-ban-take-effect.

The ensuing dramatics was political theatre at its worst starting with Lindsey Graham's contorted face and spiteful antics at the open with Kavanagh going off the rail in a partisan attack against the Clintons.

> *"This whole two-week effort has been a calculated and orchestrated political hit, fueled with apparent pent-up anger about President Trump and the 2016 election, fear that has been unfairly stoked about my judicial record. Revenge on behalf of the Clintons and millions of dollars in money from outside left-wing opposition groups. This is a circus. The consequences will extend long past my nomination. The consequences will be with us for decades."[307]*

Kavanagh is a D.C. belt swamp creature through and through. Spite and malice in his voice he brought up and accused the Clintons of derailing his ascendency to a life appointment to the Supreme Court. That needed context. Kavanagh as an associate counsel for independent counsel Kenneth Starr has extreme prejudice against the Clintons, as he tried to take down then President Bill Clinton for his affair with intern Monica Lewinsky. While I agree that Presidents lying about affairs should be impeached, the Supreme Court's integrity and luster was forever tarnished as this extremely prejudiced jurist eventually was seated.[308]

In the end, it was Ford's quiet testimony that rang true, not the at times nearly screaming theatrics of the ring master of the circus Brett Kavanagh that set my mind about what happened. Ford's description of the two boys laughing at her as he attempted to restrain her were the lasting impression of the Kegmaster High School Brett I will always remember. Still, people change. Beyond the accusation his testimony that day disqualified him as unfit to sit on the bench, as he cannot be impartial about something that he was involved in twenty years ago, not the heavy drinking and allegations of assault from High School, with his aggression towards the Clintons and Democrats he put on

---

[307] Haltiwanger, John. "Kavanaugh Delivers Fiery, Emotional Opening Remarks in Senate Hearing, Claims His Life Has Been 'Totally and Permanently Destroyed.'" *Business Insider*, Business Insider, 27 Sept. 2018, www.businessinsider.com/brett-kavanaugh-opening-statement-transcript-senate-christine-ford-2018-9.

[308] Gambino, Lauren. "Brett Kavanaugh Had Graphic Questions for Bill Clinton about Lewinsky Affair." *The Guardian*, Guardian News and Media, 20 Aug. 2018, www.theguardian.com/law/2018/aug/20/brett-kavanaugh-bill-clinton-questions-1998-memo-trump.

display. But it was Trump's October 2, 2018, response that will be more memorable in the long run:

> *"Well, I say that it's a very scary time for young men in America, when you can be guilty of something that you may not be guilty of. This is a very, very—this is a very difficult time.*
>
> *"What's happening here has much more to do than even the appointment of a Supreme Court Justice. It really does. You could be somebody that was perfect your entire life and somebody could accuse you of something. It doesn't necessarily have to be a woman, as everybody say—but somebody could accuse you of something, and you're automatically guilty.*
>
> *"But in this realm, you are truly guilty until proven innocent. That's one of the very, very bad things that's taking place right now."[309]*

Trump's incredible lack of filter and incidental self-projection on the whole Kavanagh hearings just made men the victims of the entire Me Too movement. Trump has a staggering number of women accusing him of all sorts of sexual things, many with other witnesses or recorded evidence which he denies. He knows which are true as well as the occasional ones that are not, so in a sense he identifies with Brett and all his other friends like Roger Ailes caught up in the Me Too movement.

It would not be a scary time for young men in America if they would simply treat women with respect and dignity. Of course doing so precludes sleeping around on your first, second and third wives so it isn't probably part of Trump's underlying value system he is capable of generating a positive example. Kavanagh was seated securing many 5-4 votes could potentially go Trump's way in his efforts to reimage America to reflect his own soul. With Kavanagh's swearing onto the Court the fabric that held the Constitution together was significantly torn, leaving just the integrity of Congress left to corrupt. However, that branch of government too was long compromised under Trump's leadership and demanded abeyance from most Republicans. Only the House remains independent of his influence.

---

[309] Canty, Jennifer. "Transcript Quote - Press Gaggle: Donald Trump Speaks to the Press Before Marine One Departure - October 2, 2018." *Factbase*, CantyMedia, factba.se/transcript/donald-trump-press-conference-marine-one-departure-october-2-2018.

Perhaps the most telling of how precarious the threat Donald is to the Constitution was his creation of a national emergency on February 15, 2019, then promptly got on the plane and headed to Mar Lago for yet another vacation.[310] Trump had failed on his key Nationalist agenda, to build a wall to keep non-whites out. Let's be clear, the problems Trump names as the reasons he wants the wall expanded (the wall was built in nearly every location it was needed) do not constitute a sudden imminent threat like say gun violence in our schools. Border crossings are well below historic highs. [311] Crime rates for non-citizens are lower than the general population. [312] Drugs are locally manufactured, and the foreign stuff comes as much from the North as it does from the South, with most carried via trains, cars and boats at legal points of entry according to his own government.[313] The only "emergency" is that Trump didn't get what he wanted and couldn't sit down with people he did not already "control" to make a deal.

Donald for greater part of more than two years has stayed mostly within his comfort zone. Being intolerant of being made the butt of a friendly roast at the Correspondent dinner, he held a rally that was more suited to his personal needs of praise and flattery. Then once burned by Lester Holt who got him to admit he fired James Comey over the *"And in fact, when I decided to just do it I said to myself, I said, you know, this Russia thing with Trump and Russia is a made-up story,"* Trump restricted his behavior as tight as any autistic could. He would then almost exclusively watch in his boxers and only be interviewed by those who would treat him "well" with his control of the questioning thus excluding the vast majority of the networks and limiting his reach. [314]

All of Don's shutting down and then sheltering himself whenever he faced adversity should be obvious in that each and every report where he was "in-

---

[310] Dodson, Marianne. "Trump Heads to His Florida Golf Resort after Declaring National Emergency." *Image*, The Week, 15 Feb. 2019, theweek.com/speedreads/824042/trump-heads-florida-golf-resort-after-declaring-national-emergency.

[311] "National Emergency: Is There a Crisis on the US-Mexico Border?" *BBC News*, BBC, 15 Feb. 2019, www.bbc.com/news/world-us-canada-44319094.

[312] Flagg, Anna. "The Myth of the Criminal Immigrant." *The New York Times*, The New York Times, 30 Mar. 2018, www.nytimes.com/interactive/2018/03/30/upshot/crime-immigration-myth.html.

[313] Winter, Jana. "Trump Says Border Wall Will Stop Drugs. Here's What a DEA Intel Report Says." *Foreign Policy*, Foreign Policy, 29 Aug. 2017, foreignpolicy.com/2017/08/29/trump-says-border-wall-will-stop-drugs-heres-what-a-dea-intel-report-says/.

[314] Factbase. "Transcript Quote - NBC News: Lester Holt Interviews Donald Trump at The White House - May 11, 2017." *Factbase*, factba.se/transcript/donald-trump-interview-nbc-lester-holt-may-11-2017.

volved" in discussions with Congress he failed to include those who might oppose or criticize him that would later need to pass a bill. Sure, he Tweeted. That is a SAFE thing to do. He can turn off the feed and ignore the blowback and think himself smart completely safe in his cocoon encircled with bubble wrap. None of this stuff he did worked well at all to get his wall money. He begged McConnell to go nuclear so his agenda would not require him to make deals. He even shut down the government and failed to get what he wanted, though at least he did invite Pelosi and Schumer over to be schooled on governance. Trump had one last chance. Make something up and hope that his people in the Senate and/or in the courts would back him up. Here are some of his arguments he gave to the American people:

> *"There are so many examples. In El Paso, they have close to 2,000 murders right on the other side of the wall. And they had 23 murders. It's a lot of murders, but it's not close to 2,000 murders right on the other side of the wall, in Mexico. So everyone knows that walls work. And there are better examples than El Paso, frankly."*

Walls don't work. Ask the Mongols. Heck, ask Israel. They have walls and fences everywhere with heavily armed guards and still bad guys get in. A shovel, another medieval object for Trump to ponder about in his walls and wheels thoughts, can indeed undermine a wall.

> *"You just take a look. Almost everywhere. Take a look at Israel. They're building another wall. Their wall is 99.9 percent effective, they told me—99.9 percent. That's what it would be with us, too. The only weakness is they go to a wall and then they go around the wall. They go around the wall and in. Okay?"*[315]

Yes, Israel is building another wall. Somehow that last wall didn't keep out threats because as Don explains it, the threat went around the wall. I know Trump is making up bull for his base, and they believe it, but really, Israel with likely the most barriers and best trained security in the world still hasn't had

---

[315] Factbase. "Transcript Quote - Remarks: Donald Trump Announces Border National Emergency at The White House - February 15, 2019." *Factbase*, factba.se/transcript/donald-trump-remarks-border-wall-emergency-february-15-2019.

full success with their walls keeping out Hezbollah. The tunneling has gone back for years with recent incursions into Israel under the wall reported several times, including December 4, 2018, by NPR.[316]

> *"That's what it is. It's very simple. And a big majority of the big drugs—the big drug loads—don't go through ports of entry. They can't go through ports of entry. You can't take big loads because you have people—we have some very capable people; the Border Patrol, law enforcement—looking."*

According to the Trump administration, not to be confused with Donald Trump who makes stuff up to create a false argument, most drugs are smuggled at legal ports of entry.[317]

> *"You can't take human traffic—women and girls—you can't take them through ports of entry. You can't have them tied up in the backseat of a car or a truck or a van. They open the door. They look. They can't see three women with tape on their mouth or three women whose hands are tied. They go through areas where you have no wall. Everybody knows that. Nancy knows it. Chuck knows it. They all know it. It's all a big lie. It's a big con game. You don't have to be very smart to know: You put up a barrier, the people come in, and that's it. They can't do anything unless they walk left or right, and they find an area where there's no barrier, and they come into the United States."*

Trump, who may have trafficked women and girls through his Trump Models establishment to work illegally as indentured servants indebted to his company, is probably more of an expert on how to do this than I. From reports of his victims, he used ports of entry and coerced girls from countries that could visit without a VISA.

---

[316] Dwyer, Colin, and Bill Chappell. "Israel's Army Says It Found Tunnels Dug By Hezbollah Beneath Border With Lebanon." *NPR*, NPR, 4 Dec. 2018, www.npr.org/2018/12/04/673181288/israels-army-says-it-found-tunnels-dug-by-hezbollah-beneath-border-with-lebanon.

[317] Carranza, Rafael. "Meth, Cocaine, Heroin: Most Gets Smuggled through Ports of Entry. A Wall Won't Stop It." *Azcentral*, Arizona Republic, 10 Jan. 2019, www.azcentral.com/story/news/politics/border-issues/2019/01/08/most-hard-drugs-get-smuggled-into-u-s-through-ports-entry/2517586002/.

"So I'm going to be signing a national emergency. And it's been signed many times before. It's been signed by other Presidents from 1977 or so. It gave the Presidents the power. There's rarely been a problem. They sign it; nobody cares. I guess they weren't very exciting. But nobody cares. They sign it for far less important things, in some cases, in many cases. We're talking about an invasion of our country with drugs, with human traffickers, with all types of criminals and gangs."

It is all about the power, isn't it? Trump lacks the power to get funding as he has been "impotent" in the deal-making department, so he ignores Congress as a Constitutional branch of Government, then finds the only way he can to "win." Trump took questions and "shot his argument in the foot" about his emergency with this:

> *"But on the wall, they skimped. So I did—I was successful, in that sense, but I want to do it faster. I could do the wall over a longer period of time. I didn't need to do this. But I'd rather do it much faster. And I don't have to do it for the election. I've already done a lot of wall, for the election—2020. And the only reason we're up here talking about this is because of the election, because they want to try and win an election, which it looks like they're not going to be able to do. And this is one of the ways they think they can possibly win, is by obstruction and a lot of other nonsense. And I think that I just want to get it done faster, that's all. Okay."*

Can a national emergency be created to do a political promise faster? This is Trump, king of Cons. There is a very good chance that his precedent that Congress's power of the purse no longer counts will stand. He has enough thugs under control to prevent an override in the Senate and can steal military funds for his wall before the courts will intervene. The vote to end the Emergency Declaration passed in the Senate with twelve Republicans signing on with their colleagues. Trump vetoed on March 15.

Ah, the courts. While the sing-song part of his speech happened early, just before he took questions from reporters, it was his way of showing his annoyance with the lower courts he doesn't fully control, especially the ninth apparently.

> *"So the order is signed. And I'll sign the final papers as soon as I get into the Oval Office. And we will have a national emergency, and*

*then we will then be sued, and they will sue us in the Ninth Circuit,
even though it shouldn't be there. And we will possibly get a bad
ruling, and then we'll get another bad ruling. And then we'll end
up in the Supreme Court, and hopefully we'll get a fair shake. And
we'll win in the Supreme Court, just like the ban. They sued us in
the Ninth Circuit, and we lost, and then we lost in the appellate division, and then we went to the Supreme Court, and we won."[318]*

Trump then went into how he prevailed in his so-called Muslim ban in the
Supreme Court, something he sees as more in his control now with Brett on
board. Trump understands this as evidenced from this Fox News interview
quote on July 1, 2018:

*"Honestly, if the Democrats would have won the election, first of
all, you would have a lot of different—if you look at the last four
decisions on the Supreme Court, at 5-4, they would have all been
reversed."[319]*

On March 14, 2019, the Senate followed suit with the House voting to end
Trump's guised money grab in the form of a national emergency declaration.
Neither did so with a veto-proof majority ensuring Trump's first Presidential
veto on March 15 would sustain his absolute power to ignore one-full branch
of "co-equal" government while facing the likely prolonged showdown with
the other he had successfully stacked.

*"I look forward to VETOING the just passed Democrat inspired
Resolution which would OPEN BORDERS while increasing
Crime, Drugs, and Trafficking in our Country. I thank all of the
Strong Republicans who voted to support Border Security and our
desperately needed WALL!"*

2:43 P.M., March 14, 2019[320]

---

[318] Factbase. "Transcript Quote - Remarks: Donald Trump Announces Border National Emergency at The White House - February 15, 2019." *Factbase*, factba.se/transcript/donald-trump-remarks-border-wall-emergency-february-15-2019.

[319] Factbase. "Transcript Quote - Interview: Maria Bartiromo Interviews Donald Trump on Fox News - July 1, 2018." *Factbase*, factba.se/transcript/donald-trump-interview-maria-bartiromo-fox-july-1-2018.

[320] Shaw, Adam. "Senate Votes to Block Trump's Border Emergency Declaration, in Bipartisan Rebuke

Trump, while generally limited in his thinking ability, wields an enormous amount of power. As President he has taken security clearances away from those who critique him, as well as give those to who are loyal to him. It is in this capacity he "forced" security clearances be given to at least two individuals, Ivanka and Jared Kushner that should likely not have access to national secrets. Jared is the more troubling of the two as he has had multiple failures to pass basic screening and application requirements, and had his temporary clearance revoked. While Kushner is a person of importance in the Trump orbit, his questionable ethics raised flags that Trump overrode, making he responsible as authorizer of any misdeeds Jared undertook with that access. He did so intentionally to push the Middle East agenda of the Marshall Plan discussed in the next chapter, though undoubtedly Kushner would access that data to further other global interests that he and his father-in-law want to pursue. While Trump can "get away with" giving our enemies documents, Kushner could not. That he has this access when he could not pass the screening requirements is like allowing a person who has only played video games then is given a license to fly a plane. [321]

With Trump and his corrupt mob organization, we have seen a complete and thorough carving out of nearly all of our nation's core values, laws and governance. In a sense, the Constitution, a sacred document is hanging by a thread. The President seeking loyalty and obedience cleaned out his government of those whom would disrupt his goals from both the executive and congressional side of his party, while simultaneously packing judges into the courts at a record pace with as many same-minded interpreters of the law.

The most concerning evidence that our Constitution is dangling by a thread is that Trump and his administration seeks to sell nuclear technology to Saudi Arabia, fast-tracking the sale and bypassing regulations. As I said earlier, the Russia story is a nothing-burger compared to the Saudi conspiracy.

Teeing up Veto." *Fox News*, FOX News Network, www.foxnews.com/politics/senate-republicans-join-dems-in-voting-to-rebuke-trumps-border-emergency-declaration.

[321] "Trump Reportedly Ordered That Jared Kushner Get His Security Clearance." *MSNBC*, NBCUniversal News Group, www.msnbc.com/11th-hour/watch/trump-reportedly-ordered-that-jared-kushner-get-his-security-clearance-1450286147727.

Chapter Twenty-two

"Tut-beer Erqei"
The "Ethnic Cleansing" of the Shia Houthi People

There have been quite a few actions and non-actions by Trump and his administration that have cost people around the world dearly, and America too distracted by all the smoke and mirrors put out by Trump's spokespeople deflecting from his Russia conspiracy has missed most of it. The carnage began in 2017. Rules were removed prohibiting weapon sales to Nigeria and Saudi Arabia, two countries that would put those weapons to use to cleanse entire villages full of people, making this administration likely complicit in at least two different genocides. Then there is Syria.

Syria was already pretty messed up before Trump took office with a long Civil War that served as a proxy for world powers to test their militaries without fighting directly with each other. Trump had ceded full decision making to the generals and on March 16, 2017, the US targeted a Syrian Mosque leveling it with three hundred people inside just before the commencement of night prayer at 6:55 P.M. local time.

> *"My lower half was buried under the rubble. I couldn't move my head. Someone's legs were beneath me. Half an hour later we started hearing a faint voice, people were calling out, so we shouted back. The civil defense started digging us out, using only their hands. Two hours later they got us through a hole. There was rubble*

as high as four meters above us. They stayed there working till the following morning, trying to rescue as many people as possible. I had wounds all over."

-Mosque Massacre Survivor

A second strike hit shortly after the first. In all hundreds were injured with thirty-eight confirmed dead in an intentional targeting that might not have happened had Trump repealed targeting rules and the troops followed international law.[322]

The Omar Ibn al-Khatab Mosque massacre in Aleppo, Syria, at first was denied by the US military, saying that they had targeted a community hall. Upon further review the US military recognized that the building was not a legal target as they had thought it had been. The fighting continued with many more lives snuffed out by US forces and bombing.

On May 9, 2017, Trump opted to train and arm Kurdish forces for an assault of Raqqah, Syria, the capital of the ISIS caliphate, some of which were designated by the US department as terrorist organizations, to fight ISIS and other terror groups in Syria and northern Iraq. This would increase friction with US ally Turkey who views both these groups as separatists. After the Raqqah offensive the Trump administration continued to support these Kurdish groups until Trump decided he was bored and pulling the US troops out without consulting his generals during the shutdown on December 19, 2018.[323] [324] [325]

Considering US abandonment of these people happened in Iraq after the first Gulf War without a no-flight zone or a warning to Saddam Hussein, allowing them to be gassed and suppressed by the Iraqi militia, this second abandonment with Turkish and Russian forces ready to sweep in and clean up, was

---

[322] "Attack on the Omar Ibn Al-Khatab Mosque | US Authorities' Failure to Take Adequate Precautions." *Human Rights Watch*, 6 June 2017, www.hrw.org/report/2017/04/18/attack-omar-ibn-al-khatab-mosque/us-authorities-failure-take-adequate-precautions#.

[323] Hennigan, W.J. "Trump Approves Pentagon Plan to Arm Syrian Kurds despite Turkish Objections." *Los Angeles Times*, Los Angeles Times, 9 May 2017, www.latimes.com/politics/washington/la-na-essential-washington-updates-trump-approves-pentagon-plan-to-arm-1494355283-htmlstory.html.

[324] Landler, Mark, et al. "Trump to Withdraw U.S. Forces From Syria, Declaring 'We Have Won Against ISIS.'" *The New York Times*, The New York Times, 19 Dec. 2018, www.nytimes.com/2018/12/19/us/politics/trump-syria-turkey-troop-withdrawal.html.

[325] Bender, Bryan, et al. "Trump to Unleash More Global Arms Sales." *POLITICO*, 29 Sept. 2017, www.politico.com/story/2017/09/29/trump-global-arms-sales-243282.

unconscionable. Just one more group of Trump "people" casually discarded once they had no more use.

> *"....going to be there for three months, and that was seven years ago—we never left. When I became President, ISIS was going wild. Now ISIS is largely defeated and other local countries, including Turkey, should be able to easily take care of whatever remains. We're coming home!"*
>
> *11:30 A.M., December 22, 2018*[326]

A slow pull-out was arranged by the generals, while a conspicuous change March 1, 2019, on the State Department website lists of FTO, Foreign Terror Organization, groups appeared, reviewing and maintaining the status of the PKK, the Kurdistan Workers' Party, originally designated as a Foreign Terror Organization in 1997. With that posted those Kurds left on the ground to die in Syria are "easily" justified as a Trump sacrifice branded conveniently as terrorists. [327]

With a derelict commander in chief, there has been a systemic breakdown in communication and follow through on Constitutional obligations that has led to at least three military blunders—two separate ship to ship deadly collisions on the high seas and the Nigerian ambush. The Nigerian ambush, on October 4, 2017, a country the troops do not have Congressional authorization to be deployed to, lost four servicemen. Mistakes that led to the ambush were detailed in a 6,300-page report.

The mission was a capture-or-kill mission, something they were not authorized to perform. Inadequate training and improper paperwork were also cited as problems. Thirty Nigerian troops and a Green Beret unit headed to the capture site, found no one, then departed where they then were beset by enemy combatants that had them severely outnumbered. Only one side had been doing proper surveillance, as the US scrapped aerial support due to weather and just sent in the troops on the ground. The side that had done

---

[326] Trump, Donald J. "....Going to Be There for Three Months, and That Was Seven Years Ago - We Never Left. When I Became President, ISIS Was Going Wild. Now ISIS Is Largely Defeated and Other Local Countries, Including Turkey, Should Be Able to Easily Take Care of Whatever Remains. We're Coming Home!" *Twitter*, Twitter, 22 Dec. 2018, twitter.com/realdonaldtrump/status/1076515352249597954?lang=en.

[327] "State Department Maintains Foreign Terrorist Organization (FTO) Designation of the Kurdistan Workers' Party (PKK)." *U.S. Department of State*, U.S. Department of State, 1 Mar. 2019, www.state.gov/r/pa/prs/ps/2019/03/289833.htm.

their work outnumbered the American and Nigerian group four to one. Three soldiers' remains were lifted by French troops that night along with other troops, while one soldier's remains stayed missing till the morning of October 6. Two other US soldiers were wounded. More troops likely were spared thanks to the rescuing French and Nigerian troops.[328] [329]

While the Nigerian ambush was bad, like the level of Benghazi bad, there were much worse things going on as Trump voided weapon sales bans to the country, similar to how he voided ones to Saudi Arabia. Nigeria has been having a field day with US arms support, one of the reason they winded up on the do not sell list under Obama. The ongoing conflict has had so many uncorroborated accounts involving US weapons and mass killings that Trump really should have steered clear despite Boko Haran and other dangerous groups that roam the country.

The worst of the worst military deals are Trump's mostly hidden agreements with Saudi Arabia, the country where its nationals along with neighbor and ally UAE orchestrated the September 11, 2001, attacks on New York. I previously mentioned the Mideast roadmap, the Trump-Kushner arrangement for "peace" in the Middle East, and how it is wreaking havoc in the region. Essentially there are three parties to the agreement, Israel, the US and Saudi Arabia, with Kushner being the main point of connection between each party. The details are mostly hidden, while the following are suggested:

The Saudis get weapons and military support against "proxy" Iranians and terror groups. In return they have stayed mum on Israel's advancements.

Israel gets recognition of claim over Jerusalem and cover for other actions that Saudi Arabia normally would condemn such as a recent assassination of a general by an Israeli elite force in the Gaza strip.

The US gets money. More than likely there are "benefits" going to the Kushner and Trump families that are not as easy to track. Saudi Arabia as an example, could frequent Trump businesses, buy real estate or do other things that pay Trump back. We do know they are spending money on Trump which suggests ethics breaches. During the campaign, in 2015 at Mobile Alabama he said this of the Saudis:

---

[328] *Niger Ambush Summary of Investigation*, Department of Defense, 2018, dod.defense.gov/portals/1/features/2018/0418_niger/img/Oct-2017-Niger-Ambush-Summary-of-Investigation.pdf.

[329] Rempfer, Kyle. "Two-Star General, Green Berets Punished for Deadly Niger Ambush That Killed 4 US Soldiers." *Army Times*, Army Times, 5 Nov. 2018, www.armytimes.com/news/your-army/2018/11/05/two-star-general-green-berets-punished-for-deadly-niger-ambush-that-killed-4-us-soldiers/.

> *"I get along great with all of them; they buy apartments from me.*
> *They spend $40 million, $50 million. Am I supposed to dislike*
> *them? I like them very much!"*

Money drives Trump as he views the amount he gets as winning. His wallet has beefed up with increased bookings from Saudi nationals staying at his hotels and properties, so yeah, there is something likely there. It is one of the problems with Trump's refusal to divest of his businesses and his frequent comingling of US interests with his own personal ones. Trump supports MbS as MbS supports him:

> *"King Salman and Crown Prince Mohammad bin Salman vigor-*
> *ously deny any knowledge of the planning or execution of the mur-*
> *der of Mr. Khashoggi. Our intelligence agencies continue to assess*
> *all information, but it could very well be that the Crown Prince*
> *had knowledge of this tragic event—maybe he did and maybe he*
> *didn't!"[330]*

He did. There is no other man in the Kingdom who had the authority to execute such an order other than the Crown Prince. Trump knows that, but sides with him as a way to castigate the intelligence community that is investigating him. He also doesn't want to insult the man who is enriching him. Selling nuclear technology takes national security threats to a whole other level. In a dated February 2019 report to the Oversight and Reform committee headed by Elijah E. Cummings enters this Report:

Whistleblowers Raise Grave Concerns with Trump Administration's Efforts to Transfer Sensitive Nuclear Technology to Saudi Arabia

> *"This interim staff report was prepared for Rep. Elijah E.*
> *Cummings, the Chairman of the Committee on Oversight and Re-*
> *form, after multiple whistleblowers came forward to warn about*
> *efforts inside the White House to rush the transfer of highly sensi-*

---

[330] Bryan, Bob. "Trump Said He Has 'No Financial Interests in Saudi Arabia.' But His Businesses Have Made Millions from the Saudi Government, and the Crown Prince Gave His New York City Hotel a Huge Boost." *Business Insider*, Business Insider, 21 Nov. 2018, www.businessinsider.com/trump-saudi-arabia-financial-interests-ties-hotel-bookings-sales-2018-10.

tive U.S. nuclear technology to Saudi Arabia in potential violation of the Atomic Energy Act and without review by Congress as required by law—efforts that may be ongoing to this day."

"These whistleblowers provided a snapshot of events at the beginning of the Trump Administration, but it is limited. While serving as Ranking Member of the Committee, Rep. Cummings tried to investigate these actions for years, without Republican support."

"Without Republican support" suggests how bad the "whole" GOP is, willing to keep deals like this one hidden to protect the President's own interests while launching an Obama-era nuclear investigation over something significantly less than selling nuclear technology, selling rocks from a Canadian Uranium mine to Russia.

Fox News and the GOP circled around like vultures decrying the Uranium One Clinton-Russia conspiracy. [331] It was all the rage and had intense coverage for months on their airways then the news just stopped right? I even recall "treason" and "collusion" being muttered fairly frequently. Then silence. The probe found nothing improper with the sale of a mostly depleted Canadian Uranium mine's rights being sold to Russia as the Obama administration followed all laws and regulations that cover nuclear material. Laws and regulations ARE strict for a reason. Generally, when these exist, they either grant rights or give consumers protections. When they are weakened or not followed, bad things happen such as trains falling off of tracks on their first trip December 18, 2017, [332] or possibly newly approved 2017 airplanes falling out of the sky. Sure, the President could blame Obama, which he did, but when the news checks on when things were approved and finds the date saying anything after January 20, 2019, it falls on his administration's safety cutting shoulders.

Trump's administration has been tearing up regulation whenever they can, so it should surprise no one that they appear to have circumvented or ignored those that were not as easy to rewrite regarding "nuclear" when the Middle East Marshall Plan was decided upon. The plan was even supposed to bypass Congress via executive order.

---

[331] "Uranium One." *Newsweek*, www.newsweek.com/topic/uranium-one.

[332] Lindblom, Mike, and David Gutman. "NTSB Report: Amtrak Engineer Missed Speed-Limit Signs before Train Crashed South of Tacoma." *The Seattle Times*, The Seattle Times Company, 26 Jan. 2018, www.seattletimes.com/seattle-news/transportation/ntsb-report-amtrak-engineer-missed-speed-limit-sign-before-the-train-crashed-on-a-curve-south-of-tacoma/.

"The white paper stated that the President should implement the Middle East Marshall Plan through an executive order. It described the Special Envoy as building 'long-line relationships with U.S. private sector leaders acting as their expediter in clearing the traditional regional and regulatory hurdles to their participation' and 'trusted relationships with top leaders of GCC countries, Israel, Egypt, Jordan, and Iraq.'"

The Middle East Marshall Plan was a scheme connected to Michael Flynn (and his former employer IP3) to build nuclear plants, up to forty in Saudi Arabia, UAE and Egypt, because if the US didn't, surely the Russians or French would. From a Trump mindset, those are dollars lost. He is unable to see the potential for harm in such a move and people around him including Flynn, Kushner and personal friend Thomas Barrack had long since convinced him to do the deals. Don's mind is set on the issue. As many of the Trump administration dealings with Russia, meetings with Saudi Arabia were held before January 20, 2017, to arrange the sale of nuclear technology. The plan was on the fast track as early as January 27, 2017, when regulators began to push back and raise concerns.

"When Congress passed the Atomic Energy Act, it imposed stringent controls on the export of U.S. technology to a foreign country that could be used to create nuclear weapons. Under Section 123 of the Act, the U.S. may not transfer nuclear technology to a foreign country without the approval of Congress, in order to ensure that the agreement reached with the foreign government meets nine specific nonproliferation requirements."[333]

The administration allegedly pushed forward with the atomic plan without following required laws and procedures according to whistleblowers. The President, however, has not as of yet issued an executive order to force this. When Rex Tillerson speaking on December 7, 2018, referred that he told Trump no we can't do something because it violated a law or a treaty, this nuclear agreement was likely the main cause:

---

[333] "Trump Saudi Nuclear Report." *Oversight.house.gov*, 19 Feb. 2019, oversight.house.gov/sites/democrats.oversight.house.gov/files/Trump%20Saudi%20Nuclear%20Report%20-%202-19-2019.pdf.

"Part of it was obviously we are starkly different in our styles. We did not have a common value system. When the president would say, 'Here's what I want to do, and here's how I want to do it.' And I'd have to say to him, 'Mr. President, I understand what you want to do, but you can't do it that way, it violates the law. It violates treaty.'"[334]

As one can imagine, there are quite a lot of regulations one needs to jump through for anything nuclear. Cue the attack on "excessive" Obama regulation in a Memorandum for the President from Bud McFalrlane of IP3 to Flynn then Trump on January 28, 2017:

"Further, execution of the plan will involve the rebirth of the U.S. nuclear power industry with all that implies for job-creation. (Over the past thirty years the industry has atrophied—thanks to over-regulation and misguided environmental opposition.) The rebuilding of that industry will provide a major boost to our economy and a major reduction in carbon-based pollution."[335]

The point of regulation is to prevent bad things from happening. With the nuclear power industry the problem hasn't been "over-regulation" or misguided environmental opposition, otherwise Idaho Falls would not have had six nuclear accidents since 2011 at the Idaho National Laboratory. This lie is just a sales pitch along with these five objectives from the *White Paper* by Tom Barrack on March 10, 2017:[336]

The Trump Plan's Five Objectives:
Stop the exportation of radical Islamic terrorism.

---

[334] Stewart, Emily. "Rex Tillerson Had to Warn Trump Not to Break the Law as Secretary of State." *Vox*, Vox, 7 Dec. 2018, www.vox.com/policy-and-politics/2018/12/7/18130476/rex-tillerson-interview-bob-schieffer-donald-trump.

[335] "Trump Saudi Nuclear Report Appendix." *Oversight.house.gov*, 19 Feb. 2019, oversight.house.gov/sites/democrats.oversight.house.gov/files/Appendix%20A.pdf.

[336] Malone, Patrick, and Peter Cary. The Center for Public Integrity. "Unheeded Warnings, Repeated Mistakes Put Workers' Health at Risk at Idaho Nuclear Lab." *Idahostatesman*, Idaho Statesman, 11 Aug. 2017, www.idahostatesman.com/news/northwest/idaho/article166418912.html.

> *This goal will be accomplished by supporting our "benevolent Islamic allies" in creation and implementation of a viable economic development plan which will provide hope and shared prosperity.*
>
> *Aid in a peaceful resolution between Israel and Palestine.*
>
> *Egypt is paramount to this process, and Egypt must support an Israeli solution if any peace process is to be successful*
>
> *However, Egypt can only survive the Muslim Brotherhood and other Internal attacks if it develops a viable economic plan for hopeful prosperity for its people executed in a co-operative but not corrupt manner with its military.*
>
> *Maintain the regional balance of power by countering Iranian and Russian Intervention through USA economic cooperation.*
>
> *Russia, China and Iran have filled the voids created by American foreign policy missteps of the past.*
>
> *Generate USA economic stimulus and growth by expanding International opportunities for our domestic industries and service providers, thereby creating jobs, reduction our trade deficit and providing investment for research and development.*
>
> *American-made Engineering, Construction, Power, Water, Agricultural, Healthcare, Security, Legal, Logistics, and Financial Industries will pave a new path of economic development.*
>
> *Provide a countervailing and compassionate foreign policy initiative as the USA becomes more scrutinizing and firm with immigration and national defense policy across the Middle East.*[337]

Does Tom Barrack "get" his intended audience of Donald Trump? You bet he does. Barrack was chairman of Trump's inaugural committee, and connects Gates, Manafort, and Flynn as the guy who probably pushed each towards the Trump orbit. Tom, a billionaire, has had many dealings with the President since the mid-eighties, with Barrack playing Trump like a fiddle on more than one occasion. His best-buying the Plaza Hotel for $350m and convincing Trump to take it off his hands months later for $400! Trump defaulted on that one in 1992, likely never having the money to buy it in the first place, but able to get the loan due to his reputation as a "rich" dude. Tom still can sucker

---

[337] "Trump Saudi Nuclear Report Appendix." *Oversight.house.gov*, 19 Feb. 2019, oversight.house.gov/sites/democrats.oversight.house.gov/files/Appendix%20A.pdf.

Trump into a bad deal using the right dose of charm and phrases like benevolent Islamic allies.[338]

"Benevolent Islamic allies" is probably not the best description of a country that has since gained a reputation for killing and cutting up a journalist, bombing a full school bus, or starving millions. The only Middle East actor that has been strictly benevolent for decades towards the US has been Qatar, the country Trump would go on to accuse of supporting terrorism at the insistence of those who actually did support terrorism. Tom said just enough about China, Iran and Russia to get buy-in from others. What is perhaps the most interesting "red flag statement" that Egypt with "internal threats" such as the named Muslim Brotherhood, could only be protected by giving them nuclear power. To a group of generals or others with high-level security, such a statement of "suspected" instability, would normally end such a proposal. If that wasn't bad enough, Tom dropped this line after fearmongering that Russia and Iran would build the plants if the US did not with this added disastrous consequences:

> *"thus setting off a potential nuclear arms race in the years ahead."* [339]

Let me explain the logic flaw. Tom is saying if Russia builds a nuclear power plant in Saudi Arabia, it will lead to a nuclear weapon, so we must be the ones to build the power plant instead. The Cause-Effect relationship isn't who builds the plant. The correct logic is that if the plant is built, so will a bomb be built. Additionally, Tom argued both that regulation was a problem AND that US regulation would prevent a bomb coming from such a deal. It is either one or the other. Is regulation really the problem here? No. The actual problem is that people like Tom and Kushner decided to make money off a largely incompetent President, while bringing him along for the ride, making sure he got his cut too. Whether the Middle East sees nuclear proliferation isn't an actual concern.

IP3 documents really sold Trump on speeding things up, and to potentially bypass laws with the concept of regulation-killing, job creation and

---

[338] *Bloomberg.com*, Bloomberg, www.bloomberg.com/news/features/2018-10-26/tom-barrack-got-trump-right-then-things-went-wrong.

[339] "Trump Saudi Nuclear Report Appendix." *Oversight.house.gov*, 19 Feb. 2019, oversight.house.gov/sites/democrats.oversight.house.gov/files/Appendix%20A.pdf.

money as the buy-in. There were line items of 200,000 jobs and $250 billion in revenue in the key US objectives. Additionally, Money flows into corrupt officials pockets with these types of backroom deals:

> *"In January 2018, Brookfield Business Partners, a subsidiary of Brookfield Asset Management, announced its plans to acquire Westinghouse Electric for $4.6 billion. Westinghouse Electric is the bankrupt nuclear services company that is part of IP3's proposed consortium to build nuclear reactors in Saudi Arabia, and which stands to benefit from the Middle East Marshall Plan. In August 2018, Brookfield Asset Management purchased a partnership stake in 666 Fifth Avenue, a building owned by Jared Kushner's family company."*

Is this a possible thank-you for insider information? Kushner had been trying to off-load 666 to a number of potential buyers for at least two years, as the loan was likely at high risk of default.

> *"Also in March 2018, Crown Prince Mohammed bin Salman undertook a 'last-minute visit to New York,' where he housed his entourage at the Trump International Hotel in Manhattan for five days, a stay that reportedly 'was enough to boost the hotel's revenue' by 13 percent 'for the entire quarter.'"*[340]

How nice to see the Trump Organization turn-in such a nice "unexpected" uptick in profit.

Trump's first foreign trip was to Saudi Arabia for a reason. The plans for "rebirth" of the Saudi kingdom as a dual center of tech and energy had incredible potential for deals, with a large military industrial complex purchase announced with pride, and this secret deal being discussed in detail behind closed doors. Both are incredibly scary deals. The weapon sales allow continued genocide, while nuclear power has problems of its own.

There is a stark difference in selling unrefined and rock-bound Uranium than selling working nuclear reactors as Trump planned to sell to the Saudis.

---

[340] "Trump Saudi Nuclear Report." *Oversight.house.gov*, 19 Feb. 2019, oversight.house.gov/sites/democrats.oversight.house.gov/files/Trump%20Saudi%20Nuclear%20Report%20-%202-19-2019.pdf.

The ore must be processed, taking several tons of material to produce a rod or plate. Then you have to make sure to keep the refined ore separated to prevent radiation bursts, something my grandfather George Jarvis was credited with discovering as a nuclear physicist in Los Alamos.

When he described the experiment, clearing out the safety pads in the room and hand stacking Uranium plates carefully measured, up to the "flash point" where a radiation burst would occur, I asked him if it was dangerous. He said he wasn't worried because he had done the math. Then he thought for a moment then explained that a competing lab working on the same question had failed in their calculations and went above the flashpoint. The red light in the room went on indicating a radiation burst occurred. The scientist died about a week later, heavily radiated. Math can be life and death, and working towards such weaponry costs many American lives. Most of my limited nuclear knowledge came from him. I even "read" his research paper he was proud of, but frankly it was well above my own understanding to get besides the most basics.

Trump also "knows nuclear" because of his conversations with an uncle, according to his childlike speech with PM May given on July 13, 2018:

> *"But the proliferation is a tremendous—I mean, to me, it's the biggest problem in the world: nuclear weapons. Biggest problem in the world. I understand nuclear. Look up Dr. John Trump at MIT. He was my uncle. Many, many years a professor. I used to talk nuclear with him. And this is many years ago. It's the biggest problem, in my opinion, this world has. Nuclear weapons. So if we could do something to substantially reduce them—I mean, ideally, get rid of them. Maybe that's a dream. But certainly it's a subject that I'll be bringing up with him. And it's also a very expensive thing. But that's the least important. So if we can—if we can do something."[341]*

Given that Trump has withdrawn on February 1, 2019. from the INF Treaty with Russia that was designed to limit nuclear weapons, and his selling of US reactors to risky "allies" I think he was bluffing that day on both the knowing nuclear, and being worried about nuclear proliferation.

---

[341] Factbase. "Transcript Quote - Press Conference: Donald Trump Holds a Joint Press Conference With Theresa May - July 13, 2018." *Factbase*, factba.se/transcript/donald-trump-press-conference-united-kingdom-july-13-2018.

Reactors aren't that far removed from warheads in concept, as the radioactive material must have weight calculated and arranged a certain distance from each other to prevent or control radiation bursts in both bombs and reactors. The main difference is creating a maximized energy burst in a bomb that ignites the radioactive material generating large explosions released in a radiative wave. My grandfather spoke of occasions where warheads had been accidentally dropped in the lab. None exploded, and for good scientific reasons. They needed additional elements, which I won't be discussing nor understand. The point is, having pure radioactive rods AND the information of how to handle them can lead to the quick creation of nuclear warheads able to fit on top of missiles we already sell to the Saudis. At the bare minimum, "dirty bombs" leaving radioactive contamination harming large areas full of people can be made from "spent" rods or other radioactive contaminants. Transferring nuclear technology to the Middle East can and would likely backfire on the US over time even with US protocols. The whistleblowers pointed this out using MbS's own words:

> *"However, experts worry that transferring sensitive U.S. nuclear technology could allow Saudi Arabia to produce nuclear weapons that contribute to the proliferation of nuclear arms throughout an already unstable Middle East. Saudi Crown Prince Mohammed bin Salman conceded this point in 2018, proclaiming: 'Without a doubt, if Iran developed a nuclear bomb, we will follow suit as soon as possible.'"[342]*

With access to nuclear weapons, the only people that will die from it are generally the ones that it has been launched towards or in the vicinity of the radioactive cloud. Let's say Trump manages to transfer the tech, and bombs are developed, either full-fledged nukes or of the dirty bomb variety. Who will be the target of an eventual attack?

Right now it would be Yemen. MbS is likely to end the Houthi "threat" in one nuclear strike instead of this forced attrition through starvation caused by his blockading of ports and US supported bombing campaigns. As I said in an earlier chapter, the numbers dead from Trump's genocidal agreement could

---

[342] "Trump Saudi Nuclear Report." *Oversight.house.gov*, 19 Feb. 2019, oversight.house.gov/sites/democrats.oversight.house.gov/files/Trump%20Saudi%20Nuclear%20Report%20-%202-19-2019.pdf.

surpass what Hitler accomplished in the Holocaust, with at least eight million people of the same religious group deceased through mass murder and starvation. MbS could also hit Qatar, Iran, Turkey or even Israel, but Yemen makes the most sense as it will not provoke other powers into engaging. MbS is intelligent and brutal. He is rumored to be connected with all sorts of chaos in the Middle East besides the headlines that hit US papers including bombings in Iran and arming terrorists. He understands how to operate, who he wants in power in each of the Gulf States, and already has "permission" on forcing changes in Yemen and Qatar from the United States President. MbS pretty much has the green light to make a bomb if we or anyone else sells him refined uranium. What he really doesn't like, besides an honest press or other internal threat to his power, is the country of Iran. It is a religious thing with hostility on both sides to put it mildly. His war with Yemen is a proxy war with Iran, explaining his barbarism and *"tut-heer Erqei"* of the Shia Houthi.

Hitting Yemen would be better than striking Iran whom he despises the most as the message to Iran and others would have been delivered. Several small Arabian countries, he presently lacks sway with would quickly fall in-line with the Crown Prince after such a strike, consolidating power collectively without bringing Russia or the United States into the conflict.

If MbS does what he has with other US weapons, he could give "spent" nuclear material to ISIS, which can easily be fashioned into a dirty bomb. While Saudi Arabia would not likely attack Israel or other countries, ISIS and many other groups MbS wants to gain favor with would. I fear one of those rebel tunnels under the walls of Israel will lead such a weapon into a heavily populated area, detonating and spreading a noxious radioactive cloud harming tens of thousands of the Israeli people. The likelihood radioactive material winds up in ISIS or another dangerous group's hands is inevitable if the US builds nuclear power plants as even the waste presents a danger.

Many US weapons Saudi Arabia has bought have either been abandoned or given as "currency" to buy allegiance from the very groups the US opposes such as Al-Qaeda and ISIS. In an exclusive CNN report by Nima Elbagir, Salma Abdelaziz, Mohamed Abo El Gheit and Laura Smith-Spark, posted February 2019, they detailed the weapons markets full of US weaponry for sale in Yemen, sales that have been ongoing at least back to 2015. Now, Saudi Arabia and UAE supply the weapons, including the "good stuff" for help in cleansing the Houthi "scourge":

"Saudi Arabia and the United Arab Emirates, its main partner in the war, have used the US-manufactured weapons as a form of currency to buy the loyalties of militias or tribes, bolster chosen armed actors, and influence the complex political landscape, according to local commanders on the ground and analysts who spoke to CNN.

"By handing off this military equipment to third parties, the Saudi-led coalition is breaking the terms of its arms sales with the US, according to the Department of Defense. After CNN presented its findings, a US defense official confirmed there was an ongoing investigation into the issue." [343]

From these markets Iran, Russia and others are also buying and learning from our military technology, finding ways to exploit weakness or to make tech similar to our own. Not only do we run the risk of our troops being killed by older US weapons, our defensive ones aren't as protective when their flaws are known, yet the sales revived under Trump to the Middle East have continued.

---

[343] "US Arms Sold to Saudi Arabia and UAE End up in Wrong Hands." *CNN*, Cable News Network, www.cnn.com/interactive/2019/02/middleeast/yemen-lost-us-arms/.

Chapter Twenty-three

"We Are Better Than This"

When an exasperated Elijah Cummings shouted this phrase after the main Cohen hearing I could sense that he was both right and wrong when looking at the different actors on Don's scripted United States of America show that we have all played unwitting part of these past several years. Yes, the vast majority is better than this, however many in positions of power within this great nation has been acting criminally working to undermine democracy, laws, and humanity for at least two years.

The media needs to change to be "better than this," both the "fake" social media that most Americans rely on and the "real" media of print and TV journalism. Too often the "left" and "right" media have settled for the lowest-hanging fruit that narrowly focus only on what their audience wants to hear, sacrificing honest open dialogue and common ground. This is why Trump's railing on CNN, *Washington Post* and others on the right of coverage was and is so effective. Instead of presenting information and requiring thought, our polarized media presents thought in place of information, hence "fake." I have seen Trump edited out of context, perhaps because few understand his language irregularities such as a Sped Teacher does, that nevertheless change his whole argument negatively much further than it should had the "power statement" been provided full context. While imperfect, I am very appreciative at those journalists who do great American work, dredging through the documents and asking the questions that are needed in today's world.

The Republicans in Congress and in positions of power, the vast majority of them aren't "better than this. Many still work towards their own interests over those whom they were elected to serve while others do not dare to go against the majority of their party, afraid of the Trump mob or other retribution. Few condemn the daily lies of the administration and are either tacitly complicit or overly obvious in their zeal to support the "Commander in Chief." McConnell, Ryan, and others failed in their Constitutional duties weakening the framework of our government. With such callous behavior and disregard for patriotism over party, they emboldened Trump's cult, many of them armed and indoctrinated, ready to support MAGA and the Nationalist Republican party, reformed by Trump. With the "dumb laws" of the Constitution in peril, our "fake" media, "witch hunting" law enforcement and "conflicted" Intelligence communities under constant derision too many Republican voices parrot the same attacks that boom from our authoritarian minded President who only is able to keep this ruse up because of them. While some occasionally stand with America, it seems that they are usually few and easily beaten down by the MAGA mobs or fearing the Cult of Trump given their eerie silence.

America isn't safe. That threat does not come from families clutching small children walking hundreds of miles away from violence. It is the administration led by a threatening criminal leader who is willing to gas, shoot and/or kidnap children with mostly full support of the government, "conservatives" and "his people" to appease his cult:

> *"Anybody throwing stones, rocks—like they did to Mexico and the Mexican military, Mexican police, where they badly hurt police and soldiers of Mexico—we will consider that a firearm. Because there's not much difference, where you get hit in the face with a rock— which, as you know, it was very violent a few days ago—very, very violent—that break-in. It was a break-in of a country. They broke into Mexico."*
>
> *-Individual 1*
> *November 1, 2018*[344]

---

[344] Factbase. "Transcript Quote - Remarks: Donald Trump Delivers a Statement on Immigration and Border Security - November 1, 2018." *Factbase*, factba.se/transcript/donald-trump-remarks-immigration-border-security-november-1-2018.

One of my esteemed colleagues, a phenomenal 7th grade Social Studies teacher and humanitarian, on his last day at my present Austin, Texas, area school asked the assembled sixth-graders to raise their hand if something that the President or his administration had done had caused harm to themselves, their family or somebody they knew. Some students paused and looked at each other and hands began to go up. All hands were in the air as what this administration has done with reckless abandon on our rights and democracies have harmed each and every child. He went on to express how important it was for them to get their educations, to have voices, to stand up be counted and vote, so what America is presently facing is not allowed to happen again, ever.

We are two Americas. One is an ugly America turned backwards inspired by Nazi-era rhetoric and that Make America (White-Power) Great Again nationalist zeal wearing the red hats, hanging nooses in workplaces, and threatening to call the cops on their neighbors simply because they are offended by the color of their skin, their difference of religion or their sexuality. Then there are the bombers, shooters and murders that when they act, are dismissed as mentally ill simply because they are white. The other America is kneeling peacefully, marching in record numbers in Washington pushing for change while still having renewed hope to make the world a better, cleaner and safer world for our children.

To see the United States, a country that once fought hand in hand with its Democratic allies to fight Nationalist movements in Japan, Italy and Germany to be going through such changes, is disheartening. Racism and hate is rampant, with recruitment no longer subtle but open. In 30s Germany, indoctrinated youth wore the "uniform" of the Nazi party. In the present day, youth groups mirror that such as those Catholic school boys wearing MAGA hats blocking the steps leading up to Mr. Lincoln in Washington, D.C.

That flashpoint of racism in America, boy in Trump's Nationalist "uniform," staring down sneering unmoving at a soon surrounded drumming native American, unleashed a firestorm of early partial reporting, followed by a backlash that had one added fact yet lacked the fuller context by the right-wing media, then little follow-up by the left. The school and general public sided with the boys being "misrepresented," yet everyone has formed their own opinions of all the actors involved. All three groups should take ownership of their own actions, the Indigenous Peoples group, the Hebrew Israelites and the MAGA Covington High boys. All probably agree that the

Hebrew Israelites were by far the worst behaved group seeking constant provocation with anyone. The second worse behaved group was Covington, due to lack of adult supervision.

My own opinion on what happened and why was based on watching a number of videos from different angles, reading the principle student's own statements, the other stories about the high school involving racism at a basketball game and then considering all the evidence.

The boys attended a protest wearing the Trump Nationalist Uniform (MAGA hat) with inadequate adult to student ratio support. Many boys had been loitering in the area for some time as were the four Hebrew Israelites and the Indigenous People Marchers. Many of the kids were long since misbehaving.

A boy in the group was filmed saying, "It's not rape if you enjoy it," standing next to a group of girls, then turns around and walks off. An interesting statement given the context of attending a rally that sought to remove women's reproductive rights.[345]

The boys were engaging with another verbally hostile and profane group of mostly black men called Hebrew Israelites, according to the main student's statement got "permission" to engage those men further by shouting school chants. The boys MOVED TOWARDS the Hebrew Israelites and began blocking the stairs shouting chants, escalating the situation. I heard during the chant a voice shout, "Build the wall," among the other shouts while reports alleged a student was actually calling to a classmate named Jamal. "Wall" and "Jamal" do sound similar. The real problem is that another short clip exists from two girls walking by some of the same red-hat group dated January 22, 2019, purported to be about an hour before the main incident. A boy shouting build the wall was VERY clear instead of the muffled ones in other videos. It sounds like the same voice in the main clip, meaning probably only one boy was using the phrase. Sadly the clip was only 8 seconds long with one girl saying "MAGA" sarcastically and the other, *"I'm so tired already."* With her post she claimed these boys had been behaving that way for quite some time. With multiple times the main event had been reported and recorded, someone in the group had clearly been using the racist slur. Yes, "Build the wall" is a racist slur as it is derogatory against immigrants from Central and South America. Any time a word or phrase is used so ex-

---

[345] Arriveria, Top. "Covington MAGA Teens on Abortion Due to Rape: 'It's Not Rape If You Enjoy It.'" *YouTube*, YouTube, 22 Jan. 2019, www.youtube.com/watch?v=CqUh7nlXn2k.

cessively against a group of people alongside other epithets such as rapists, murders, criminals, etc., it is a racist slur.[346]

Nathan Phillips, a native-American and frequent activist, "attempted" to diffuse the situation between the Hebrew Israelites and MAGA boys who were shouting at each other. He went towards the group of students on the stairs beating the drum and singing a song. It worked initially.

Students "mocking" Native American culture began jumping up and down swinging arms in a tomahawk chop and whooping it up. This low-level form of racism can be an incredible teaching opportunity about showing respect to cultures and people that are different. That is how my Order of the Arrow (Boy Scouts of America) friends would always react when similar behaviors occurred at our drum circles.

The main student and Nathan Phillips came face to face after Phillips moved gradually opening a pathway up the stairs. The boy had been standing there the whole time as most of the boys had been, yet instead of moving respectfully to the side as all others did when Nathan approached, chose to remain standing still and stare down Phillips silently while smirking.

For a couple minutes Phillips beat the drum holding it at the same leveled height he had the entire time he had been drumming. The boy smirked and stared mostly directly, and angled slightly downward at Phillips. Phillips looked in the direction of the boy, but not at his "dominating" eyes.

As a teacher I have witnessed that smirk dozens of times. ALWAYS a flurry of punches follows because it is rude, challenging behavior when it is two students doing it. His classmates reacted to it in different ways. Some appeared to enjoy it. Others felt the intensity. Then the group collapsed in closely around the two individuals as the drumming and smirking continued. One Native American stood on the steps with the boys arguing with a leveled-voice intermittent with "careless" profanity with a couple of students.

The boy's finally began to leave the area, then shortly the song ended and people began to disperse. One student who had been arguing earlier on the steps said something about how "lands get stolen, that is how it works." He didn't seem to get that the lands being taken by the white man was only accomplished

---

[346] scallly. "'MAGA' & 'Build A Wall' Shouted by Covington Catholic Boys." *YouTube*, YouTube, 22 Jan. 2019, www.youtube.com/watch?v=wrnqHPxoBrc.

by mass genocide of the native populations, hence why they were in Washington for their own rally.[347]

There was a ton to process from all this. Both Phillips and the boy have differing yet valid views of what happened to them personally. For Phillips, being shouted at, "Build the wall," and then having the whole group collapse around him heightened his emotions and credible fear for his safety. His video shortly after the incident was not feigned, rather a genuine emotional response to a stressful situation. The boy with his posturing stated he was showing he would not be intimidated by staring directly at the "protestor." Once he made that mistake and no one bailed him out (where are the teachers), well, he became the face of the whole group despite not saying a word in any video that day.

The young man's statement given to Jake Tapper had some interesting points. One, the students obtained permission to engage as a group the four African-American protestors chanting from an adult (they already HAD some students engaging back and forth). Two he did not hear the "Build the Wall" slur, giving "distance" to what was being said in reports. Three, he only referred to Nathan Phillips as a "Native American protestor." Odd considering this young man likely knew Phillips name if he thought to include the "distance" statement of not hearing the slur. Four, he felt he behaved entirely appropriately.

He didn't. And it really isn't his fault.

I blame the teachers and the school ENTIRELY for this one, not the young man or the students as they are just kids that make bad mistakes. Had adults done their job, pulled the group away to the left or right of the memorial instead of blocking the stairway access AND engaging the four vulgar protestors there would be NO story. In a public school these faculty would all have been written up, perhaps fired for their inactions as well as the poor decisions leading up to the confrontation that made things worse. I also question the logic of taking students to a protest in the first place and allowing them to wear the hats, which are just as offensive as swastikas these days.

The young man did smirk and did block the stairs. He wore a racist hat. He is entitled to do two of those three things under the Constitution (hint— you can't block others' public access). However as he is a child, the school is responsible for him, the hats and his classmates actions that day, including the rape comment, the harassment of those two girls, the build the wall (though

[347] "'Land Gets Stolen. That's How It Works.'" *Sierra Club*, 25 Jan. 2019, www.sierraclub.org/sierra/land-gets-stolen-s-how-it-works-native-covington-catholic-lincoln-memorial.

WHO was yelling it is not clear in any of the videos, just that someone with the group is likely doing it), the insults about taking land, blocking the stairs and the fallout days later.

I personally have never seen an apology from any of the boys in the group, only deflection and blame being placed on others to justify their own actions. While not all the boys behaved badly, a great deal of them did, but they are children who hopefully can change and turn away from MAGA, racism and misogyny that was evident on multiple videos taken that day. The Trump-youth MAGA boys do not deserve threats for their intentional actions, only the strongest scrutiny and criticism, as even racists and antagonists have the right to be here and assemble under the Constitution. Outside of the day of protest that the school kids were involved in were other stories of racism. A picture with at least four full-bodied black-faced students and a boy flashing the "white power" hand sign towards a black student from another school at a basketball game surfaced quickly, clearly showing the school has always had a race problem.[348]

Trump ecstatic about the "victimized" MAGA youth invited "his" boys to the White House as well as lathered on praise in this Tweet (child's name omitted by me):

"[NAME WITHHELD] and the students of Covington have become symbols of Fake News and how evil it can be. They have captivated the attention of the world, and I know they will use it for the good—maybe even to bring people together. It started off unpleasant, but can end in a dream!"

4:32 A.M., January 22, 2019[349]

The Covington kid in the video whose name I withheld has since sued multiple media outlets seeking a quarter of a billion in damages each against Trump media targets CNN and *Washington Post*. More lawsuits are expected according to Fox News against HBO, AP and others. These challenges to the First Amendment have been in the works since late January has a "Trump feel" to them, using lawsuits to silence and intimidate. Is money what Trump meant, by end in a dream?

---

[348] 2019, pbs.twimg.com/media/DxiAAC3W0AAFISh.jpg.

[349] Trump, Donald J. "Nick Sandmann and the Students of Covington Have Become Symbols of Fake News and How Evil It Can Be. They Have Captivated the Attention of the World, and I Know They Will Use It for the Good - Maybe Even to Bring People Together. It Started off Unpleasant, but Can End in a Dream!" *Twitter*, Twitter, 22 Jan. 2019, twitter.com/realDonaldTrump/status/1087689415814795264.

When something doesn't seem right, ask questions, take some time and get answers. In this case the question is why has the young man targeted CNN and *Washington Post* first? That actually might be a bigger story than Covington High and racism as Trump and his media have maliciously gone after those that provide critical and usually correct reporting of the President. By filing the lawsuits, another avenue of attack in the overall war on the press Donald J. Trump has waged has been opened, this time by proxy via supporters.

When it comes to controversy and racism, Trump has always jumped in to support those that share his beliefs. Covington was one of those moments where he could publicly harm another US company as President that he has sought to destroy, and appeal to his MAGA nationalist base. The Don approved the MAGA hit job as evidenced by this "Presidential" Tweet after the first lawsuit for a quarter-of-a-billion hit:

> *The Washington Post ignored basic journalistic standards because it wanted to advance its well-known and easily documented biased agenda against President Donald J. Trump. Covington student suing WAPO. Go get them [Name Removed]. Fake News!*
>
> *3:44 A.M. EST, February 20, 2019*[350]

As the incident unfolded online and in Twitter-verse CNN was a VERY late reporter on the intense standoff, posting the story online in the mid to late afternoon with specific language stating they could not independently verify the reports that other news outlets had issued. How do I know? I was online on Twitter and began checking both Fox and CNN when I saw the video first pop up and propagate like wildfire in the morning. By the time CNN had posted their very late coverage, I had already read five or six other reports including WaPo, watched two hours of video, heard the build the wall, lands taken and rape comments from other Covington students.

If CNN produces their internal timeline of coverage and my "perception" of when they began reporting (I do not own cable so cannot verify what they did on TV) is accurate, the intent to harm CNN by the suing parties to show

---

[350] Trump, Donald J. "'The Washington Post Ignored Basic Journalistic Standards Because It Wanted to Advance Its Well-Known and Easily Documented Biased Agenda against President Donald J. Trump." Covington Student Suing WAPO. Go Get Them Nick. Fake News!" *Twitter*, Twitter, 20 Feb. 2019, twitter.com/realDonaldTrump/status/1098201685518893056?ref_src=twsrc%5Etfw%7Ctwcamp%5Etweetembed&ref_url=https%3A%2F%2Ffactba.se%2Fsearch.

support of the President is clear. I would assume *Washington Post* was also targeted for political retribution simply because CNN has likely been, meaning both have a legitimate case for their own damages including lawyer fees if what I am saying is true.

As the basis of such a lawsuit is that CNN caused this kid harm, it is on the suing party to prove intent and harm was directly caused by the company. I was also on when Jake Tapper's Twitter account lit up posting Covington Kid's "factual account" and they also issued several "pro-Covington" stories when the right-wing media backlash began. CNN additionally posted the longer narrative, which blamed the Hebrew Israelites (they DO share blame). The problem with that report is CNN never put the whole story of what these "innocent choir boys" had done together, and stayed mostly on the side as a casual secondary observer while other smaller outlets did the legwork. I also remember the first time I saw the kid's name pop up it was in a comment section of a post. That happened hours before CNN's initial report. The "fake" Covington Mom story, which isn't the boy's mom, was the only hitch I spotted in the first couple days of the event. That one appeared on "news" site Heavy, which originally attributed blame to black Muslims. The identity was never confirmed and a correction was issued.[351]

---

[351] Santiago, Ellyn. "WATCH: Covington Catholic Students Wearing MAGA Hats Encounter Native Americans [VIDEO]." *Heavy.com*, 4 Feb. 2019, heavy.com/news/2019/01/ky-catholic-teens-maga-native-american/.

Chapter Twenty-four

We'll See What Happens[353]

Donald J. Trump is not going to change. He is an elderly man that has always without question done what he wanted to do. As President he was going to make the world change to conform to him as he did in business. That is his nature, and an unfortunate one. His extreme rigidity and cognitive inflexibility make him as obstinate as any child, generally unable to complete the affairs required of an adult, let alone the affairs of the country. No one, friend or foe, can persuade him to do what he doesn't want to do, though everyone has tried. That stubbornness, a quality expressively Autistic, has made Donald specifically unfit to hold the office of the President, not even considering the clusters of criminal behaviors discussed in these pages.

Keep in mind Donald's Autism disability DOES NOT directly cause his criminality, which he alone controls, rather explains his inability to properly communicate, understand and convey emotion and behave in a socially appropriate way.

There are many avenues that I can see how the Trump era ends. He could be voted out of office, impeached, removed by his cabinet applying the Twenty-fifth Amendment or with the help of his media, cult, mob and foreign actors subvert a second US election taking four more years off of American luster, integrity and prestige. I worry most for the latter as our election security doesn't feel as secure with Republicans alleged behaviors of fixing one Federal election in North Carolina during the midterms being so fresh on my mind.

The most likely scenario is that Donald J. Trump will be voted out of office then indictments against him for a host of crimes and possibly others I haven't suggested can be unsealed in 2021.

There is a strong case for removal of any President who is cognitively unfit for office under the Twenty-fifth Amendment. While in general I believe most high-functioning individuals with Autism Spectrum Disorders function well enough to run companies, or the Presidency of the United States and are productive law-abiding individuals, Trump has shown himself extensively disabled and limited cognitively due to the severity of his unique sets of deficits connected to the disorder. His cabinet as required by the Constitution should act given the President's behavior and limited functioning, removing him from where he has been allowed to do the most harm.

Trump's stereotypical behavior of tearing up documents violates the Presidential Records Act. His abysmal executive functioning skills means he spends most of his day disregarding nearly all executive duties, instead Tweeting, vacationing, golfing and watching TV. Trump's restricted patterns of behavior have been such prevalent and pervasive problems for the White House that his presence usually stymies others administrative work, or frequently endanger our national security. He trusts the wrong people, makes poor decisions and says things everybody else knows are false, yet he adamantly believes them. He can't take criticism and views anything that differs from what he believes as a personal attack against him demanding a rebuttal. Being this behaviorally restrictive is incompatible with public service as he has offended nearly every US ally to the point none trusts him to keep his word or to share intelligence for the fear he will again hand it over to our shared foes.

Then we have his communication and emotional/social deficits. Trump's language that measures on a fourth-grade level for oral language added to poor literacy skills both for fluency and comprehension means he can't access any governmental report independently. Heck, he can't even read and understand the US Constitution, it seems. Even if a report is read to him, it is unlikely he can fully understand it beyond literal comprehension as he appears to have extremely limited attention and high distractibility when others are speaking. This is why Trump is a "one-pager" kind of guy, as he can't process longer material. Emotionally those deficits mean he can't connect with the American people when they are suffering. He has no empathy, because he has not been taught explicitly step-by-step how to show it from his parents or a special education teacher. He only connects on a rudimentary level socially looking at friendship as what he can extract by his knowing you. He is unable to "read" people and is genuinely vulnerable to influence by foreign actors that have been able to build a relationship of trust with him such as Vladimir Putin. He can't help these things as his disability; Autism-Pervasive Developmental Disorder Not Otherwise Specified is so severe. Trump is essentially a man with a twelve-year-old brain, and the emotional temperament of a four-year-old. Isn't that enough of a reason to invoke the Twenty-fifth? Trump is so handicapped by his disability most of what has been done that he was required to do was done by others. All Donnie seems to do is show up to events and sign things after everyone else did the work, and that isn't functioning at all.

Then we have this whole issue of his making a fake National Emergency as a scheme to achieve a political goal of branding a wall with his name on it. Reports are that people tried to work with Trump, to let him have options that would lessen political harm of his poor decisions and restricted behavior. GOP Senators Ted Cruz, Lindsey Graham and Ben Sasse strolled over to see Trump on March 13 to chat at dinner time.

"We just kind of barged in on his supper," said Graham. Trump had already said no, and wasn't going to be convinced any more than if they had been trying to give him veggies when he has his heart set on chocolate cake. According to reports Trump blew up at them, just another meltdown in a series of Trump's characteristic autistic behavior. They should have seen that coming as Trump is triggered whenever he sees someone challenging him.

"I said I don't expect you to give up any powers of the president that you think is necessary but if you could find a way to sit down and bridge the gap here prospectively it would be in everybody's best interest," replied Graham.[352]

The only interest is Trump's interest as he has limited ability to view things from another's perspective. He doesn't foresee how his actions harm others, hence his incredibly poor judgement in most of his choices.

While Trump is truly disabled cognitively and should be removed via the Twenty-fifth, he probably will just fire his cabinet if he thinks they will act as he had been warned that this was the greatest threat to ending his Presidency by Steve Bannon. This is why Congress needs to proceed with Impeachment proceedings.

---

[352] Collins, Kaitlan, et al. "An Interrupted Dinner Followed by a Rebuke: How GOP Senators Failed to Stop the Emergency Resolution Vote." *CNN*, Cable News Network, 14 Mar. 2019, www.cnn.com/2019/03/14/politics/white-house-trump-national-emergency/index.html.

Speaker Nancy Pelosi is a smart scary woman. I mean who "vacations" in war zones other than Chuck Norris and Nancy Pelosi? She was also very much right on her statements given to *The Washington Post*'s Joe Heim on March 6, 2019:

> *"I'm not for impeachment. This is news. I'm going to give you some news right now because I haven't said this to any press person before. But since you asked, and I've been thinking about this: Impeachment is so divisive to the country that unless there's something so compelling and overwhelming and bipartisan, I don't think we should go down that path, because it divides the country. And he's just not that worth it."*

She also considers him unfit for these three: ethics, intellect, and curiosity-wise. We all see those problems, at least those who aren't emotionally invested in him.[353]

While Trump is not worth it, our Democracy surely is. Nancy is right though in how divisive it will be as there are likely to be an insurrection from the bad hombres of Trump's Cult. Trump himself has hinted of those he expects to rise up on a March 13, 2019, interview to white nationalist favored mag Breitbart:

> *"You know, the left plays a tougher game, it's very funny. I actually think that the people on the right are tougher, but they don't play it tougher. Okay? I can tell you I have the support of the police, the support of the military, the support of the Bikers for Trump—I have the tough people, but they don't play it tough—until they go to a certain point, and then it would be very bad, very bad. But the left plays it cuter and tougher. Like with all the nonsense that they do in Congress… with all this invest[igations]—that's all they want to do is—you know, they do things that are nasty. Republicans never played this."*[354]

---

[353] "Nancy Pelosi on Impeaching President Trump: 'He's Just Not Worth It.'" *The Washington Post*, WP Company, 11 Mar. 2019, www.washingtonpost.com/news/magazine/wp/2019/03/11/feature/nancy-pelosi-on-impeaching-president-trump-hes-just-not-worth-it/.

[354] Marlow, Alexander, et al. "Exclusive-Trump: Paul Ryan Blocked Subpoenas of Democrats." *Breitbart*, 15 Mar. 2019, www.breitbart.com/politics/2019/03/13/exclusive-president-donald-trump-paul-ryan-

Never? January 28, 2019, John Bolton intentionally has the not-so-hidden message of *"5000 troops to Columbia"* written clearly on the back on a yellow notepad, holding it outwards towards the press.[355]

Yes, Trump has many supporters who will get violent with his removal from office, some with large munitions and caches of guns similar to the Coast Guard terrorist. They will rise up at some point anyway if a Democrat wins or something else frustrates their dreams of MAGA, walls and a white dominant heavily armed and militant America. They are invested that much in the illusion Trump has created, making them the most dangerous. Just round them up and protect America from the mass murder each is likely to commit on behalf of their "favorite President."

Nancy is correct, though, there needs to be sufficient evidence Trump has committed high crimes enough to convince twenty Republican Senators to protect the country. Not an easy sale given how so many of them act arm in arm with Trump, but there is hope. The evidence is insurmountable that he committed a mass of felonies that he should be held accountable for as well as countless minor crimes.

"Individual One" will "likely" be facing the following crimes with multiple counts once investigations release their reports and/or charges (dependent on if they can indict a sitting President):

Obstruction of Justice charges, multiple charges (at least three recent clusters)

Trump "allegedly" undertook actions to "end" and "restrict" Federal investigators investigations into his activities with Russia before and during the campaign. These included firing the FBI director James Comey, making repeated false public statements to discredit the investigation and investigators that number in excess of two-hundred uses of "witch hunt" and other attacks on credibility, and comments/questions he had given to officials that "indicate" intention to stop the investigations through his own actions.

Trump "allegedly" created false and misleading statements to protect his son Donald Trump Junior after his exposure increased with setting up and conducting the Trump Tower meeting.

---

blocked-subpoenas-of-democrats/.

[355] CBS/ap. "'5,000 Troops to Colombia'? Nation Responds to Bolton's Note." *CBS News*, CBS Interactive, 18 Feb. 2019, www.cbsnews.com/news/colombia-confused-by-boltons-note-on-5000-troops/.

Trump "allegedly" sought to cover his affairs with two women then made repeated false claims and statements regarding his campaign's payments to the parent company of the *National Enquirer*.

Conspiracy Charges, multiple charges
Trump, Cohen and David Pecker of the *National Enquirer* "likely" entered into an illegal agreement to support his candidacy during the 2016 election by a catch-and-kill scheme.

Trump and other election officials Mike Flynn, Tom Barrack, Paul Manafort, Jared Kushner, etc., "likely" entered into a scheme to sell nuclear reactors to Saudi, UAE and Egypt, bypassing Federal law.

Trump "allegedly" publically requested campaign assistance in the form of targeted espionage on the Democratic National Party from the Russians, while seeking backchannels to President Putin to receive possible additional assistance. Then once the deed had been completed, Trump coordinated with Wikileaks through associate Roger Stone for the release of the stolen documents.

Campaign Finance Laws
Trump "allegedly" reimbursed Michael Cohen for the *National Enquirer* scheme using campaign donations. This is the biggest one, though hundreds of minor violations likely exist with Chinese, Russian and Saudi Arabian "donations" possible. Those sort of minor violations happen with almost all campaigns and generally are settled with fines unless the amounts directed in the campaign are substantial. The inauguration committee's record haul of "donations" is also under investigation. Considering Tom Barrack's connections to the Middle East those dollars need to be tracked, each and every one.

Human Trafficking Charges
Trump Models is the most egregious form of indentured servitude, with many of the "employees" indebted after working for the Trump Organization. While not under the specific purvey of the Office of the Special Counsel, the accusations against the company are likely a central piece of the investigations undertaken by the Southern District capable of putting all the Trump Organization (meaning Trump's kids) behind bars for their lifetimes. The immigration law violations stack up at a pop of up to six months prison per model they illegally employed BEFORE the trafficking charges.

Banking Fraud, Money Laundering, Tax Evasion and Financial Charges
These "likely" charges could be staggering considering the scope of everything Trump has done that still is within the statute of limitations. His first known scheme of fraudulently getting on the Forbes 400 plus the banking disclosures Cohen gave Congress indicate at least a thirty-year window of these sort of criminal activities including the 2.9 billion over two defaults on the Trump Taj Mahal. Trump had essentially run the largest wealth pyramid scheme, using bankruptcy protections to shaft investors and financial institutions with junk bonds and other cash grabs. Each fund "raising" junk bond event, Trump would have accessed enough money to pay interest for a while on other properties keeping the scheme going while seeking more loans using fake reputation and inflated assets.

Congressional and Other Crimes
Trump has violated the requirement of the President to report under the Magnitski Act on the Khashoggi murder.

Trump "likely" has violated the statues of the Presidential Records Act in the case of "missing" documents of each meeting with Russian President Vladimir Putin as well as his stemming behavior of tearing up documents required to be achieved.[356]

Trump and his administration may have violated the Atomic Energy Act working to get Saudi Arabia, UAE and Egypt nuclear technology without following protocols.

I think the threshold for high crimes WAS established that day Trump said, *"Russia if you are listening…"* Congress must fulfill its Constitutional duty and *"impeach the M——- F——!"*[357]

International Law Violations
While International Law isn't part of the consideration of whether Congress initiates an Impeachment, it is only fitting to recall Trump has allowed mass genocide to be committed indirectly by supporting the Saudi massacre of the

---

[356] Ward, Alex. "The US Apparently Kept No Detailed Notes of Trump-Putin Meetings for the Past 2 Years." *Vox*, Vox, 14 Jan. 2019, www.vox.com/world/2019/1/14/18182455/trump-russia-putin-notes-wapo-wsj.

[357] O'Neil, Luke. "'We're Gonna Impeach the Motherfucker': the Democrats' New Street Fighters." *The Guardian*, Guardian News and Media, 4 Jan. 2019, www.theguardian.com/us-news/2019/jan/04/democrats-congress-trump-impeach-rashida-tlaib.

Houthi people in Yemen. His Immigration stances with zero tolerance creating a government sponsored kidnap of thousands of refugee children, and the likely illegal incarceration of tens of thousands of refugees under the pretext of entering the US illegally as most had the Constitutional right to declare asylum are serious high crimes. There are other "complaints" out there against this President he must answer for should the World Criminal Courts file charges.

If Trump manages to survive the Impeachment, the election of 2020, already likely under attack by foreign agents, will need to suffice for his removal. Convicted fellow co-conspirator in the *National Enquirer* scheme Michael Cohen on February 27, 2019's closing statement sums it up:

"And I will not sit back, say nothing, and allow him to do the same to the country. Indeed given my experience working for Mr. Trump I fear that if he loses the election in 2020 that there will never be a peaceful transition of power, and this is why I agreed to appear before you today."

Even if he loses, he wins. That is how Trump operates according to his own rulebook. This is why there is almost no scenario where Donald steps down, and instead fights on, including after losing an election.

"In closing, I'd like to say directly to the president: We honor our veterans even in the rain, you tell the truth even when it doesn't aggrandize you, you respect the law and incredible law enforcement agents, you don't villainize them, you don't disparage generals, gold star families, prisoners of war and other heroes who had the courage to fight for this country. You don't attack the media and those who question what you don't like or what you don't want them to say and you take responsibility for your own dirty deeds.

"You don't use your power of your bully pulpit to destroy the credibility of those who speak out against you. You don't separate families from one another or demonize those looking to America for a better life. You don't vilify people based on the god they pray to and you don't cuddle up to our adversaries at the expense of our allies. Finally, you don't shut down the government before Christmas and New Year's just to simply appease your base."[358]

The Democrats really need someone with the moxie and willpower to fix all this. Of the "biggest crowd" of political candidates ever, only one will

---

[358] Scott, Dylan. "Michael Cohen's Parting Shot: I Fear What Happens If Trump Loses in 2020." *Vox,* Vox, 27 Feb. 2019, www.vox.com/policy-and-politics/2019/2/27/18243686/michael-cohen-testimony-closing-statement.

emerge to face Trump. They need to be young, intelligent, charismatic and inspiring. That person also really needs to be a woman, and a woman that isn't Hillary.

Hillary was flawed, while not as fractious as Don the Con, but flawed nonetheless. I didn't vote for her. Didn't vote for Don the Con either. I voted Bill Richardson as he was the best Conservative on the ballot. She had her email servers (in hindsight now that we know that Trump officials such as Ivanka and Jared also have private server scandals, Hillary's emails were never that much of an issue) and Benghazi. My personal beef had to do with honesty and her adapting to the scenery with accents and dress to appeal to whoever she was appearing before. I wanted to vote for someone who I felt was sincere.

The midterm I vacillated back and forth between whether I would vote for Ted Cruz or Beto. Cruz, while smarmy, has responded to most of my letters and has been a good Senator. I chose Beto because Cruz fears Trump after getting manhandled and branded lying Ted, and a son of a Kennedy assassin. Ted has been TOO loyal to Trump. When I went to the polls knowing of the high incidence of calibrated machines that changed Democrat votes to Republicans in Travis County, I proceeded to do something I never thought I would do after two decades of almost uniformly voting for Republicans in high offices. I clicked Democrat. I clicked another and another. Then when I had to I clicked Libertarian because there was no Democrat. Here I was a lifelong Republican conservative having to abandon a corrupted party. Still need to change my party registration come to think of it. Doing so felt right.

I remember meeting Mia Love while I was a GOP delegate for my neighborhood in Utah County, the first African-American Representative to Congress from the State. After she had lost to Ben McAdams narrowly in 2018 Trump mocked her. *"But Mia Love gave me no love, and she lost. Too bad."*[359]

Mia responded directly when conceding to McAdams weeks later after recounts had been completed.

"The President's behavior towards me made me wonder: What did he have to gain by saying such a thing about a fellow Republican. It was not really about asking him to do more, was it? Or was it something else? Well Mr. President, we'll have to chat about that. However, this gave me a clear vision of his world as it is. No real re-

---

[359] Factbase. "Transcript Quote - Press Conference: Donald Trump Meets With Reporters After Election Day 2018 - November 7, 2018." *Factbase*, factba.se/transcript/donald-trump-press-conference-midterm-elections-november-7-2018.

lationships, just convenient transactions. That is an insufficient way to implement sincere service and policy. This election experience and these comments shines a spotlight on the problems Washington politicians have with minorities and black Americans—it's transactional, it's not personal.

"You see, we feel like politicians claim they know what's best for us from a safe distance, yet they're never willing to take us home. Because Republicans never take minority communities into their home and citizens into their homes and into their hearts, they stay with Democrats and bureaucrats in Washington because they do take them home—or at least make them feel like they have a home."[360]

She is right. Mia's speech was the final cognitive break for me, knowing that moving away from the party I belonged to for twenty-five years was the right thing to do.

I've looked at the list starting with the men, growing every couple of days. Bernie…too old and has a history of problems. Nice guy, but he isn't the one. Joe Biden, same problems, though not as bad as Bernie's campaign staff misbehaving. Biden would make a stellar official, UN ambassador or something, but he isn't the one. I like Beto, and feel he is best suited as number two. The women are mostly forgettable save Elizabeth Warren who was past her window of opportunity, made mistakes and gave in to Trump's sophomoric taunting. I've made my choice given what I need in a candidate.

That candidate for change is Kamala Harris, 46[th.]

---

[360] Cole, Devan. "Mia Love Slams Trump in Concession Speech: 'No Real Relationships, Just Convenient Transactions.'" *CNN*, Cable News Network, 26 Nov. 2018, www.cnn.com/2018/11/26/politics/mia-love-donald-trump-concession/index.html.

www.ingramcontent.com/pod-product-compliance
Lightning Source LLC
Chambersburg PA
CBHW070650250726
48662CB00001B/61